CUSTOMER
SERVICE
training

ATD Workshop Series

CUSTOMER SERVICE
training

KIMBERLY DEVLIN

atd
PRESS

Alexandria, Virginia

ATD Press is an internationally renowned source of insightful and practical information on talent development, workplace learning, and professional development.

ATD Press
1640 King Street
Alexandria, VA 22314

Ordering information for print edition: Books published by ATD Press can be purchased by visiting ATD's website at td.org/books or by calling 800.628.2783 or 703.683.8100.

Library of Congress Control Number: 2015945660 (print edition only)

ISBN-10: 1-56286-968-X
ISBN-13: 978-1-56286-968-7
e-ISBN: 978-1-60728-435-2

ATD Press Editorial Staff:
Director: Kristine Luecker
Manager: Christian Green
Community of Practice Manager, Learning & Development: Amanda Smith

Trainers Publishing House (TPH) Staff:
Publisher: Cat Russo
Project, Editorial, and Production Management: Jacqueline Edlund-Braun
TPH Copyeditor: Tora Estep
Cover and Text Design: Ana Ilieva Foreman/Design
Composition: Kristin Goble, PerfecType, Nashville, TN, and Debra Deysher, Double D Media, Reading, PA

Cover art: Shutterstock
Presentation Slide and Handout Art: Fotolia
Printed by Data Reproductions Corporation, Auburn Hills, MI, www.datarepro.com

The ATD Workshop Series

Whether you are a professional trainer who needs to pull together a new training program next week, or someone who does a bit of training as a part of your job, you'll find the ATD Workshop Series is a timesaver.

Topics deliver key learning on today's most pressing business needs, including training for communication skills, leadership, coaching, new supervisors, customer service, new employee orientation, and more. The series is designed for busy training and HR professionals, consultants, and managers who need to deliver training quickly to optimize performance now.

Each ATD Workshop book provides all the content and trainer's tools you need to create and deliver compelling training guaranteed to

- **enhance** learner engagement
- **deepen** learner understanding
- **increase** learning application.

Each book in the series offers innovative and engaging programs designed by leading experts and grounded in design and delivery best practices and theory. It is like having an expert trainer helping you with each step in the workshop process. The straightforward, practical instructions help you prepare and deliver the workshops quickly and effectively. Flexible timing options allow you to choose from half-day, one-day, and two-day workshop formats, or to create your own, using the tips and strategies presented for customizing the workshops to fit your unique business environment. Each ATD Workshop book also comes with guidance on leveraging learning technologies to maximize workshop design and delivery efficiency and access to all the training materials you will need, including activities, handouts, tools, assessments, and presentation slides.

Contents

Foreword

In 2002, we launched the ASTD Trainer's WorkShop Series—a collection of books authored by practitioners that focused on the design and delivery of training on popular soft-skills topics. The creation of this series was a departure for us. These workshops-in-a-book were created to help internal trainers expedite their program delivery by using appropriate and exceptionally designed content that could be adapted and repurposed.

These topics, dealing with issues ranging from customer service to leadership to manager skills, continue to be important training programs offered in companies and organizations of all sizes and across the globe. The ASTD Trainer's WorkShop Series has helped more than 60,000 trainers and occasional trainers deliver top-notch programs that meet business needs and help drive performance.

And while many things about the delivery of soft skills training have not changed in the last decade, there have been advances in technology and its use in training. So, when we began talking about how to refresh this popular series, we knew we needed to incorporate technology and new topics. We also wanted to make sure that the new series was cohesively designed and had input from author-practitioners who are, after all, the heart and soul of this series.

Inside *Customer Service Training,* by Kimberly Devlin, and each of the titles in the series, you'll find innovative content and fresh program agendas to simplify your delivery of key training topics. You'll also find consistency among titles, with each presented in a contemporary manner, designed by peers, and reflecting the preferences of training professionals who conduct workshops.

We hope that you find tremendous value in the ATD Workshop Series.

Tony Bingham
President & CEO
Association for Talent Development (ATD)
July 2015

Preface

"Yes!" A one-word sentence. Said with enthusiasm, it has led me to many adventures—authoring this book being just one. *Yes* has become my go-to response. Would you like to . . . ? Can you . . . ? Do you think you'd enjoy . . . ? Are you willing to try . . . ? Yes, yes, yes, and yes!

Here are some nos. Did I *know* what I was getting into? Was it easy to create learning events to fit all organizations and still be specific? Were my time estimates for completing this on target? Did I anticipate the number of scrapped approaches that would lead me to the final result? Do I regret a minute of it? No, no, no, no, no.

Typically, when asked to design a workshop (or three), my starting point is targeting the specific goals and gaps of the organization. In the case of customer service training, that would include determining whether organizational service standards exist, and either facilitating their creation or aligning the learning events to the existing standards. This project did not lend itself to that approach.

So, after multiple false starts and maybe a few frustrating afternoons at my desk, it was time to get an infusion of new perspective. One brief phone call (from my Jeep, in a parking lot, with my dog in the back) set me on track. Talking through the challenges I was encountering and listening to a mentor/business partner/friend provide an alternative approach seemed to put the pieces into place brilliantly. Until I was back at my desk! (But *you* are still brilliant, Ronnie.) The new strategy brought its own set of challenges. To quote a participant from a workshop: "When I fail, I learn." And learn I did!

Ultimately, all of this learning I experienced led to a series of workshops driven by three interrelated facets of service. I designed them with three different end goals in mind instead of by triage (that is, taking a "complete" program and whittling it down to fit ever-tighter time constraints). Each workshop has a specific purpose, and each might be appropriate to roll out to different populations in one organization. Or, each may fit best into organizations with certain support systems and cultural factors in place. (There is more on this in the Introduction.)

Saying *yes* to this invitation challenged me. It pushed me to find a new approach to what I thought I already knew. It simultaneously drew on my skills and developed them. If you have read this far (I commonly skip the preface), my hope is that by you saying *yes* to a request to implement an effective customer service training initiative, you also draw from your expertise and expand your skills too. That you not only enhance the skills of your participants, but develop yourself in ways you didn't expect. That you have as much fun with your customer service initiative as I did writing this book (even, maybe especially, when challenges arise for you too, for surely they might).

Yes still brings so much more potential for excitement, adventure, memory making, life experiences, and fun than *no*. Knowing what I do now, that I didn't know when I accepted the invitation to write this book, would I do it all again?

Yes!

Kimberly Devlin, CPLP
Ft. Lauderdale, FL
July 2015

How to Use This Book

What's in This Chapter

- Why customer service training is important
- Determining which workshop agenda will best meet your needs
- What you need to know about training
- Estimates of time required
- A broad view of what the book includes

Why Is Developing Customer Service Skills Important?

You may know the story of a letter to the editor of a newspaper on customer service. In short, the newspaper reported that a local government agency would be committing significant resources to training on customer service. It was expected to be expensive for the agency and time consuming for the staff. A resident wrote the editor that he had the solution at a mere fraction of the cost: "Tell them to be nice."

As good as that advice is, is it enough? From my experience, it isn't. Even when service providers are doing all the "right things," there are a lot of displeased customers because service *behaviors* are only one part of the equation. Equally critical are service *strategies* and service *systems*. Employees empowered to, trained to, and supported in their efforts to improve their service delivery strategies can effect significant positive change on the customer's experience. And, organizations that are committed to examining and reengineering their service systems can achieve incredible outcomes, related to both the customer experience and profitability.

This book is not limited to telling staff to be nice. Nor is it limited in focus to call center service situations. The workshops in it are applicable to any industry, to any employee, whether delivering service to external customers or to internal ones (think co-workers). The agendas and support materials are designed to

- Elicit specific techniques to manage challenging customers and situations
- Provide practice using a four-step process appropriate to any service interaction
- Prepare participants to respond to conflict
- Explore the current service environment (individually and organizationally)
- Shift employees' perspectives to that of the customer
- Lead participants to identify customers' pain points and mitigate them
- Guide participants to create mistake-proof techniques to avoid customer frustration.

Which Program Is Best?

The duration of each program will be a consideration but should not be the basis of your decision. Instead, consider these descriptions.

Half-Day Workshop: Service Behaviors That Matter

This session focuses on service behaviors: resolving difficult situations participants face, identifying conflict-causing and deescalating language, determining how to react when the customer is behaving poorly, and using a four-step HELP process when servicing any customer. It briefly introduces service strategies and service systems at the close.

The half-day workshop may be the right choice when the intended participants

- Deal extensively with angry customers
- Have little experience as service providers
- Will be limited in their authority to revise existing service strategies.

One-Day Workshop: From the Customer's Perspective

This session integrates a segment on service behaviors (specifically, using the four-step HELP process when servicing a customer) but primarily focuses on service strategies—from the *customer's* perspective. Participants will differentiate among service behaviors, strategies, and systems; be introduced to process improvement concepts and techniques; complete a self-assessment; collaborate to identify streamlining opportunities; devise improvements they can initiate; and develop action plans to implement them.

The one-day workshop may be the right choice when

- There is an organization-wide commitment to service
- Participants will be empowered to make inexpensive improvements to existing strategies
- Program sponsors and champions will look for, recognize, and reward application of the concepts following training
- A sustained approach to continuous service improvement is desired and will be supported.

Two-Day Workshop: A Total Approach to Service

As the name implies, this program covers service behaviors, strategies, and systems. Much of the half-day workshop, and many elements of the one-day workshop (above) are in this design, but it also includes creative problem-solving to take service strategies further. A key difference from the one-day agenda is this workshop's emphasis on service systems, which includes cross-functional process mapping, business reengineering, and collaborative action planning.

The two-day workshop may be the right choice when

- The organization is placing a significant priority on service
- Leadership is open to making big-picture changes in how things are done
- Time will be allocated, post-training, to continue the work of process mapping, business re-engineering, and process improvement
- The organization is pursuing external recognition/certification for being committed to quality service.

How Much Time Will Preparation Take?

Putting together and facilitating a training workshop, even when the agendas, activities, tools, and assessments are created for you, can be time consuming. For planning purposes, estimate about four days of preparation time for a two-day course.

What Do I Need to Know About Training?

The ATD Workshop Series is designed to be adaptable for many levels of both training facilitation and topic expertise. Circle the answers in the quick assessment on the next page that most closely align with your state of expertise.

QUICK ASSESSMENT: HOW EXPERT DO I NEED TO BE?			
Question	Authority	Developing Expertise	Novice
What is your level of expertise as a facilitator?	• More than 5 years of experience • Consistently receive awesome evaluations • Lead highly interactive sessions with strong participant engagement	• From 1 to 5 years of experience • Catch myself talking too much • May feel drained after training • Participants sometimes sit back and listen instead of engage	• Less than 1 year of experience • No idea what to do to be successful • Eager to develop a facilitative style
How proficient are you with the topic?	• Well-versed • Have taken courses • Read books/ authored articles • Created training materials • Am sought out by peers on this topic • And it is my passion	• On my way • Have taken courses • Read books • Created workshop materials • Would benefit from the book's support tools	• I can spell it! • Had a course in school • Receive feedback from respected colleagues that I have a natural inclination for this topic (but feel a bit like an imposter)

Two-fold novice: Your best bet is to stick closely to the materials as they are designed. Spend extra time with the content to learn as much as possible about it. Read the examples and sample stories, and plan examples of your own to share. Also, closely read Chapter 8 on training delivery, and consider practicing with a colleague before delivering the program. Take comfort in the tested materials you are holding and confidence in your ability to apply them!

Developing your expertise in one or both areas: Logical choices for you may include using the outline and materials, and then including material you have developed that is relevant to the topic *and* your participants' workplace needs. Or, take the core content of the materials and revise the learning techniques into interactive approaches you have used with success in the past. Play to your strengths and develop your growth areas using the resources in this volume that complement your existing skills.

Authority twice over: Feel free to adapt the agendas and materials as you see fit and use any materials that you have already developed, or simply incorporate training activities, handouts, and so forth from this volume into your own agenda. Enjoy the benefits of ready-to-use processes and support tools and have fun tailoring them to your preferences and organizational needs.

What Are the Important Features of the Book?

Section I includes the various workshop designs (from half-day to two days) with agendas and thumbnails from presentation slides as well as a chapter on customizing the workshop for your circumstances. The chapters included are

- Chapter 1. Half-Day Workshop (3 hours program time) + Agenda + PPT (thumbnails)
- Chapter 2. One-Day Workshop (7.5 hours program time) + Agenda + PPT (thumbnails)
- Chapter 3. Two-Day Workshop (15 hours program time) + Agenda + PPT (thumbnails)
- Chapter 4. Customizing the *Customer Service Training* Workshop.

The workshop chapters include advice, instructions, workshop at-a-glance tables, as well as full program agendas.

Section II is standard from book to book in the ATD Workshop Series as a way to provide a consistent foundation of training principles. This section's chapters follow the ADDIE model—the classic instructional design model named after its steps (analysis, design, development, implementation, and evaluation). The chapters are based on best practices and crafted with input from experienced training practitioners. They are meant to help you get up to speed as quickly as possible. Each chapter includes several additional recurring features to help you understand the concepts and ideas presented. The Bare Minimum gives you the bare bones of what you need to know about the topic. Key Points summarize the most important points of each chapter. What to Do Next guides you to your next action steps. And, finally, the Additional Resources section at the end of each chapter gives you options for further reading to broaden your understanding of training design and delivery. Section II chapters include

- Chapter 5. Identifying Needs for Customer Service Training
- Chapter 6. Understanding the Foundations of Training Design
- Chapter 7. Leveraging Technology to Maximize and Support Design and Delivery
- Chapter 8. Delivering Your Customer Service Workshop: Be a Great Facilitator
- Chapter 9. Evaluating Workshop Results.

Section III covers information about post-workshop learning:

- Chapter 10. The Follow-Up Coach.

Section IV includes all the supporting documents and online guidance:

- Chapter 11. Learning Activities
- Chapter 12. Assessments

- Chapter 13. Handouts
- Chapter 14. Online Tools and Downloads.

The book includes everything you need to prepare for and deliver your workshop:

- **Agendas,** the heart of the series, are laid out in three columns for ease of delivery. The first column shows the timing, the second gives the presentation slide number and image for quick reference, and the third gives instructions and facilitation notes. These are designed to be straightforward, simple agendas that you can take into the training room and use to stay on track. They include cues on the learning activities, notes about tools or handouts to include, and other important delivery tips. You can download the agendas from the website (see Chapter 14) and print them out for easy use.

- **Learning activities,** which are more detailed than the agendas, cover the objectives of the activity, the time and materials required, the steps involved, variations on the activity in some cases, and wrap-up or debriefing questions or comments.

- **Assessments, handouts, and tools** are the training materials you will provide to learners to support the training program. These can include scorecards for games, instructions, reference materials, samples, self-assessments, and so forth.

- **Presentation media** (PowerPoint slides) are deliberately designed to be simple so that you can customize them for your company and context. They are provided for your convenience. Chapter 7 discusses different forms of technology that you can incorporate into your program, including different types of presentation media.

All the program materials are available for download, customization, and duplication. See Chapter 14 for instructions on how to access the materials.

How Are the Agendas Laid Out?

The following agenda is a sample from the two-day workshop.

Day One: (9:00 a.m. to 4:30 p.m.)

TIMING	SLIDES	ACTIVITIES/NOTES/CONSIDERATIONS
	Slide 1 ATD Workshop A Total Approach to Service Systems · Strategies · Behaviors © 2013 Kimberly Devlin. Used with permission | SLIDE A1	**Create a Positive Learning Environment** Display this opening slide and welcome participants as they arrive.

TIMING	SLIDES	ACTIVITIES/NOTES/CONSIDERATIONS
9:00 a.m. (10 min)	Slide 2 *Service-Themed Graffiti* • Use color, images, and words to *tag* the graffiti charts • Work quickly...don't get caught!	**Welcome/** **Learning Activity 26: Wall Graffiti** Use this learning activity to create immediate involvement and to draw out the participants' perspectives, *not* as housekeeping, introductions, or generalized "welcoming" comments (you will do that later in the workshop). Set the tone for the learning event as an active, contributory, and fun experience.
9:10 a.m. (5 min)	Slide 3 Learning Objectives – Day One • Strengthen relationships and awareness of service challenges • Distinguish among service behaviors, strategies, and systems • Assess your service environment to target improvement opportunities • Document a process map for a customer-critical service system	**Program Objectives/** **Learning Activity 27: Prioritize Learning** • **Handout 27: Learning Objectives** This individual activity introduces the workshop's learning objectives for both days, encouraging participants to begin engaging with the objectives.
9:15 a.m. (10 min)	Slide 4 Social Agreements • Create a list of guidelines to adhere to for a fun, effective workshop	**Ground Rules/** **Learning Activity 28: Social Agreements** Guided by your facilitation, this activity will help participants generate a list of guidelines that will drive their behavior for the two days. During the debrief, reach consensus on how the group will monitor and correct breaches of these agreements (so that you are not placed in the role of sole enforcer).

How Do I Use This Book?

If you've ever read a "Choose Your Own Adventure" book, you will recognize that this book follows a similar principle. Think back to the self-assessment at the beginning of this introduction:

- If you chose *authority*, you can get right to work preparing one of the workshops in Section I. Use Section II as a reference. Each of the chapters in Section II features a sidebar or other information written by the author who has much experience in the topic under consideration. This advice can help guide your preparation, delivery, and evaluation of training.

- If you chose *developing expertise*, read Section II in depth and skim the topic content.

- If you chose *novice at training and the topic,* then spend some serious time familiarizing yourself with both Sections I and II of this volume as well as the topic content.

Once you have a general sense of the material, assemble your workshop. Select the appropriate agenda and then modify the times and training activities as needed and desired. Assemble the materials and familiarize yourself with the topic, the activities, and the presentation media.

Key Points

- Improving an organization's customer service climate may require more than just focusing on service behaviors.
- The service culture and service goals of your organization should factor heavily into your workshop selection and modification choices.
- The workshops in this book are designed to be effective at all levels of trainer expertise.
- Good training requires an investment of time.
- The book contains everything you need to create a workshop, including agendas, learning activities, presentation media, assessments, handouts, and tools.

What to Do Next

- Review the agendas presented in Section I and select the best fit for your requirements, time constraints, and budget.
- Based on your level of expertise, skim or read in-depth the chapters in Section II.
- Consider what kind of follow-up learning activities you will want to include with the workshop by reviewing Section III.

Additional Resources

Biech, E. (2008). *10 Steps to Successful Training.* Alexandria, VA: ASTD Press.

Biech, E., ed. (2014). *ASTD Handbook: The Definitive Reference for Training & Development,* 2nd edition. Alexandria, VA: ASTD Press.

Emerson, T., and M. Stewart. (2011). *The Learning and Development Book.* Alexandria, VA: ASTD Press.

McCain, D.V., and D.D. Tobey. (2004). *Facilitation Basics.* Alexandria, VA: ASTD Press.

Piskurich, G. (2003). *Trainer Basics.* Alexandria, VA: ASTD Press.

Stolovitch, H.D., and E.J. Keeps. (2011). *Telling Ain't Training,* 2nd edition. Alexandria, VA: ASTD Press.

SECTION I

The Workshops

Chapter 1

Half-Day Customer Service Workshop: Service Behaviors That Matter

What's in This Chapter

- Objectives of the half-day Customer Service Workshop
- Summary chart for the flow of content and activities
- Half-day program agenda

Do your workshop participants have limited experience as effective service providers? Are they routinely dealing with angry customers? Will the concept of internal customers be new to them? Is the organization's leadership asking for improved service behaviors? If you answered yes to any of these questions, then this workshop is a logical match to meet the training need. With a focus on resolving difficult situations, identifying language that deescalates conflict, reacting effectively when the customer is behaving poorly, and following a four-step HELP process, this comprehensive half-day session will provide engaging and powerful tools to help service providers improve the customer experience at your organization. Get ready to have some fun with this workshop.

Half-Day Workshop Objectives: Service Behaviors That Matter

Here are the learning objectives for the half-day workshop:

- Develop a personalized set of phrases and actions to increase customer satisfaction.

- Diffuse escalating customer situations through word choice and actions.

- Follow the four-step HELP process for customer interactions.

- Distinguish service behaviors from service strategies and service systems.

Half-Day Workshop Overview

TOPICS	TIMING
Welcome/Learning Activity 1: Intriguing Question or Story	5 minutes
Icebreaker/Learning Activity 2: Hello, My Idea Is . . .	15 minutes
Program Objectives and Social Agreements/Learning Activity 3: Prioritize Learning	5 minutes
Learning Objective 1/Learning Activity 4: I'm Stumped	30 minutes
Learning Objective 2/Learning Activity 5: Keep a Cool Head	20 minutes
BREAK	**15 minutes**
Learning Objective 2/Learning Activity 6: Quit Taking It Personally (Q-Tip)	20 minutes
Learning Objective 3/Learning Activity 7: The HELP Process for Customer Interactions	15 minutes
Learning Objective 3/Learning Activity 8: HELP the Customer	40 minutes
Learning Objective 4/Learning Activity 9: Interconnected Service Facets	10 minutes
Course Closure	5 minutes
TOTAL	**180 minutes (3 hours)**

A Word About Presentation Slides and Handouts

The presentation slides for this workshop have been animated to enhance their effectiveness. They can be used effectively in the pdf format (which are static), but if you choose to use the fully customizable versions and display the slides in slide show mode, many will have motion and builds. These animations are not merely movement; they are structured to enhance the visuals' effectiveness, provide greater facilitative control of group discussions, manage cognitive load by chunking content in keeping with activity instructions, and in some instances, even provide feedback to the participants. Some animations are controlled by advancing the slides, and others are automated for you. This is intentional to guide certain activities and to offer you facilitative flexibility in others. Make time to familiarize yourself with the animations and plan how you will leverage them. You can run the workshop effectively using the pdf versions; however, if you are accessing the presentation slides in their native format through an optional license, be sure to display them in slide show mode to derive their full benefit!

Please note that some slides in this workshop may also appear in the one-day or two-day workshops. Their animations here may be a bit different, in support of this workshop's structure. Please be sure to familiarize yourself with these animations, even if you previously reviewed a different workshop's visuals.

Each workshop has been designed as a continuous event. If facilitated that way, it may be logical for you to assemble all of the associated handouts into one bound workbook to distribute to participants when they arrive. In this case, where the learning activities direct you to distribute a handout, you may want to make note of and refer to the appropriate workbook pages during the workshop.

Half-Day Workshop Agenda

Even in a half-day workshop, time can get away from you. Interesting questions, lengthy group discussions, and tangential concerns can all potentially enhance or derail a workshop agenda. You are encouraged to keep this table readily available for reference during the workshop and to support you in remaining on schedule while being responsive to participants' unique needs. You will also want a reference set of the handouts (Chapter 13) and the details of the workshop design included in the learning activity pages (Chapter 11)—be sure to have those pages available during your facilitation.

Half Day: (9:00 a.m. to 12:00 p.m.)

TIMING	SLIDES	ACTIVITIES/NOTES/CONSIDERATIONS
9:00 a.m. (5 min)	Slide 1 ATD Workshop Service Behaviors That Matter	**Welcome/** **Learning Activity 1: Intriguing Question or Story** Plan an opener that sets the tone for the learning event—ideas are included in the learning activity; choose one or create your own. Start strong, grab your learners' interest, and let them see the value of this learning event to their workplace performance. Use this learning activity to establish the learners' expectations, *not* as housekeeping, introductions, or generalized "welcoming" comments (you will do that later in the workshop).
9:05 a.m. (15 min)	Slide 2 Hello, My Idea Is… • Take an "idea tag" • Think of a service behavior you want to be remembered by • Write the idea on your sticker • Meet 3-5 new "ideas" (and their people too!)	**Icebreaker/** **Learning Activity 2: Hello, My Idea Is . . .** • **Handout 1: Hello, My Idea Is . . .** This large group activity will help participants meet other participants and share their strategies for effectively delivering customer service. To help them get started, share an example of an effective customer service idea from your own best practices. Use the instructions in the learning activity to guide the exercise. Following the debrief, integrate a complete self-introduction, focusing on your experience and expertise with customer service.
9:20 a.m. (5 min)	Slide 3 Learning Objectives • Develop a set of phrases/actions to increase customer satisfaction • Diffuse escalating situations through word choice and actions • Follow the four-step HELP process for customer interactions • Distinguish among service behaviors, strategies, and systems	**Program Objectives and Social Agreements/** **Learning Activity 3: Prioritize Learning** • **Handout 2: Learning Objectives** This individual activity introduces the workshop's learning objectives. You are encouraged to share a prepared chart of social agreements (ground rules) appropriate to your group after the activity.

TIMING	SLIDES	ACTIVITIES/NOTES/CONSIDERATIONS

9:25 a.m.
(30 min)
	Slide 4
	
	I'm Stumped
	• Think of a customer service interaction that "stumps" you
	• Maybe…
	  – it gets you every time
	  – you are dissatisfied with the outcome
	  – you just don't know how to handle it
	  – you want a new strategy
		Learning Objective 1/
		Learning Activity 4: I'm Stumped
		• **Handout 3: I'm Stumped Idea Starters**
		
		This team activity supports the first learning objective—develop a personalized set of phrases and actions to use to increase customer satisfaction.
		
		Following a brief discussion of barriers to delivering quality service to every customer, ask participants to write a service challenge that "stumps" them on an envelope. Encourage them to choose a challenge for which they would like fresh ideas from the group.
		
		Use the instructions in the learning activity and on these two slides to conduct the activity. Lead a large group discussion to debrief the exercise (questions are included at the end of the learning activity).
		
		(Slide 1 of 2)

	Slide 5 • Write your situation on the outside of an envelope • Pass envelopes as directed • Write a suggested action on an index card and place it inside the envelope • Pass envelopes again…	(Slide 2 of 2)
9:55 a.m. (20 min)	Slide 6 Some words have a tendency to cause conflict Others reduce (or avoid) the conflict effectively	**Learning Objective 2/** **Learning Activity 5: Keep a Cool Head** • **Handout 4: Keep a Cool Head** This large group activity supports the second learning objective—diffuse escalating customer situations through word choice and actions. In this activity, participants identify terms and phrases that increase conflict, strategize on how to respond to them to reduce their conflict-causing effects, and list alternative phrases so that *they* do not create the conflict. Use the instructions in the learning activity and these three slides to conduct the exercise. (Slide 1 of 3)

TIMING	SLIDES	ACTIVITIES/NOTES/CONSIDERATIONS
	Slide 7 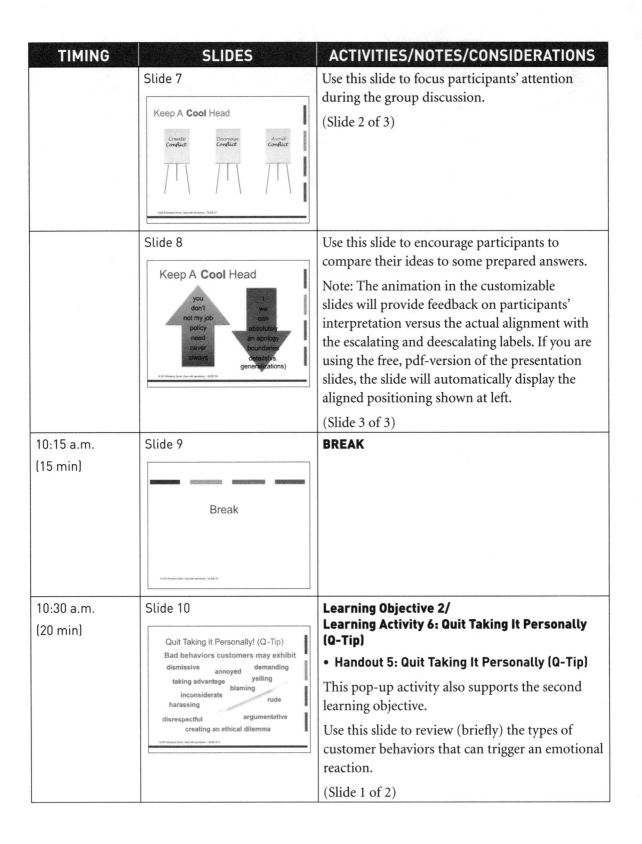	Use this slide to focus participants' attention during the group discussion. (Slide 2 of 3)
	Slide 8	Use this slide to encourage participants to compare their ideas to some prepared answers. Note: The animation in the customizable slides will provide feedback on participants' interpretation versus the actual alignment with the escalating and deescalating labels. If you are using the free, pdf-version of the presentation slides, the slide will automatically display the aligned positioning shown at left. (Slide 3 of 3)
10:15 a.m. (15 min)	Slide 9 Break	**BREAK**
10:30 a.m. (20 min)	Slide 10	**Learning Objective 2/** **Learning Activity 6: Quit Taking It Personally (Q-Tip)** • **Handout 5: Quit Taking It Personally (Q-Tip)** This pop-up activity also supports the second learning objective. Use this slide to review (briefly) the types of customer behaviors that can trigger an emotional reaction. (Slide 1 of 2)

TIMING	SLIDES	ACTIVITIES/NOTES/CONSIDERATIONS
	Slide 11 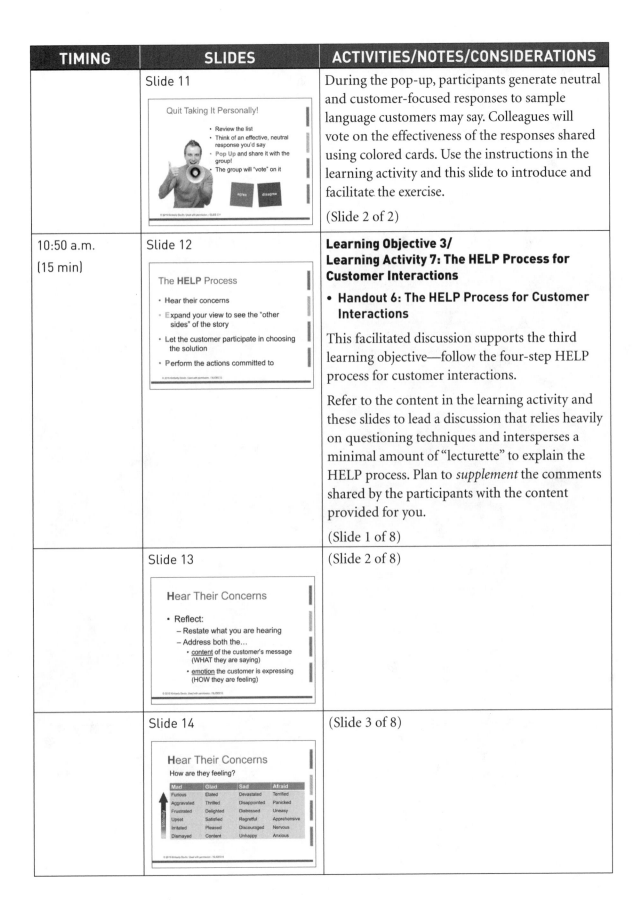	During the pop-up, participants generate neutral and customer-focused responses to sample language customers may say. Colleagues will vote on the effectiveness of the responses shared using colored cards. Use the instructions in the learning activity and this slide to introduce and facilitate the exercise. (Slide 2 of 2)
10:50 a.m. (15 min)	Slide 12	**Learning Objective 3/** **Learning Activity 7: The HELP Process for Customer Interactions** • **Handout 6: The HELP Process for Customer Interactions** This facilitated discussion supports the third learning objective—follow the four-step HELP process for customer interactions. Refer to the content in the learning activity and these slides to lead a discussion that relies heavily on questioning techniques and intersperses a minimal amount of "lecturette" to explain the HELP process. Plan to *supplement* the comments shared by the participants with the content provided for you. (Slide 1 of 8)
	Slide 13	(Slide 2 of 8)
	Slide 14	(Slide 3 of 8)

TIMING	SLIDES	ACTIVITIES/NOTES/CONSIDERATIONS
	Slide 15	(Slide 4 of 8)

	Hear Their Concerns
	• Sentence stems:
	  – "It sounds like…"
	  – "Am I right that you are feeling… about…"
	  – "Is it correct that…"
	  – "Can I make sure I have this correct…"
	  – "I'd like to make sure I have this right…"
	  – "I hear that you are… over the…"	

	Slide 16	(Slide 5 of 8)

	Expand Your View to See Other Sides
	• Probing Questions and Statements:
	  – Are open-ended
	  – Provide a bigger picture of the situation
	  – Uncover information the customer didn't think to share
	  – Shed light on the "other sides" of the story	

	Slide 17	(Slide 6 of 8)
	Expand Your View to See Other Sides *(table of Probing Stems and Sample Open-Ended Questions/Statements: What, When, Where, How, Why, Tell Me/Give Me)*	
	Slide 18	(Slide 7 of 8)
	Let the Customer Participate in Choosing the Solution **What does this mean to you?**	
	Slide 19	(Slide 8 of 8)
	Perform the Actions Committed To Details · Deadlines · Follow through · Follow up	

TIMING	SLIDES	ACTIVITIES/NOTES/CONSIDERATIONS
11:05 a.m. (40 min)	Slide 20 HELP Interviews • Find a partner you don't know well • Partner 1 interviews Partner 2 • Partner 2 interviews Partner 1	**Learning Objective 3/** **Learning Activity 8: HELP the Customer** • **Handout 7: HELP the Customer—Interview Tool** • **Handout 8: HELP the Customer—Planning Worksheet** • **Handout 9: HELP the Customer—Observer Worksheet** This two-part activity also supports the third learning objective. Part one involves partner interviews to elicit real-world challenges. Part two provides an opportunity to role play the challenges surfaced during the interviews. Use the instructions in the learning activity and this slide to pair up participants for interviews. (Slide 1 of 3)
	Slide 21 Role Play with HELP 1. **Plan:** Use 12 minutes to plan both role plays 2. **Role Play:** Use 4 minutes to role play one situation, using HELP (with two observers) 3. **Feedback:** Use 3 minutes to give feedback to the service provider **REPEAT steps 2 and 3** to work through all four scenarios	Use the instructions in the learning activity and this slide to lead participants to prepare for quad role plays. (Slide 2 of 3)
	Slide 22 HELP the Customer • Hear their concerns • Expand your view to see the "other sides" of the story • Let the customer participate in choosing the solution • Perform the actions committed to	Display this slide during the quad role plays as a support tool participants may want to reference. (Slide 3 of 3)

TIMING	SLIDES	ACTIVITIES/NOTES/CONSIDERATIONS
11:45 a.m. (10 min)	Slide 23 Interconnected Service Facets • Behaviors – person-to-person skills • Strategies – a step in a system (within your control) • Systems – processes	**Learning Objective 4/** **Learning Activity 9: Interconnected Service Facets** • **Handout 10: Interconnected Service Facets** This facilitated discussion supports the fourth learning objective—distinguish service behaviors from service strategies and service systems. Use the content in the learning activity and this slide to introduce the idea that there are three service facets and this workshop focused on just one (service behaviors).
11:55 a.m. (5 min) End at noon.	Slide 24 ATD Workshop Service Behaviors That Matter	**Course Closure** • **Handout 11: Course Evaluation—Service Behaviors That Matter** Share next steps (if program is part of a larger organizational initiative). Collect completed course evaluations. Distribute certificates (if provided).

What to Do Next

- Review Chapter 10 and create your workshop support plan:
  - Select the most effective pre- and post-workshop communication strategies.
  - Involve participants' managers early on.
  - Choose the follow-up coaching strategies that most efficiently align with your workshop rollout.
- Manage workshop logistics:
  - Identify participants.
  - Schedule the workshop date, reserve an appropriate location, and invite participants.
  - Inform participants about any pre-work, if you are adding it to the workshop.
  - Prepare copies of the participant handouts (refer to Chapter 14 for information about how to access and use the supplemental materials provided for this workshop).
  - Coordinate catering, if being provided.

- Prepare yourself for the workshop:
  - Review the workshop objectives, learning activities, and handouts to plan the content you will use.
  - Confirm that you have addressed scheduling and personal concerns so that you can be fully present to facilitate the class.
  - Set an out-of-office email auto response for the day of the workshop.
- Pack your bag:
  - Gather the workshop essentials: participant materials, slide show file, facilitator notes (learning activity pages in Chapter 11), and any activity materials noted in the learning activities (such as customized manipulatives, index cards, envelopes, or others).
  - Coordinate or bring audio-visual equipment: laptop, projector, speakers, and remote control for presentation slides.
  - Pack training room basics: markers, tape, easels, flip charts, and tactile items, such as Koosh balls, Play-Doh, or others, to place on the tables for tactile learners.
  - See Chapter 8 for other ideas to enhance the learning environment of your workshop.

Chapter 2

One-Day Customer Service Workshop: From the Customer's Perspective

What's in This Chapter

- Objectives of the one-day Customer Service Workshop
- Summary chart for the flow of content and activities
- One-day program agenda

This workshop's primary focus is on service strategies—from the *customer's* perspective. Throughout the activities and discussions, be prepared to drive home the importance of that point. Participants may be tempted to look at service strategies from the perspective of what is easiest or best for them, rather than for the customer. Redirect participants when needed, by asking questions such as "I hear you, I am just wondering how that is best for the customer?" or "And the way that benefits the customer is . . . ?" An effectively worded redirection statement or question will have greater impact than "telling participants they are wrong."

Participants leave this workshop with a service delivery model to apply immediately and a set of newly created process improvements to implement, making it a rewarding workshop to facilitate. Have fun with it and be sure to be prepared with concrete examples of where and how *you* are using the strategies in the workplace.

One-Day Workshop Objectives: From the Customer's Perspective

Here are the learning objectives for the one-day workshop:

- Distinguish service behaviors from service strategies and service systems.
- Assess your service environment to target improvement opportunities.
- Follow the four-step HELP process for efficient customer interactions.
- Improve existing service strategies from the customer's perspective.
- Examine the organization's service systems for breakdowns from the customer's perspective.
- Create implementation plans with a peer support component.

One-Day Workshop Overview

TOPICS	TIMING
Welcome/Learning Activity 10: Initial Reactions	15 minutes
Icebreaker/Learning Activity 11: Services Heroes	20 minutes
Program Objectives and Social Agreements/Learning Activity 12: Prioritize Learning	5 minutes
Learning Objective 1/Learning Activity 13: Interconnected Service Facets	15 minutes
Learning Objective 1/Learning Activity 14: Do They Agree?	25 minutes
BREAK	**15 minutes**
Learning Objective 2/Learning Activity 15: Performance Improvement Service Levels	20 minutes
Learning Objective 2/Learning Activity 16: Where Are We Now?	15 minutes
Transition to Service Behaviors	
Learning Objective 3/Learning Activity 17: The HELP Process for Customer Interactions	10 minutes
Learning Objective 3/Learning Activity 18: HELP the Customer: Interviews and Role Plays	40 minutes
LUNCH	**60 minutes**
Morning Review and Transition to Afternoon/Learning Activity 19: Quick Start	10 minutes
Transition to Service Strategies	
Learning Objective 4/Learning Activity 20: Mistake Proofing	20 minutes

TOPICS	TIMING
Learning Objective 4/Learning Activity 21: Creating Mistake-Proof Techniques	40 minutes
BREAK	**15 minutes**
Learning Objective 4/Learning Activity 21: Creating Mistake-Proof Techniques (Take 2)	30 minutes
Learning Objective 4/Learning Activity 22: Critiquing Mistake-Proof Techniques	20 minutes
Transition to Service Systems	
Learning Objective 5/Learning Activity 23: Our Service Systems	30 minutes
Learning Objective 5/Learning Activity 24: Where and How Can I Help?	20 minutes
Learning Objective 6/Learning Activity 25: Where We Go From Here	20 minutes
Course Closure	5 minutes
TOTAL	**450 minutes (7.5 hours)**

A Word About Presentation Slides and Handouts

The presentation slides for this workshop have been animated to enhance their effectiveness. They can be used effectively in the pdf format (which are static), but if you choose to use the fully customizable versions and display the slides in slide show mode, many will have motion and builds. These animations are not merely movement; they are structured to enhance the visuals' effectiveness, provide greater facilitative control of group discussions, manage cognitive load by chunking content in keeping with activity instructions, and in some instances, even provide feedback to the participants. Some animations are controlled by advancing the slides, and others are automated for you. This is intentional to guide certain activities and to offer you facilitative flexibility in others. Make time to familiarize yourself with the animations and plan how you will leverage them. You can run the workshop effectively using the pdf version; however, if you are accessing the presentation slides in their native format through an optional license, be sure to display them in slide show mode to derive their full benefit!

Please note that some slides in this workshop may also appear in the half-day or two-day workshops. Their animations here may be a bit different, in support of this workshop's structure. Please be sure to familiarize yourself with these animations, even if you previously reviewed a different workshop's visuals.

Each workshop has been designed as a continuous event. If facilitated that way, it may be logical for you to assemble all of the one-day workshop handouts and the assessment into a single, bound workbook to distribute to participants when they arrive. In this case, where the learning activities direct you to distribute a handout or assessment, you may want to make note of and, during the workshop, refer to the appropriate workbook pages. TIP: The assessment for Learning Activity 16 should fall between Handouts 17 and 18 if you choose to bind the participant materials.

For ease of navigation throughout the book, learning activities and handouts for all three workshops are numbered sequentially. Therefore, this workshop begins with Learning Activity 10 and the first handout is number 12. Each handout has a name as well. For a seamless participant experience, I suggest you refer to the handouts and assessment by name, page number (if bound), or renumber them to begin with number 1.

One-Day Workshop Agenda

You can use the agenda on the following pages as a quick-reference, birds-eye view to the workshop while you are facilitating. The learning activity pages in Chapter 11 will provide the detail in support of the workshop design, so be sure to have those pages available during your facilitation, as well as a reference set of the handouts.

One Day: (9:00 a.m. to 4:30 p.m.)

TIMING	SLIDES	ACTIVITIES/NOTES/CONSIDERATIONS
9:00 a.m. (15 min)	Slide 1 ATD Workshop From the Customer's Perspective	**Welcome/** **Learning Activity 10: Initial Reactions** Plan an opener that sets the tone for the learning event. Start strong, grab your learners' interest, and let them see the value of this learning event to their workplace performance. Use this learning activity to establish the learners' expectations, *not* as housekeeping, introductions, or generalized "welcoming" comments (you will do that later in the workshop). Or, if you choose, the learning activity gives an alternate activity involving customer service statistics to substitute for the initial reactions exercise. Use the opener that will be most engaging for your particular group.

TIMING	SLIDES	ACTIVITIES/NOTES/CONSIDERATIONS
9:15 a.m. (20 min)	Slide 2 Service Heroes • A customer service strength I have is_____ • Two ways I demonstrate it are: 1. 2.	**Icebreaker/Learning Activity 11: Service Heroes** • **Handout 12: Service Heroes** This large group activity will help participants meet other participants and highlight their strengths in and strategies for effectively delivering customer service. Use the instructions in the learning activity to guide the exercise. To help participants get started, share an example of your own to demonstrate how they might complete Part 1 of the handout. Following the debrief, integrate a complete self-introduction, focusing on your experience and expertise with customer service. See the learning activity notes for ideas on what to include to establish your credibility.
9:35 a.m. (5 min)	Slide 3 Learning Objectives - Morning • Distinguish between service behaviors, strategies, and systems • Assess your service environment to target improvement opportunities • Follow the four-step HELP process	**Program Objectives and Social Agreements/ Learning Activity 12: Prioritize Learning** • **Handout 13: Learning Objectives** • **Handout 14: Participant Journal** This individual activity introduces the workshop's learning objectives and provides participants with a personal journaling tool. Use this slide to introduce the objectives you will explore during the morning session. (Slide 1 of 2)
	Slide 4 Learning Objectives - Afternoon • Improve existing service strategies… from the customer's perspective • Examine the organization's service systems for breakdowns…from the customer's perspective • Create implementation plans with a peer support component	Use this slide to present the objectives you will explore during the afternoon session of the workshop. You are encouraged to share a prepared chart of social agreements (ground rules) appropriate to your group after the activity. (Slide 2 of 2)

TIMING	SLIDES	ACTIVITIES/NOTES/CONSIDERATIONS
9:40 a.m. (15 min)	Slide 5 Interconnected Service Facets • Behaviors — person-to-person skills • Strategies — a step in a system (within your control) • Systems — processes	**Learning Objective 1/** **Learning Activity 13: Interconnected Service Facets** • **Handout 15: Interconnected Service Facets** This facilitated discussion supports the first learning objective—distinguish service behaviors from service approaches and service systems. Lead a discussion of the three elements that contribute to the customer's overall experience, referring to the content in the learning activity. Be sure to use questioning to draw information, ideas, and examples from the participants. Plan to *supplement* the comments shared by the participants with the content provided for you to avoid turning this into lecture.
9:55 a.m. (25 min)	Slide 6 Do They Agree? • Brainstorm examples of: — service behaviors — service strategies — service systems • Choose your top 5-7 in each category to be used in the challenge activity	**Learning Objective 1/** **Learning Activity 14: Do They Agree?** • **Handout 16: Do They Agree?** Learning Activity 14 also supports the first learning objective. During this team challenge, participants create a card sorting activity (and answer key) to be completed by participants at the next table. Use this slide and the learning activity instructions to start the activity. (Slide 1 of 3)
	Slide 7 • Record your selected examples on the Answer Key handout • Write each example on an index card • Place the shuffled cards and folded answer key inside the envelope • Pass your envelope to the next table	Continue to guide participants through the activity with this slide and the learning activity instructions. (Slide 2 of 3)

TIMING	SLIDES	ACTIVITIES/NOTES/CONSIDERATIONS
	Slide 8	Use this slide and the learning activity instructions to provide direction on what to do with the activity materials created by other table groups. During the debrief, guide table groups to rotate from one table to the next, where they review each other's work and ideas. (Slide 3 of 3)
10:20 a.m. (15 min)	Slide 9	**BREAK**
10:35 a.m. (20 min)	Slide 10	**Learning Objective 2/ Learning Activity 15: Performance Improvement Service Levels** • **Handout 17: Performance Improvement** This partner talk activity supports the second learning objective—assess your service environment to target improvement opportunities. Ask participants to team up and discuss their interpretations of As Is, Should Be, and Could Be based on the slide image. Then lead a large group discussion to clarify and expand on the partner talk content. (Slide 1 of 5)
	Slide 11	Use this slide and the learning activity instructions to provide additional context for As Is, Should Be, and Could Be, and as a transition into a large group discussion. (Slide 2 of 5)

TIMING	SLIDES	ACTIVITIES/NOTES/CONSIDERATIONS

	Slide 12
	
	As Is Level
	As Is
	• Where we are right now
	  – objective assessment
	  – no justifications
	  – no explanations
	  – just a true assessment
	
	If we don't know where we **are**…how can we **measure** our **progress?**
		Begin a large group discussion on As Is, referring to the slide and learning activity for content.
		
		(Slide 3 of 5)

	Slide 13
	
	Should Be Level
	Should Be
	• What is possible with…
	  – existing resources
	  – creative thinking
	  – streamlining
	  – asking (and answering) how can we/I do this more effectively/efficiently
		Continue the large group discussion on Should Be, referring to the slide and learning activity for content.
		
		(Slide 4 of 5)

	Slide 14
	
	Could Be Level
	Could Be
	• What we might achieve if…
	  – resources are reallocated
	  – departments collaborate
	  – we stop worrying about who gets credit for ideas
	  – updates are made
	  – processes are redesigned
		Wrap up the large group discussion with the Could Be level, referring to the slide and learning activity for content.
		
		(Slide 5 of 5)

10:55 a.m. (15 min)	Slide 15 Assessment	**Learning Objective 2/** **Learning Activity 16: Where Are We Now?** • **Assessment 1: Where Are We Now?** This assessment activity also supports the second learning objective. There are three sections to the assessment aligned with the three service facets. In each section there is space or a question allowing participants to personalize the assessment. NOTE: Be sure to integrate the instrument for this activity (in Chapter 11) with the other handouts (in Chapter 13).

TIMING	SLIDES	ACTIVITIES/NOTES/CONSIDERATIONS
	Slide 16 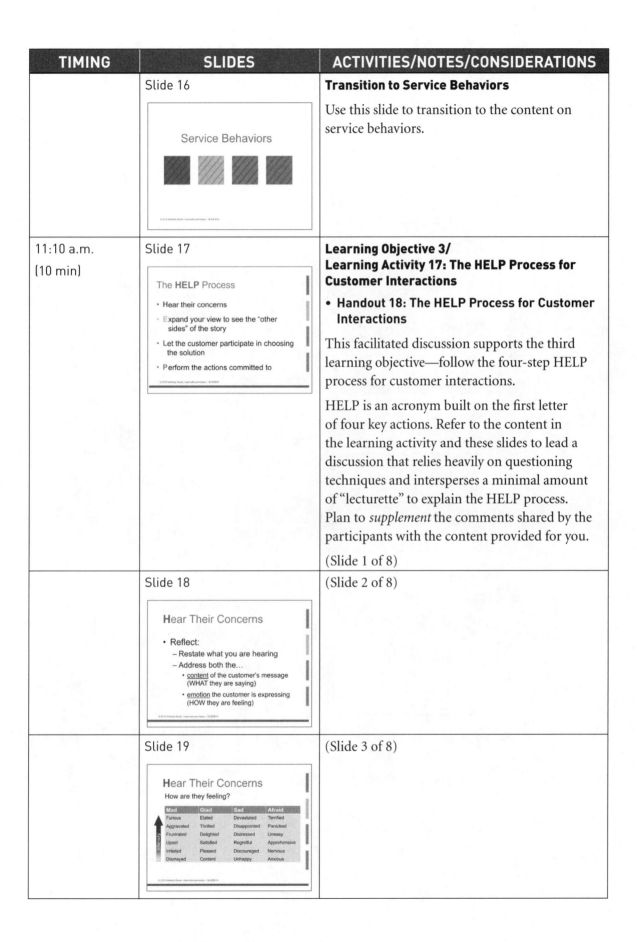	**Transition to Service Behaviors** Use this slide to transition to the content on service behaviors.
11:10 a.m. (10 min)	Slide 17	**Learning Objective 3/** **Learning Activity 17: The HELP Process for Customer Interactions** • **Handout 18: The HELP Process for Customer Interactions** This facilitated discussion supports the third learning objective—follow the four-step HELP process for customer interactions. HELP is an acronym built on the first letter of four key actions. Refer to the content in the learning activity and these slides to lead a discussion that relies heavily on questioning techniques and intersperses a minimal amount of "lecturette" to explain the HELP process. Plan to *supplement* the comments shared by the participants with the content provided for you. (Slide 1 of 8)
	Slide 18	(Slide 2 of 8)
	Slide 19	(Slide 3 of 8)

TIMING	SLIDES	ACTIVITIES/NOTES/CONSIDERATIONS
	Slide 20 **H**ear Their Concerns • Sentence stems: – "It sounds like…" – "Am I right that you are feeling… about…" – "Is it correct that…" – "Can I make sure I have this correct…" – "I'd like to make sure I have this right…" – "I hear that you are… over the…"	(Slide 4 of 8)
	Slide 21 Expand Your View to See Other Sides • Probing Questions and Statements: – Are open-ended – Provide a bigger picture of the situation – Uncover information the customer didn't think to share – Shed light on the "other sides" of the story	(Slide 5 of 8)
	Slide 22 Expand Your View to See Other Sides	(Slide 6 of 8)
	Slide 23 Let the Customer Participate in Choosing the Solution **What does this mean to you?**	(Slide 7 of 8)
	Slide 24 Perform the Actions Committed To Details Deadlines Follow through Follow up	(Slide 8 of 8)

TIMING	SLIDES	ACTIVITIES/NOTES/CONSIDERATIONS
11:20 a.m. (40 min)	Slide 25 HELP Interviews • Find a partner you don't know well • Partner 1 interviews Partner 2 • Partner 2 interviews Partner 1	**Learning Objective 3/ Learning Activity 18: HELP the Customer: Interviews and Role Plays** • Handout 19: HELP the Customer—Interview Tool • Handout 20: HELP the Customer—Planning Worksheet • Handout 21: HELP the Customer—Observer Worksheet This two-part activity also supports the third learning objective. Part one involves partner interviews to elicit real world challenges. Part two provides an opportunity to role play the challenges surfaced during the interviews. Use the instructions in the learning activity and this slide to pair up participants for interviews. (Slide 1 of 3)
	Slide 26 Role Play with HELP 1. **Plan:** Use 12 minutes to plan both role plays 2. **Role Play:** Use 4 minutes to role play one situation, using HELP (with two observers) 3. **Feedback:** Use 3 minutes to give feedback to the service provider **REPEAT steps 2 and 3** to work through all four scenarios	Use the instructions in the learning activity and this slide to lead participants to prepare for quad role plays. (Slide 2 of 3)
	Slide 27 **HELP** the Customer • Hear their concerns • Expand your view to see the "other sides" of the story • Let the customer participate in choosing the solution • Perform the actions committed to	Display this slide during the quad role plays as a support tool participants may want to reference. (Slide 3 of 3)
12:00 p.m. (60 min)	Slide 28 Lunch	**LUNCH**

TIMING	SLIDES	ACTIVITIES/NOTES/CONSIDERATIONS

1:00 p.m.
(10 min)
	Slide 29
	
	Quick Start
	• Remove the cards from the envelope on your table
	• Working together, sort the cards into three piles:
	  – Service Behaviors
	  – Service Strategies
	  – Service Systems
		Morning Review and Transition to Afternoon/ Learning Activity 19: Quick Start
		
		Use this post-lunch review activity as a soft-start to open the afternoon. Display this slide and follow the learning activity instructions to invite table groups to complete a card sort review of service behaviors, service strategies, and service systems.
		
		After the activity, provide an overview of the remaining learning objectives for the afternoon.

	Slide 30 Service Strategies	**Transition to Service Strategies** Use this slide to signal a transition from service behaviors to service strategies.
1:10 p.m. (20 min)	Slide 31 Mistake Proof! Process mis-steps result in annoyance Oh no Uh-oh Really? Well that makes no sense... That did *not* just happen Whoops! AGAIN? There has to be a better way	**Learning Objective 4/ Learning Activity 20: Mistake Proofing** • **Handout 22: Mistake Proofing to Improve Customer Service** Learning Activity 20 supports the fourth learning objective—improve existing service strategies from the customer's perspective. Lead the group through a facilitated discussion of what mistake proofing is and how it supports customer service. Provide samples of how mistake-proof techniques can be used by a trainer to support servicing the participant "customer." Direct participants to document how they are already using mistake proofing and partner to share their examples. (Slide 1 of 5)

TIMING	SLIDES	ACTIVITIES/NOTES/CONSIDERATIONS
	Slide 32 Mistake-Proofing Traits Techniques • Simple — Streamline — Color code • Inexpensive — Templates — Checklists • Creative — Layout/arrangement — Regulate behavior • Easy to implement — Correct misinformation — Others	(Slide 2 of 5)
	Slide 33 Color Coding	(Slide 3 of 5)
	Slide 34 Checklists	(Slide 4 of 5)
	Slide 35 Regulate Behavior	(Slide 5 of 5)

TIMING	SLIDES	ACTIVITIES/NOTES/CONSIDERATIONS
1:30 p.m. (40 min)	Slide 36 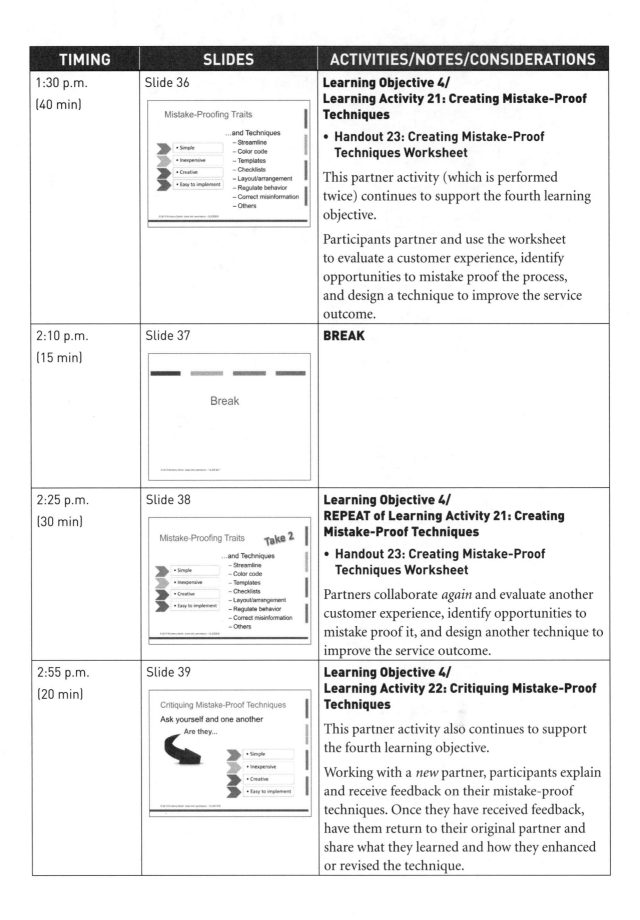	**Learning Objective 4/ Learning Activity 21: Creating Mistake-Proof Techniques** • **Handout 23: Creating Mistake-Proof Techniques Worksheet** This partner activity (which is performed twice) continues to support the fourth learning objective. Participants partner and use the worksheet to evaluate a customer experience, identify opportunities to mistake proof the process, and design a technique to improve the service outcome.
2:10 p.m. (15 min)	Slide 37	**BREAK**
2:25 p.m. (30 min)	Slide 38	**Learning Objective 4/ REPEAT of Learning Activity 21: Creating Mistake-Proof Techniques** • **Handout 23: Creating Mistake-Proof Techniques Worksheet** Partners collaborate *again* and evaluate another customer experience, identify opportunities to mistake proof it, and design another technique to improve the service outcome.
2:55 p.m. (20 min)	Slide 39	**Learning Objective 4/ Learning Activity 22: Critiquing Mistake-Proof Techniques** This partner activity also continues to support the fourth learning objective. Working with a *new* partner, participants explain and receive feedback on their mistake-proof techniques. Once they have received feedback, have them return to their original partner and share what they learned and how they enhanced or revised the technique.

TIMING	SLIDES	ACTIVITIES/NOTES/CONSIDERATIONS
	Slide 40	**Transition to Service Systems**
	Service Systems	Use this slide as a signal to transition from service strategies to service systems.
3:15 p.m. (30 min)	Slide 41	**Learning Objective 5/ Learning Activity 23: Our Service Systems** This large group activity supports the fifth learning objective—examine the organization's service systems for breakdowns from the customer's perspective. Everyone will contribute input to a facilitator-led creation of a cross-functional process map of an organization-specific service system. Choosing a process that is not complex (or a subsection of a process) will make this exercise easier. (TIP: I strongly encourage you to work with subject matter experts, or SMEs, to map the service system ahead of time to reference during the activity and to guide the group.)
3:45 p.m. (20 min)	Slide 42	**Learning Objective 5/ Learning Activity 24: Where and How Can I Help?** • Handout 24: Where and How Can I Help? This individual activity also supports the fifth learning objective. Considering the cross-functional process map just created, individuals determine where they have Control–No Control–Influence (C–NC–I) in the service system.

TIMING	SLIDES	ACTIVITIES/NOTES/CONSIDERATIONS
4:05 p.m. (20 min)	Slide 43 Where We Go From Here... © 2015 Kimberly Devlin. Used with permission. / SLIDE43	**Learning Objective 6/** **Learning Activity 25: Where We Go From Here** • **Handout 25: Where We Go From Here** This action planning activity supports the sixth learning objective—create implementation plans with a peer support component. To help participants take the learning back to the workplace, encourage them to independently create an action plan. Once drafted, have them pair up, and ask them to share their plans, take notes on their partner's plan, and commit to following up with each other at designated times to receive progress updates.
4:25 p.m. (5 min) End at 4:30 p.m.	Slide 44 ATD Workshop From the Customer's Perspective © 2015 Kimberly Devlin. Used with permission. / SLIDE 344	**Course Closure** • **Handout 26: Course Evaluation—From the Customer's Perspective** Share next steps (if program is part of a larger organizational initiative). Collect completed course evaluations. Distribute certificates (if provided).

What to Do Next

- Review Chapter 10 and create your workshop support plan:
  - Select the most effective pre- and post-workshop communication strategies.
  - Involve participants' managers early on.
  - Choose the follow-up coaching strategies that most efficiently align with your workshop rollout.
- Manage workshop logistics:
  - Identify appropriate participants.
  - Schedule the workshop date, reserve an appropriate location, and invite participants.
  - Inform participants about any pre-work, if you are adding it to the workshop.
  - Prepare copies of the participant handouts and assessment (refer to Chapter 14 for information about how to access and use the supplemental materials provided for this workshop).
  - Coordinate catering, if being provided.

- Prepare yourself for the workshop:
  - Review the workshop objectives, learning activities, handouts, and assessment to plan the content you will use.
  - Confirm that you have addressed scheduling and personal concerns so that you can be fully present to facilitate the class.
  - Set an out-of-office email auto response for the day of the workshop.
- Pack your bag:
  - Gather the workshop essentials: participant materials, slide show file, facilitator notes (learning activity pages in Chapter 11), and any activity materials noted in the learning activities (customized manipulatives, index cards, envelopes, or others).
  - Coordinate or bring audio-visual equipment: laptop, projector, speakers, and remote control for presentation slides.
  - Pack training room basics: markers, tape, easels, flip charts, and tactile items, such as Koosh balls, Play-Doh, or others, to place on the tables for tactile learners.
  - See Chapter 8 for other ideas to enhance the learning environment of your workshop.

Chapter 3

Two-Day Customer Service Workshop: A Total Approach to Service

What's in This Chapter

- Objectives of the two-day Customer Service Workshop
- Summary chart for the flow of content and activities
- Two-day program agenda

Congratulations! If this is the workshop you are choosing to facilitate, you are working with an organization that places a priority on service, has leadership that is open to making big-picture changes in processes and systems, and supports investing time in learning and development. That is significant. Now, it will be your turn to put an emphasis on preparing to lead this workshop. In addition to being the lengthiest of the three workshops, it is also the most fluid. There is a greater need in this design for you to refine the timings based on dynamics of your unique group. You may need to dedicate more time to planning and preparation for this workshop. Be sure to thoroughly review the agenda and learning activities *before* conducting your needs assessment and subject matter expert (SME) interviews to be certain you ask all the necessary questions.

Two-Day Workshop Objectives: A Total Approach to Service

The two-day agenda covers service behaviors, strategies, and systems, with an emphasis on systems, including cross-functional processes. The learning objectives for Day One of the two-day workshop are

- Strengthen internal relationships and awareness of lateral service challenges
- Distinguish service behaviors from service strategies and service systems
- Assess the three aspects of your service environment to target improvement opportunities
- Document a process map for a customer-critical service system.

The learning objectives for Day Two of the workshop are

- Examine the organization's service systems for breakdowns from the customer's perspective
- Improve existing service strategies through mistake-proofing techniques
- Follow a framework for creative problem-solving
- Create team action plans to enhance the service systems documented on Day One
- Identify strategies for managing conflict.

Two-Day Workshop Overview

Overview of Day One

TOPICS	TIMING
Welcome/Learning Activity 26: Wall Graffiti	10 minutes
Program Objectives/Learning Activity 27: Prioritize Learning	5 minutes
Ground Rules/Learning Activity 28: Social Agreements	10 minutes
Learning Objective 1/Learning Activity 29: Now You Know	35 minutes
Learning Objective 1/Learning Activity 30: Group Résumé	25 minutes
BREAK	**15 minutes**
Learning Objective 2/Learning Activity 31: Interconnected Service Facets	10 minutes
Learning Objective 2/Learning Activity 32: The Root Issue Is?	20 minutes
Learning Objective 3/Learning Activity 33: Performance Improvement Service Levels	15 minutes
Transition to Service Systems	
Learning Objective 3/Learning Activity 34: Field Trip	20 minutes
LUNCH (AND FIELD TRIP)	**105 minutes**

TOPICS	TIMING
Learning Objective 3/Learning Activity 35: Quick Start—Field Trip Debrief	15 minutes
Learning Objective 4/Learning Activity 36: Working With Cross-Functional Process Mapping	30 minutes
Learning Objective 4/Learning Activity 37: Cross-Functional Process Mapping Our Processes	60-90 minutes
BREAK	**included above**
Learning Objective 4/Learning Activity 38: Cross-Functional Process Map Reviews	30 minutes
Closing/Learning Activity 39: Day-One Workshop Closure	15 minutes
TOTAL	**450 minutes (7.5 hours)**

Overview of Day Two

TOPICS	TIMING
Reconnect/Learning Activity 40: Welcome Back!—Quick Start	20 minutes
Learning Objective 5/Learning Activity 41: Control–No Control–Influence (C–NC–I)	30 minutes
Transition to Service Strategies	
Learning Objective 6/Learning Activity 42: Mistake Proofing	20 minutes
Learning Objective 6/Learning Activity 43: Mistake-Proofing Process Map Elements	30 minutes
BREAK	**15 minutes**
Learning Objective 6/Learning Activity 44: Critiquing Mistake-Proof Techniques	30 minutes
Learning Objective 7/Learning Activity 45: Creative Problem-Solving	35 minutes
LUNCH	**60 minutes**
Transition to Afternoon/Learning Activity 46: Quick Start	15 minutes
Learning Objective 8/Learning Activity 47: Next Steps to Improve Our Systems	45 minutes
BREAK	**15 minutes**
Transition to Service Behaviors	
Learning Objective 9/Learning Activity 48: Keep a Cool Head	30 minutes
Learning Objective 9/Learning Activity 49: Quit Taking It Personally (Q-Tip)	30 minutes
STRETCH BREAK	**10 minutes**
Personalizing the Learning/Learning Activity 50: Living My Legacy	40 minutes
Closing/Learning Activity 51: Day-Two Workshop Closure	25 minutes
TOTAL	**450 minutes (7.5 hours)**

A Word About Presentation Slides and Handouts

The presentation slides for this workshop have been animated to enhance their effectiveness. They can be used effectively in the pdf format (which are static), but if you choose to use the fully customizable versions and display the slides in slide show mode, many will have motion and builds. These animations are not merely movement; they are structured to enhance the visuals' effectiveness, provide greater facilitative control of group discussions, manage cognitive load by chunking content in keeping with activity instructions, and in some instances, even provide feedback to the participants. Some animations are controlled by advancing the slides, and others are automated for you. This is intentional to guide certain activities and to offer you facilitative flexibility in others. Make time to familiarize yourself with the animations and plan how you will leverage them. You can run the workshop effectively using the pdf versions; however, if you are accessing the presentation slides in their native format through an optional license, be sure to display them in slide show mode to derive their full benefit!

Please note that some slides in this workshop may also appear in the half-day or one-day workshops. Their animations here may be a bit different, in support of this workshop's structure. Please be sure to familiarize yourself with these animations even if you previously reviewed a different workshop's visuals.

Each workshop has been designed as a continuous event. If facilitated that way, it may be logical for you to assemble all of the associated handouts into one bound workbook to distribute to participants when they arrive. In this case, where the learning activities direct you to distribute a handout, you may want to make note of and refer to the appropriate workbook pages during the workshop.

For ease of navigation through the book, learning activities and handouts for all three workshops are numbered sequentially. Therefore, this workshop begins with Learning Activity 26 and the first handout is number 27. Each handout has a name as well. For a seamless participant experience, I suggest you refer to the handouts by name, page number (if bound), or renumber them to begin with number 1.

Two-Day Workshop Agenda: Day One

With all that you are focused on when facilitating a workshop, it can be useful to have a quick-reference, birds-eye view to the workshop. This agenda is intended for that purpose. If you are customizing the timings in the learning activities, be sure to update them here too. While I typically use the agenda below as my main reference, I also always have two other tools available to me: the learning activity pages in Chapter 11, which provide the detail in support of the workshop design, and a reference set of the handouts.

When you tailor these materials to your needs, be sure to carry any changes through all three resources for a seamless facilitation.

Day One: (9:00 a.m. to 4:30 p.m.)

TIMING	SLIDES	ACTIVITIES/NOTES/CONSIDERATIONS
	Slide 1 ATD Workshop A Total Approach to Service Systems - Strategies - Behaviors	**Create a Positive Learning Environment** Display this opening slide and welcome participants as they arrive.
9:00 a.m. (10 min)	Slide 2 *Service-Themed Graffiti* • Use color, images, and words to *tag* the graffiti charts • Work quickly…don't get caught!	**Welcome/** **Learning Activity 26: Wall Graffiti** Use this learning activity to create immediate involvement and to draw out the participants' perspectives, *not* as housekeeping, introductions, or generalized "welcoming" comments (you will do that later in the workshop). Set the tone for the learning event as an active, contributory, and fun experience.
9:10 a.m. (5 min)	Slide 3 Learning Objectives – Day One • Strengthen relationships and awareness of service challenges • Distinguish among service behaviors, strategies, and systems • Assess your service environment to target improvement opportunities • Document a process map for a customer-critical service system	**Program Objectives/** **Learning Activity 27: Prioritize Learning** • Handout 27: Learning Objectives This individual activity introduces the workshop's learning objectives for both days, encouraging participants to begin engaging with the objectives.
9:15 a.m. (10 min)	Slide 4 Social Agreements • Create a list of guidelines to adhere to for a fun, effective workshop	**Ground Rules/** **Learning Activity 28: Social Agreements** Guided by your facilitation, this activity will help participants generate a list of guidelines that will drive their behavior for the two days. During the debrief, reach consensus on how the group will monitor and correct breaches of these agreements (so that you are not placed in the role of sole enforcer).

TIMING	SLIDES	ACTIVITIES/NOTES/CONSIDERATIONS
9:25 a.m. (35 min)	Slide 5 Now You Know	**Learning Objective 1/ Learning Activity 29: Now You Know** • **Handout 28: Now You Know** Learning Activities 29 and 30 act as icebreakers while supporting the first learning objective—strengthen internal relationships and your awareness of lateral service challenges. Through one-on-one interviews, this large group activity will help participants meet others and develop deeper understandings of one another's work and how it affects the organization's ability to deliver customer service. Use the instructions in the learning activity to guide the exercise. To help participants get started, share examples of how you might complete the worksheet statements and sentence stems. Following the debrief, integrate a complete self-introduction, including your experience and expertise with customer service.
10:00 a.m. (25 min)	Slide 6 Group Résumé • Take stock of your group's skills and strengths • Create a resume to sell yourselves as service improvement gurus!	**Learning Objective 1/ Learning Activity 30: Group Résumé** Working in small groups, teams will chart the collective strengths of the members of their group in the form of a wall chart résumé. These will be useful to refer back to at points in the workshop where the groups' strengths are being drawn upon.
10:25 a.m. (15 min)	Slide 7 Break	**BREAK**

TIMING	SLIDES	ACTIVITIES/NOTES/CONSIDERATIONS
10:40 a.m. (10 min)	Slide 8 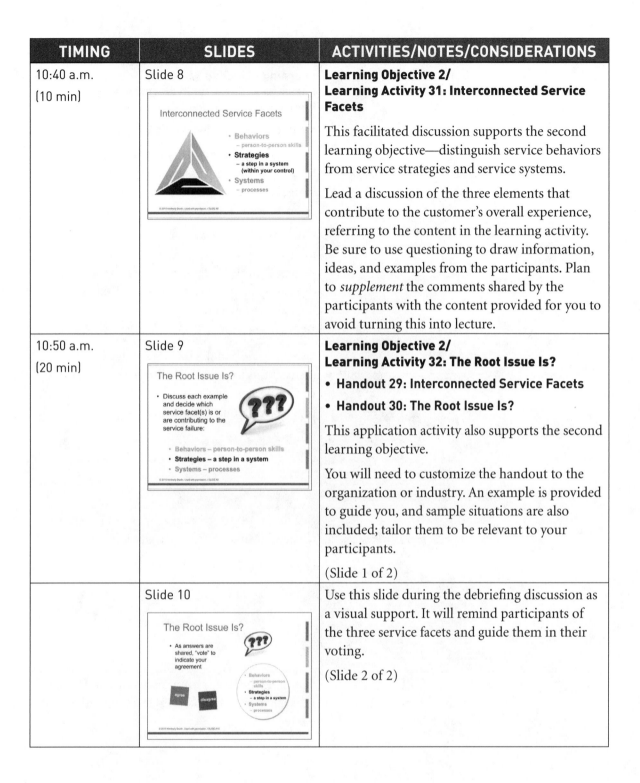	**Learning Objective 2/** **Learning Activity 31: Interconnected Service Facets** This facilitated discussion supports the second learning objective—distinguish service behaviors from service strategies and service systems. Lead a discussion of the three elements that contribute to the customer's overall experience, referring to the content in the learning activity. Be sure to use questioning to draw information, ideas, and examples from the participants. Plan to *supplement* the comments shared by the participants with the content provided for you to avoid turning this into lecture.
10:50 a.m. (20 min)	Slide 9	**Learning Objective 2/** **Learning Activity 32: The Root Issue Is?** • **Handout 29: Interconnected Service Facets** • **Handout 30: The Root Issue Is?** This application activity also supports the second learning objective. You will need to customize the handout to the organization or industry. An example is provided to guide you, and sample situations are also included; tailor them to be relevant to your participants. (Slide 1 of 2)
	Slide 10	Use this slide during the debriefing discussion as a visual support. It will remind participants of the three service facets and guide them in their voting. (Slide 2 of 2)

TIMING	SLIDES	ACTIVITIES/NOTES/CONSIDERATIONS
11:10 a.m. (15 min)	Slide 11	**Learning Objective 3/ Learning Activity 33: Performance Improvement Service Levels** • **Handout 31: Performance Improvement** This partner talk activity supports the third learning objective—assess the three aspects of your service environment to target improvement opportunities. Direct participants to team up and discuss their interpretations of As Is, Should Be, and Could Be based on the slide image. Lead a large group discussion afterwards to clarify and expand on the partner talk content. (Slide 1 of 5)
	Slide 12	Use this slide and the learning activity instructions to provide additional context for As Is, Should Be, and Could Be, and as a transition into a large group discussion. (Slide 2 of 5)
	Slide 13	Begin a large group discussion on As Is, referring to the slide and learning activity for content. (Slide 3 of 5)
	Slide 14	Continue the large group discussion on Should Be, referring to the slide and learning activity for content. (Slide 4 of 5)

TIMING	SLIDES	ACTIVITIES/NOTES/CONSIDERATIONS
	Slide 15	Wrap up the large group discussion with the Could Be level, referring to the slide and learning activity for content.

	Could Be Level
	 • What we might achieve if…
	 Could Be
	   – resources are reallocated
	   – departments collaborate
	   – we stop worrying about who gets credit for ideas
	   – updates are made
	   – processes are redesigned
		(Slide 5 of 5)

	Slide 16	**Transition to Service Systems** Display this slide to signal the transition from service strategies to service systems.
	Service Systems	
11:25 a.m. (20 min)	Slide 17 Field Trip Examine the service interaction by walking in the customer's shoes	**Learning Objective 3/ Learning Activity 34: Field Trip** • **Handout 32: Field Trip Log** • **Handout 32b: Virtual Field Trip Map (optional)** • **Assessment 1: Where Are We Now? (optional)** In support of the third learning objective—assess the three aspects of your service environment to target improvement opportunities—ask participants to visit their service delivery environment as a *customer* and assess and document the customer experience. This activity is scheduled to span the lunch hour plus 45 minutes of workshop time to allow flexibility for varying field trip needs. The field trips will be debriefed after lunch through the quick start activity. Handout 32b and Assessment 1 are optional resources to use with activity variations noted in the learning activity.

TIMING	SLIDES	ACTIVITIES/NOTES/CONSIDERATIONS
11:45 a.m. (105 min) NOTE: Includes 45-minute field trip and 60-minute lunch.	Slide 18 Lunch	**LUNCH (AND FIELD TRIP)**
1:30 p.m. (15 min)	Slide 19 Quick Start • Review your Field Trip Log • Grab a marker and add your answers to the posted charts: – What I didn't know... – Why customers are fortunate – How we aren't helping customers – I felt... – Number of POCs I hit	**Learning Objective 3/ Learning Activity 35: Quick Start—Field Trip Debrief** Use this slide to initiate the self-directed debrief of the field trips as participants return from lunch.
1:45 p.m. (30 min)	Slide 20 Process Mapping vs. Flowchart Cross-Functional Process Map	**Learning Objective 4/ Learning Activity 36: Working with Cross-Functional Process Mapping** This activity supports the fourth learning objective—document a process map for a customer-critical service system. Use this slide to show examples of a flowchart and a cross-functional process map and to help you highlight the differences between the two. (Slide 1 of 2)
	Slide 21 Cross-Functional Process Map Me Spouse Child 1 Child 2	Working with a generic process, groups will process map the steps involved in a family of four going out to dinner at a restaurant. Display this slide to model how their process map should be set up. (Slide 2 of 2)

TIMING	SLIDES	ACTIVITIES/NOTES/CONSIDERATIONS
2:15 p.m. (60-90 min) NOTE: This includes a 15-minute break.	Slide 22 Process Mapping Our Systems • Choose a customer-critical service system to map • Identify the roles that touch the system; create "swim lanes" on your map • Record the steps on index cards and post them in the appropriate swim lanes	**Learning Objective 4/ Learning Activity 37: Cross-Functional Process Mapping Our Processes** Transition the group from the generic process mapping exercise to an organization-specific, customer-critical one. Groups will apply the lessons learned from the mini, generic process map to their selected organization-specific one. Use learning activity notes to guide the exercise.
3:45 p.m. (30 min)	Slide 23 Process Map Review • Use assigned sticky note color • Guidelines: — Don't move/change map's index cards — Leave feedback on sticky notes — Adhere sticky notes close to relevant point on map — You can comment on other sticky notes as well	**Learning Objective 4/ Learning Activity 38: Cross-Functional Process Map Reviews** Groups will review one another's process maps and revise their maps based on feedback received. Use learning activity notes to guide the activity.
4:15 p.m. (15 min) End at 4:30 p.m.	Slide 24 Research Assignment • Find and bring to Day Two a resource related to customer service, such as: — video — article — blog — social media site — RSS feed	**Closing/Learning Activity 39: Day-Two Workshop Closure** Time has been built into this activity for you to share a simple assignment that will serve as the basis of the quick start activity for the morning of Day Two. It will also gather quick feedback on Day One, preview and potentially revise the agenda for Day Two, set a date for Day Two (if not already established), and devise a group strategy for having all of the output of Day One available on Day Two. Based on your customization and length of time between workshop days, you may also want to capture any additional expectations you have of the participants from now until Day Two.

What to Do Between Workshop Days

- Follow up on any questions or parking lot issues presented during Day One.
- Note facilitator lessons learned from the first day of the workshop. Adjust materials for Day Two accordingly, if needed.

- Address any equipment, room setup, or other learning environment issues you weren't able to address during the workshop.

- Debrief with your co-facilitator, if applicable.

Two-Day Workshop Agenda: Day Two

The second day of this workshop is where the greatest fluidity comes into play. Based on the feedback participants shared at the end of Day One, the time available to you between workshop days, and your customization of the workshop design, the following agenda overview may require adjustments and fine tuning.

Day Two: (9:00 a.m. to 4:30 p.m.)

TIMING	SLIDES	ACTIVITIES/NOTES/CONSIDERATIONS
	Slide 25 **ATD** Workshop A Total Approach to Service Systems · Strategies · Behaviors	**Transition to Day Two** This slide is primarily intended as an aid for *you*, to mark the crossover to Day Two, not as a visual support for the participants.

9:00 a.m.
 	
 (20 min)
	Slide 26
	
	 Welcome Back! – Quick Start
	 • Form a trio
	 • Share the resource you brought
	   – video
	   – article
	   – blog
	   – social media site
	   – RSS feed
	   – other
		Reconnect/
		 Learning Activity 40: Welcome Back!—Quick Start
		
		 Display this slide as participants arrive to engage them in the self-directed workshop opening activity. Welcome participants and individually direct their attention to the quick start if needed.
		
		 (Slide 1 of 2)

	Slide 27 Learning Objectives – Day Two • Examine service systems for breakdowns • Improve service strategies with mistake-proofing techniques • Follow a creative problem solving framework to address business re-engineering issues that may arise • Create team action plans to enhance service systems documented on Day One • Identify strategies for managing conflict	Revisit and remind participants of the learning objectives for Day Two. (Slide 2 of 2)

TIMING	SLIDES	ACTIVITIES/NOTES/CONSIDERATIONS
9:20 a.m. (30 min)	Slide 28 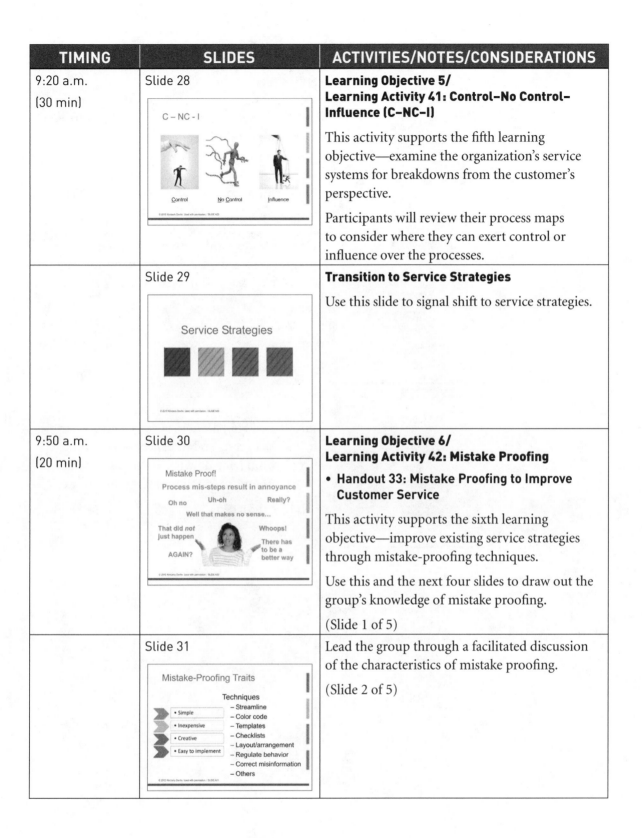	**Learning Objective 5/ Learning Activity 41: Control–No Control– Influence (C–NC–I)** This activity supports the fifth learning objective—examine the organization's service systems for breakdowns from the customer's perspective. Participants will review their process maps to consider where they can exert control or influence over the processes.
	Slide 29	**Transition to Service Strategies** Use this slide to signal shift to service strategies.
9:50 a.m. (20 min)	Slide 30	**Learning Objective 6/ Learning Activity 42: Mistake Proofing** • **Handout 33: Mistake Proofing to Improve Customer Service** This activity supports the sixth learning objective—improve existing service strategies through mistake-proofing techniques. Use this and the next four slides to draw out the group's knowledge of mistake proofing. (Slide 1 of 5)
	Slide 31	Lead the group through a facilitated discussion of the characteristics of mistake proofing. (Slide 2 of 5)

TIMING	SLIDES	ACTIVITIES/NOTES/CONSIDERATIONS
	Slide 32 Color Coding	Solicit their examples of how mistake-proof techniques can be used to support customer service. Supplement discussion with examples from your experience (or from examples provided in learning activity notes). Consider replacing Slides 32-34 with slides depicting organization-specific examples, if applicable. (Slide 3 of 5)
	Slide 33 Checklists	Checklists are another example of mistake-proofing techniques. Ask participants to cite an example of their use in their current processes. (Slide 4 of 5)
	Slide 34 Regulate Behavior	Yet another technique is regulating behavior through design (size/dimension). Other examples include arm rests on bus benches to discourage people from lying down or counter height of courtesy computer stations to limit use time. (Slide 5 of 5)
10:10 a.m. (15 min)	Slide 35 Break	**BREAK**

TIMING	SLIDES	ACTIVITIES/NOTES/CONSIDERATIONS
10:25 a.m. (30 min)	Slide 36 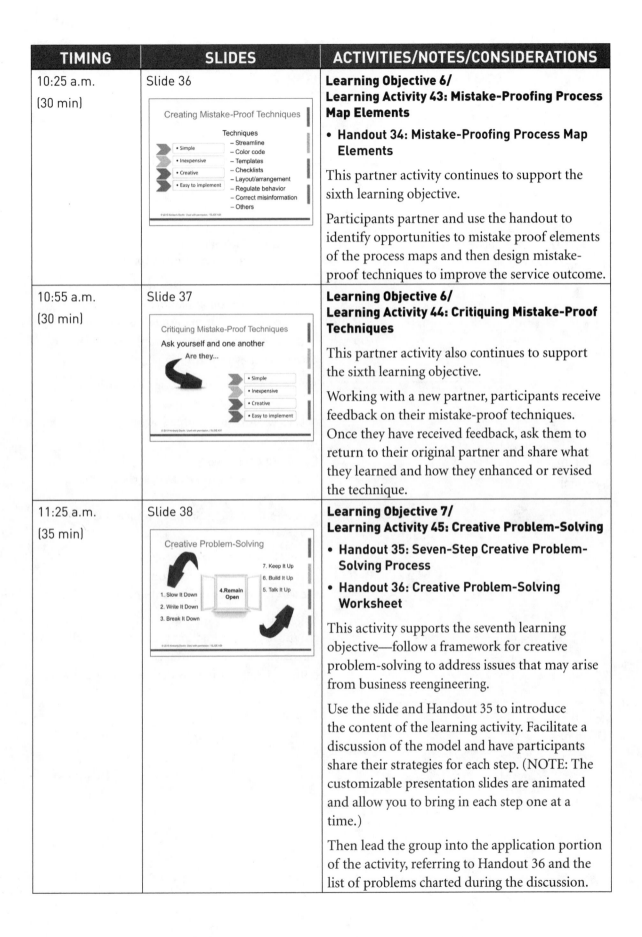	**Learning Objective 6/ Learning Activity 43: Mistake-Proofing Process Map Elements** • **Handout 34: Mistake-Proofing Process Map Elements** This partner activity continues to support the sixth learning objective. Participants partner and use the handout to identify opportunities to mistake proof elements of the process maps and then design mistake-proof techniques to improve the service outcome.
10:55 a.m. (30 min)	Slide 37	**Learning Objective 6/ Learning Activity 44: Critiquing Mistake-Proof Techniques** This partner activity also continues to support the sixth learning objective. Working with a new partner, participants receive feedback on their mistake-proof techniques. Once they have received feedback, ask them to return to their original partner and share what they learned and how they enhanced or revised the technique.
11:25 a.m. (35 min)	Slide 38	**Learning Objective 7/ Learning Activity 45: Creative Problem-Solving** • **Handout 35: Seven-Step Creative Problem-Solving Process** • **Handout 36: Creative Problem-Solving Worksheet** This activity supports the seventh learning objective—follow a framework for creative problem-solving to address issues that may arise from business reengineering. Use the slide and Handout 35 to introduce the content of the learning activity. Facilitate a discussion of the model and have participants share their strategies for each step. (NOTE: The customizable presentation slides are animated and allow you to bring in each step one at a time.) Then lead the group into the application portion of the activity, referring to Handout 36 and the list of problems charted during the discussion.

TIMING	SLIDES	ACTIVITIES/NOTES/CONSIDERATIONS
12:00 p.m. (60 min)	Slide 39 Lunch	**LUNCH**
1:00 p.m. (15 min)	Slide 40 Quick Start • Pick two cards from the pile on the table • Choose the one yo answer • Share your card and answer with your tablemates	**Transition to Afternoon/ Learning Activity 46: Quick Start** Use this self-directed pulse-check activity to open the afternoon and address any questions or concerns. Set out materials, display the slide, and invite participants to complete the learning activity as they return. After the activity, answer questions from the group and clarify content as needed. Provide an overview of the remaining learning objectives for the afternoon.
1:15 p.m. (45 min)	Slide 41 Next Steps…	**Learning Objective 8/ Learning Activity 47: Next Steps to Improve Our Systems** • **Handout 37: Next Steps to Improve Our Systems** This activity supports the eighth learning objective—create team action plans to enhance the service systems documented on Day One. You have a great deal of flexibility in how you choose to form the action planning teams. Be sure each team member takes an active role both in documenting the action plan and in the actions committed to in the plan.
2:00 p.m. (15 min)	Slide 42 Break	**BREAK**

TIMING	SLIDES	ACTIVITIES/NOTES/CONSIDERATIONS
	Slide 43 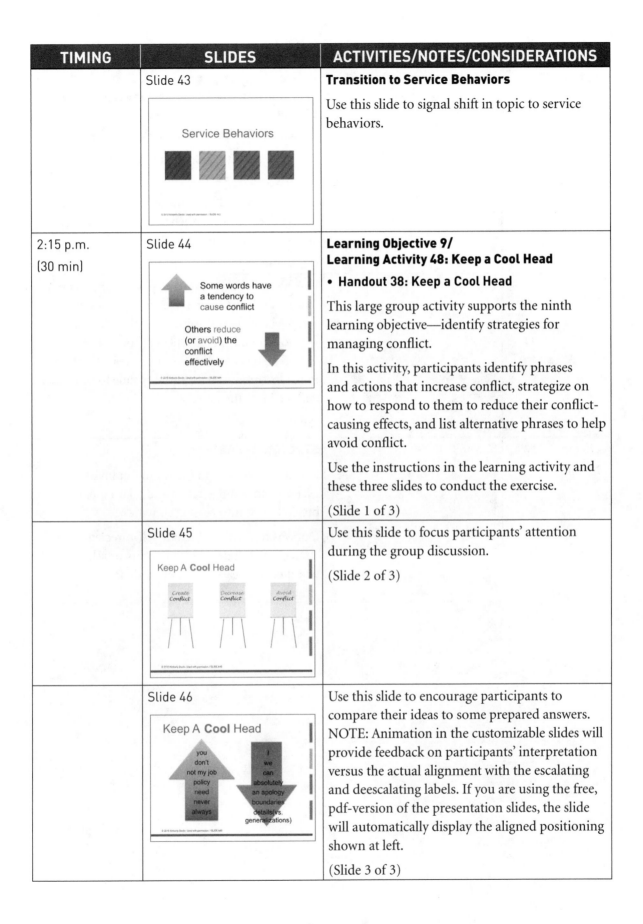	**Transition to Service Behaviors** Use this slide to signal shift in topic to service behaviors.
2:15 p.m. (30 min)	Slide 44	**Learning Objective 9/** **Learning Activity 48: Keep a Cool Head** • **Handout 38: Keep a Cool Head** This large group activity supports the ninth learning objective—identify strategies for managing conflict. In this activity, participants identify phrases and actions that increase conflict, strategize on how to respond to them to reduce their conflict-causing effects, and list alternative phrases to help avoid conflict. Use the instructions in the learning activity and these three slides to conduct the exercise. (Slide 1 of 3)
	Slide 45	Use this slide to focus participants' attention during the group discussion. (Slide 2 of 3)
	Slide 46	Use this slide to encourage participants to compare their ideas to some prepared answers. NOTE: Animation in the customizable slides will provide feedback on participants' interpretation versus the actual alignment with the escalating and deescalating labels. If you are using the free, pdf-version of the presentation slides, the slide will automatically display the aligned positioning shown at left. (Slide 3 of 3)

TIMING	SLIDES	ACTIVITIES/NOTES/CONSIDERATIONS
2:45 p.m. (30 min)	Slide 47	**Learning Objective 9/** **Learning Activity 49: Quit Taking It Personally (Q-Tip)** • **Handout 39: Quit Taking It Personally (Q-Tip)** This pop-up activity also supports the ninth learning objective. Use this slide and the handout to review (briefly) the types of customer behaviors that can trigger an emotional reaction. (Slide 1 of 2)
	Slide 48	During the pop-up exercise, participants generate neutral and customer-focused responses to sample language customers may say. Colleagues will vote on the effectiveness of the responses shared using colored cards. Use the instructions in the learning activity and this slide to introduce and facilitate the exercise. (Slide 2 of 2)
3:15 p.m. (10 min)	Slide 49	**STRETCH BREAK** For this break, stay in the room but invite everyone to stand, stretch, and take a mental break to lead into closing activities. Options to consider include self-directed stretching, a chair-yoga video clip, or asking volunteers to lead the group in their favorite stretch.

TIMING	SLIDES	ACTIVITIES/NOTES/CONSIDERATIONS
3:25 p.m. (40 min)	Slide 50 Service Legacy • What do you want to be known for? Listen greet Smile service service-culture simplify streamlined	**Personalizing the Learning/** **Learning Activity 50: Living My Legacy** • **Handout 40: Living My Legacy Worksheet** Take 10 minutes to field comments from participants on what a legacy is and how to plan and live your own desired service legacy. Begin shifting your tone and energy level to lower the intensity of the room's energy level. Establish a quiet learning environment for participants to contemplate and draft their service legacy plans. Allow 30 minutes. Consider adding a guided reflection prior to the handout to shift the energy of the room to one of self-reflection and introspection before they focus on their individual plans. It may also be beneficial to softly play music to establish a tone in the room, as described in a variation in the learning activity.
4:05 p.m. (25 min) End at 4:30 p.m.	Slide 51 ATD Workshop A Total Approach to Service Systems - Strategies - Behaviors	**Closing/Learning Activity 51: Day-Two** **Workshop Closure** • **Handout 41: Course Evaluation—A Total Approach to Service** Time has been built in here for you to structure a planned close to the workshop, rather than an abrupt ending. With questioning and other techniques, guide participants through a review of what they learned, their own assessment of what they learned, what they will do with what they learned, and a celebration of their achievements. If the workshop is part of a larger organizational initiative, be sure to share next steps in relation to the overall initiative too. Use the evaluation instrument to gather feedback on the workshop. Collect completed course evaluations. Distribute certificates (if provided).

What to Do Next

- Review Chapter 10 and create your workshop support plan:
  - Select the most effective pre- and post-workshop communication strategies.
  - Involve participants' managers early on.
  - Choose the follow-up coaching strategies that most efficiently align with your workshop rollout.
- Manage workshop logistics:
  - Identify appropriate participants.
  - Schedule the workshop dates, reserve an appropriate location, and invite participants.
  - Inform participants about any pre-work, if you are adding it to the workshop.
  - Prepare copies of the participant handouts (refer to Chapter 14 for information about how to access and use the supplemental materials provided for this workshop).
  - Coordinate catering, if being provided.
- Prepare yourself for the workshop:
  - Review the workshop objectives, learning activities, and handouts to plan the content you will use.
  - Confirm that you have addressed scheduling and personal concerns so that you can be fully present to facilitate the class.
  - Set an out-of-office email auto response for both days of the workshop.
- Pack your bag:
  - Gather the workshop essentials: participant materials, slide show file, facilitator notes (learning activity pages in Chapter 11), and any activity materials noted in the learning activities (customized manipulatives, index cards, envelopes, or others).
  - Coordinate or bring audio-visual equipment: laptop, projector, speakers, and remote control for presentation slides.
  - Pack training room basics: markers, tape, easels, flip charts, and tactile items, such as Koosh balls, Play-Doh, or others, to place on the tables for tactile learners.
  - See Chapter 8 for other ideas to enhance the learning environment of your workshop.

Chapter 4

Customizing the Customer Service Workshops

What's in This Chapter

- Introducing critical steps for customization success
- Integrating organizational service standards
- Ideas for customization of content, format, and delivery

Many organizations are challenged by having employees away from the workplace for an entire day or two, even if it is for professional and skill development. As a result, you may need to adjust and adapt your workshop to the scheduling needs of the organization. Additionally, the content and topics of your workshop truly must match the needs of the employees attending the training. Therefore, your training needs analysis will help you select the workshop best suited to your participants' needs and guide your decisions in customizing the content and activities. For more on needs analysis, see Chapter 5.

The materials in this ATD Workshop Series volume are designed to meet a variety of business needs. They cover multiple topics within three key aspects of customer service and can be offered in many timeframes and formats. By using the learning content and activities provided here as a foundation, you can modify and adapt the learning experience by customizing the content and activities, customizing the workshop format, and customizing the delivery with technology.

Customizing the Content and Activities

Knowing why you are making changes is fundamental to any customization. You are likely to use the agendas and support materials in this book in one of three ways: 1) pulling an activity or two into a design you are already working on; 2) deploying these workshops as tested, turn-key training events; or 3) using them as the basis of your program but tailoring them to fit your organizational needs. If you fall into the third category, I encourage you to connect the changes you make directly back to the business needs identified during your analysis. Resist the urge to make changes just so they are "different" than the off-the-shelf version.

Striking off on your own can be exciting and intimidating at the same time. If you follow three key steps in your customization efforts, you will be primed for success.

Step One: Get Real

Foundational to your customization of the workshops will be determining the organization's service culture *reality*. There may be a framed poster in the lobby citing service as a core value, but is that being demonstrated? If not, why not? And, if it is, how often and by whom? When customers call the service center, are those experiences consistent with the service levels provided by all of the technicians that come out to make repairs? Walking through the plant, can all employees tell you what the organization's service expectations are and how that relates to their roles? If asked about the lobby poster, will employees tell you that it was the pet project of the *former* administrator?

Case in point: I was leading a program in the offices of a client organization and saw an attractive and intriguing wall poster mounted in the back of the room. I referred to it and asked the group for some background on it. It was developed as a support tool for a reorganization, they told me. They quickly added they had been through *six* additional reorganizations since that one, and right beside it was a poster of another one of the reorganizations.

Just because it is on a wall, website, or company brochure doesn't mean it is in the culture of the organization. If you go into any of the workshops in this book without a true understanding of the service realities and challenges that may exist, many participants will likely view you as a cheerleader, label the workshop as flavor-of-the-month training, and disconnect. You want to avoid that!

In the most challenged of service environments, you might consider opening a workshop with a few direct questions that will shake up the status-quo, place the issues on the table, and engage your participants:

- Why isn't service a priority here?
- What indicators lead you to believe that leadership doesn't value service?
- Are you truly doing all you can to provide exceptional service? Why not?

Step Two: Be Relevant

To be effective, training must be relevant. No one wants to have their time wasted. You can build relevance into your workshop design in several ways:

- **Align content and format with organizational needs.** The introduction to this book provides a guide to choosing the best workshop to align with your organizational needs. Choose a workshop because of its alignment—not its duration. And then communicate the rationale for your choice. Communicate it to workshop sponsors and champions, communicate it to subject matter experts (SMEs) and co-facilitators, and, of course, communicate it to the participants.

- **Create custom scenarios for role plays.** During your needs analysis, inquire about the types of challenging situations that employees in the organization encounter in delivering customer service. Drawing from that information and then fictionalizing it, draft scenarios to use as a learning lab during the workshop. They can be integrated as case studies, role plays, match-a-strategy activities (where participants connect workshop tools or techniques to specific situations), and so on.

- **Share industry-specific examples and stories.** Replacing sample stories provided in this volume with content that is directly applicable to the participants instantly builds in relevance. In a large-scale rollout, that will likely mean creating multiple sets of stories and scenarios, tailored to each participant subset of the organization. Engineers, marketing specialists, sales staff, and security personnel will not all relate to the same situations even if they are employed by the same organization.

- **Use industry-specific terminology.** For customer service training, customization must carry over even to the language used to describe the people involved in the service interaction. Although the term *customer* is used to describe the recipient in the support materials provided with this volume, you may want to change that designation throughout. Your industry may use terms such as *client, guest, visitor, patron, resident, citizen, taxpayer,* or *patient.* Similarly, the people providing service may be called *employees, associates, ambassadors, client representatives, customer care agents,* or *staff.* Update terminology accordingly; give your participants as many points as possible to identify with the workshop content.

Step Three: Integrate the Organization's Service Standards

What does it *look like* to live up to the service expectations of the organization? How you answer this question depends on the organization and its service standards. Service standards set the measurable level of performance that customers should receive *under normal circumstances.* They are stated goals for service achievement and commitments to the customers—both external and internal. They have two main purposes: provide employees with performance targets ("resolve customer issues in one phone call") and set expectations for customers ("hold time for callers is under 10 minutes"). Here are several ideas to keep in mind when integrating your organization's service standards into your workshop:

- **Develop service standards if they don't already exist.** If your organization doesn't have service standards, you may want to tackle creating them. Writing effective service standards can be challenging because they require a high degree of specificity in the language and yet must be broadly applicable to all employees. The goal is to develop standards that are measurable, ambitiously realistic, and relevant to the customer. If you are leading the charge to establish standards, be sure to involve as many viewpoints and stakeholders as possible in the process, including customers, managers, frontline employees, service delivery partners, and executive leaders.

- **Build service standards into workshop design.** If the organization has a set of service standards, you might consider an icebreaker activity that requires assembling all of the service standard elements, a timed game of charades to act them out, or trio exchanges in which each participant shares a two-minute story of how they applied a service standard. Then, circle back to the standards throughout the workshop as you facilitate the learning activities. Ask participants how a particular skill or behavior supports the standards. Challenge the group to look for and share connections between the workshop content and the service standards.

- **Swap out some of the learning objectives to align with service standards.** Tailoring activities alone may not be enough. Consider modifying the learning objectives as well and then pairing them with new activities. Here are examples of two easy swaps you could make:
  - For a service standard on empathy, for example, replace a service behavior learning objective with one for reflective listening. Then add a new learning activity that focuses on listening skills.
  - For a service standard on timeliness, replace a service strategy learning objective with one for effective time management practices and pair it with a time management exercise.

Customizing the Workshop Format

Although extended immersion in a learning environment can increase the depth of learning experiences, workplace realities sometimes require that training be conducted in short, small doses. The resources and materials provided in this book can be used to build a variety of learning experiences. Chapter 10 includes ideas to "Continue to Offer Learning Opportunities" that include additional training topics and possible lunch-and-learn formats. Here, I offer some examples of how to modify the workshops' content for one- or two-hour sessions, or even a series of short events. (NOTE: The sample one-hour sessions that follow are not intended for use as lunch-and-learn programs, but as dedicated 60-minute learning events. As "lunch-and-learn" implies, such programs take a more informal approach and accommodate participants eating while participating.)

One-hour, Themed Sessions

To address the possible need to provide learning in shorter segments, Table 4-1 breaks down some of the content into six one-hour sessions based on selected themes to be offered as stand-alone events. You can also consider stringing a few of them together to offer as a series on a daily, weekly, biweekly, or monthly basis, depending on the scheduling needs of the organization. Note that some of the sessions contain duplicate content, so closely review the sample one-hour sessions if you are creating a customized delivery schedule. Some of these sessions may also require additional transitions or openers to deliver a seamless learning event or series.

Table 4-1. Sample One-Hour Formats

	Learning Activity	Timing	Notes
Variation 1	**Theme: Decreasing Conflict and Increasing Satisfaction**		
	Learning Activity 2: Hello, My Idea Is . . .	--*	Modify. Invite participants to make idea badges instead of name badges upon arrival. Skip the mix/mingle.
	Learning Activity 5: Keep a Cool Head	20 min	
	Learning Activity 6: Quit Taking It Personally (Q-Tip)	20 min	
	Learning Activity 4: I'm Stumped	20 min*	Select one of the "if time is tight" variations to shorten this from 30 to 20 minutes.
Variation 2	**Theme: The Service Delivery Framework**		
	Learning Activity 16: Where Are We Now?	--*	Use as pre-work.
	Learning Activity 13: Interconnected Service Facets	20 min	
	Learning Activity 14: Do They Agree?	25 min	
	Add in: Personal Action Planning	15 min	

Continued on next page

Table 4-1. Sample One-Hour Formats, *continued*

	Learning Activity	Timing	Notes
Variation 3	**Theme: Mistake Proofing Service Strategies**		
	Learning Activity 20: Mistake Proofing	20 min	
	Learning Activity 21: Creating Mistake-Proof Techniques	40 min	
Variation 4	**Theme: Isolating and Resolving Service Issues**		
	Learning Activity 29: Now You Know	30 min*	Distribute Handout 28 as pre-work to shorten activity time.
	Learning Activity 31: Interconnected Service Facets	10 min	
	Learning Activity 32: The Root Issue Is?	20 min	
Variation 5	**Theme: A Model for Service Delivery (A)**		
	This variation uses participant-generated scenarios for role play.		
	Learning Activity 1: Intriguing Question or Story	5 min	
	Learning Activity 7: HELP Process for Customer Interactions	15 min	
	Learning Activity 8: HELP the Customer	40 min	
Variation 6	**Theme: A Model for Service Delivery (B)**		
	This variation uses prepared scenarios for role play, allowing time for creative problem-solving.		
	Instruct participants to think of and bring with them a problem they face in providing quality customer service.	--*	Use as pre-work.
	Learning Activity 45: Creative Problem-Solving	25 min*	At Step 4, participants apply the Creative Problem-Solving Process to their pre-work challenge to reduce time to 25 minutes.
	Learning Activity 7: HELP Process for Customer Interactions	15 min	
	Learning Activity 8: HELP the Customer	20 min*	Use the second variation (skip interviews and provide scenarios) to reduce time to 20 minutes.
* Indicates that timing has been changed from what is in the learning activities (see the Notes column for additional direction).			

Two-hour, Themed Sessions

These sample two-hour sessions may work best when time is constrained, but the service challenges are *not*. They will delve deeper into a theme, provide participants with a greater complement of tools and strategies, and afford more time for participant-generated challenges, scenarios, and action planning than their one-hour counterparts. Table 4-2 presents three two-hour sessions that can be offered as standalone learning events. Some of these sessions may require additional transitions or openers to deliver a seamless program.

Table 4-2. Sample Two-Hour Formats

	Learning Activity	Timing	Notes
Two-Hour Variation 1	**Theme: A Model for Service Delivery (C)**		
	This variation uses participant-generated scenarios for role play and introduces creative problem-solving.		
	Handout 12: Service Heroes	--*	Use as pre-work.
	Learning Activity 11: Service Heroes	15 min*	Timing reduced to 15 minutes due to pre-work.
	Learning Activity 45: Creative Problem-Solving	35 min	
	Learning Activity 7: The HELP Process for Customer Interactions	15 min	
	Learning Activity 8: HELP the Customer	40 min	
	Learning Activity 46: Quick Start	15 min*	Modify. Participants draw and answer questions on multiple cards (at table groups or to large group), extending this activity to a modified reflection/action planning/probing activity.
Two-Hour Variation 2	**Theme: Mistake Proofing for Performance Improvement**		
	Learning Activity 16: Where Are We Now?	--*	Use as pre-work.
	Learning Activity 13: Interconnected Service Facets	20 min	
	Learning Activity 14: Do They Agree?	25 min	
	Learning Activity 15: Performance Improvement Service Levels	20 min	
	Invite participants to review pre-work and adjust rankings	5 min	Add in time to review pre-work.
	Learning Activity 20: Mistake Proofing	20 min	
	Learning Activity 21: Creating Mistake-Proof Techniques	40 min	

Continued on next page

Table 4-2. Sample Two-Hour Formats, *continued*

	Learning Activity	Timing	Notes
Two-Hour Variation 3	**Theme: Problem-Solving in a Hostile Environment**		
	Learning Activity 1: Intriguing Question or Story	5 min	
	Learning Activity 45: Creative Problem-Solving	35 min	
	Learning Activity 48: Keep a Cool Head	30 min	
	Learning Activity 49: Quit Taking It Personally (Q-Tip)	20 min	
	Learning Activity 4: I'm Stumped	30 min	
* Indicates that timing has been changed from what is in the learning activities (see the Notes column for additional direction).			

Customizing the Workshop Delivery with Technology

Learning technologies can play an important role in adapting workshops to fit your organization. They have the potential to enhance learners' abilities to apply workshop concepts and can be especially useful when participants work in different locations. Examples include webinars, wikis, email groups, and teleconferencing, to name just a few. Here are several ideas for incorporating technology into the custom delivery of your workshop:

- **Blended learning.** Depending on your comfort level and the technology resources available at your organization, you could consider a blended learning approach. Some activities can be done virtually; others cannot. Lead the workshop at least once as instructor-led training so that you understand the flow of the material and to give you ideas about what portions could be conducted effectively online.

- **Before the workshop.** Before your participants ever walk into your session, consider sending them a link to a great article or video clip to get them thinking about the workshop content.

- **After the workshop**. Use surveys and polling tools to assess how workshop skills are or are not being applied so you can address any gap. Continue the participants' focus on the training topic with blog posts that can be pushed out to email boxes using an RSS feed for those who wish to receive them. Create a group site, social network, or SharePoint site to share just-in-time online resources such as reference sheets or job aids.

Learn more about how to use technology to maximize learning in Chapter 7 of this book.

The Bare Minimum

With any of these customization options, always keep in mind the essentials of training design (Chapter 6) and delivery (Chapter 8). At a bare minimum, remember these basics:

- **Relevancy!** Ensure your scenarios and examples are relevant not just to the organization as a whole but also to the specific participant group in your workshop. After all, the service challenges that a school district's custodial staff deals with are different than those of its bus drivers, administrative personnel, or teachers. Each subaudience's environment should be considered when gathering analysis data; designing follow-up activities; and preparing stories, scenarios, and examples for the workshops.

- **Less is more.** When customizing, avoid the common tendency of packing more "stuff" into the workshop schedule for fear there won't be enough material. Prioritizing adequate time for participant application is *essential* because it is during engaging and interactive activities that the learning actually takes place.

- **Check yourself . . . and your materials.** The materials in this book have been designed, proofread, tested, and reviewed. Once you begin to make alterations, you will need to compile and carefully review all agendas, activities, handouts, assessments, and slides. Be sure that you ask—and answer—these questions: Have you introduced any contradictions? Do references within your materials match up? Are slides consistent with edits you made to printed materials? Do activity instructions (on handouts, assessments, slides, or facilitator notes) need to be updated? Do the timings on your agenda add up to the total time of your workshop? Have you maintained sufficient time in the agenda for breaks? Double-check. Then triple-check!

What to Do Next

- When customizing a workshop it is important to have a clear understanding of the learning objectives. Conduct a needs analysis to identify the gap between what the organization needs and what the employees are able to do and then determine how best to bridge the gap. At a minimum, identify who wants the training, how the results will be defined, why the training is being requested at this time, and what the budget is. Chapter 5 provides more guidance on identifying training needs.

- Modify or add your own content to an existing agenda from Chapters 1-3 or create your own agenda using the learning support documents included in this book. There is no one way to flow customer service content, but you must ensure that the topics build on one another and that you solidly connect the concepts and ideas together to leverage the most of the learning opportunity.

- Make sure to maintain an emphasis on interactive practice activities in the final design of your workshop.

- Build a detailed plan for preparing for your session, including scheduling and room reservations, invitations, supply list, facilitation notes, and time estimates. A starting point is included for you at the end of each agenda in Chapters 1-3.

SECTION II

ESSENTIALS OF EFFECTIVE CUSTOMER SERVICE TRAINING

Chapter 5

Identifying Needs for Customer Service Training

What's in This Chapter

- Discovering the purpose of needs analysis
- Introducing some data-gathering methods
- Determining the bare minimum needed to deliver training

Ideally, you should always carry out a needs analysis before designing and creating a workshop to address a performance gap. The cost of *not* identifying and carefully considering the performance requirement can be high: wasted training dollars, unhappy staff going to boring or useless sessions, increased disengagement of employees, and so forth. But the world of training is rarely ideal, and the existence of this book, which essentially provides a workshop in a box, is testament to that. This chapter describes the essential theory and techniques for a complete needs analysis to provide the fundamentals of the process and how it fits into designing learning. However, because the decision to train may already be out of your hands, the last part of this chapter provides a bare-bones list of things you need to know to train effectively even if someone just handed you this book and told you to put on a workshop.

Why Needs Analysis?

In short, as a trainer, learning professional, performance consultant, or whatever job title you hold, your role is to ensure that the employees of your organization know how to do the work that will make the organization succeed. That means you must first identify the skills, knowledge, and abilities that the employees need for optimal performance and then determine where these are lacking in the employee population to bridge that gap. However, the most important reason for needs assessment is that it is not your learning experience. You may deliver it, but the learning belongs to the learner. Making decisions for learners about what performance they need without working with them is inappropriate. If you are an experienced facilitator, you have a large repository of PowerPoint decks at your disposal. Resist the urge while talking with your customers to listen for words that allow you just to grab what you already have. Be open to the possibilities. A training needs analysis helps you do this (see Figure 5-1). Methods to identify this information include strategic needs analysis, structured interviews, focus groups, and surveys.

Strategic Needs Analysis

An analysis of future directions usually identifies emerging issues and trends with a major potential effect on a business and its customers over a two- to three-year period. The analysis

Figure 5-1. Introducing the ADDIE Model

A needs analysis is the first step in the classic instructional design model called ADDIE, which is named after its steps: analysis, design, development, implementation, and evaluation. Roughly speaking, the tasks involved in ADDIE are

1. **Analysis:** Gather data about organizational and individual needs as well as the gap between the goals the organization means to accomplish and the skills and knowledge needed to accomplish those goals.
2. **Design:** Identify and plan the topics and sequence of learning to accomplish the desired learning.
3. **Development:** Create the components of the learning event, such as learning activities and materials.
4. **Implementation:** Put on the learning event or launch the learning materials.
5. **Evaluation:** Gather data to determine the outcome of the learning to improve future iterations of the learning, enhance materials and facilitation, and justify budget decisions.

Instructional design models such as ADDIE are a systematic approach to developing learning and could also be viewed as a project management framework for the project phases involved in creating learning events.

helps a business develop goals and programs that proactively anticipate and position the organization to influence the future.

To conduct such an analysis, organizations look at issues such as expected changes within the business (for example, technology and professional requirements) and expected changes outside the company (for example, the economy, demographics, politics, and the environment).

Results of an analysis provide a rationale for developing company and departmental goals and for making policy and budgetary decisions. From the analysis comes a summary of key change dynamics that will affect the business.

These questions often are asked in strategic needs analysis:

- What does the organization know about future changes in customer needs?
- Are customer surveys conducted, and if so, what do they reveal?
- How might the organization have to change to serve customers better?
- Is the company's organizational structure working to support customer service?
- What are the biggest problems?
- What information did previous organizational analyses impart?
- Are those issues and trends still relevant?
- Do the results point to what may need to be done differently in the future?
- How has the organization performed in achieving results?
- What is the present workforce like?
- How will it change or need to change?
- What are the strengths and limitations of the company?
- What are the opportunities for positive change?
- What do competitors do or say that might have implications for the organization?
- What are the most important opportunities for the future?
- Is the organization in a competitive marketplace?
- If not, how will we demonstrate the importance of customer service?
- How does the organization compare with competitors?

The results can be summarized in a SWOT analysis model (strengths, weaknesses, opportunities, threats—see Figure 5-2). Action plans are then developed to increase the strengths, overcome the weaknesses, plan for the opportunities, and decrease the threats.

Figure 5-2. SWOT Analysis Model

	STRENGTHS	WEAKNESSES
INTERNAL		
	OPPORTUNITIES	THREATS
EXTERNAL		

Structured Interviews

Start structured interviews as high up in the organization as you can go, with the CEO if possible. Make sure that you include input from human resource personnel and line or operations managers and supervisors. Managers and supervisors will want to tell you what they have seen and what they consider the most pressing issues in the organization.

Focus Groups

Focus groups can be set up to give people opportunities to brainstorm ideas about issues in the organization and to realize the potential of team involvement. One comment may spark another and so on. Focus groups should begin with questions that you prepare. It is important to record the responses and comments on a flipchart so everyone can see them. If that is not possible, you may simply take notes. Results of the sessions should be compiled.

Surveys

Surveys, whether paper or web based, gather information from a large or geographically dispersed group of employees. The advantages of surveys are speed of data collection, objectivity, repeatability, and ease of analysis.

When conducting a needs assessment around customer service, the following additional questions will be critical to have answered:

- Do service standards exist? If so,
  - What are they?
  - How are they reinforced, modeled, and rewarded when demonstrated?
  - Are they "just a poster" or are they part of the culture?
- Is customer service specifically linked to the organization's performance appraisal system?
- What service training programs have the learners participated in previously? How were they received and what follow-up actions were built into the training to avoid the perception that customer service is only the flavor-of-the-month?

Individual Learning Needs Analysis

While identifying organizational learning needs is critical to making the best use of an organization's training budget, analyzing individual learning needs is also important. Understanding the training group's current skills and knowledge can help to focus the training on those areas that require most work—this also helps to avoid going over what the individuals already know, thus wasting their time, or losing them by jumping in at too advanced a level. In addition, individual learning needs analysis can uncover unfavorable attitudes about training that trainers will be better able to address if they are prepared for them. For example, some learners may see the training as a waste of time, as an interruption to their normal work, or as a sign of potentially frightening organizational change.

Many of the same methods used to gather data for organizational learning needs are used for individual learning needs analysis. Analyzing employee learning needs should be carried out in a thoughtful, sensitive, and inclusive manner. Here are potential pitfalls to avoid:

- **Don't analyze needs you can't meet.** Training needs analysis raises expectations. It sends a message to employees that the organization expects them to be competent in particular areas.

- **Involve employees directly.** Sometimes employees don't see a value in participating in training. In assessing needs, trainers need to prepare employees to buy into the training. Asking useful questions and listening carefully to stated needs are excellent methods for accomplishing both of those goals. Ask these questions: "To what degree would you like to learn how to do [X] more effectively?" and "To what degree would you seriously consider participating in training to improve your competency in [X]?"

- **Make the identified needs an obvious part of your training design.** Participants should be able to see that they have influenced the content and emphasis of the training session. A good practice is briefly to summarize the local trends discovered in the training needs analysis when you introduce the goals of the session.

- **Don't think of training as a "magic bullet."** In the case of customer service, a key factor is whether or not emphasis is placed on quality of service beyond the training event. This may include establishing service standards and supporting a shift to a service-minded culture, setting goals for quality service in employees' development plans, measuring customer service as a specific job expectation on performance evaluation tools, creating rewards and incentives for exceptional service, and so on.

The Bare Minimum

As noted, in an ideal world, you would have gathered all this data about the needs of the organization and the employees and determined that training was the right way to connect those dots. However, even if the decision to put on this workshop has already been made, you still need a bare minimum of information to be successful:

- **Who is your project sponsor (who wants to do this, provides the budget, and so on)?** In fact, if you don't have a project sponsor, *stop* the project. Lack of a project sponsor indicates that the project isn't important to the business. Optimally, the project sponsor should come from the business side of the organization. If the project sponsor is the head of training, then the mentality behind the training—"build it and they will come"—is likely wrong. Even compliance training should have a functional sponsor.

- **What does the sponsor want the learners to be able to do when they are done with training?** How does the sponsor define measures of success? Answering these critical questions brings clarity to the sponsor's expectations and thus to the workshop design.

- **What are the objectives of the training?** What, specifically, do you want participants to be able to *do* after the workshop? Build clear, specific, and measurable learning objectives and then develop learning activities that directly support them. A good resource for writing objectives is Bloom's Taxonomy; if you use it, aim to create Application-level or higher objectives. Knowledge- and Comprehension-level objectives have their place, but learning events need to go beyond these levels of learning to effectively change behaviors in the workplace.

- **Why does the sponsor want this right now?** Is something going on in the organization of which you should be aware?

- **What is the budget?** How much time and money will be invested in the training?

Key Points

- Needs analysis identifies the gap between what the organization needs and what the employees are able to do and then determines how best to bridge that gap.

- Methods of data gathering for needs analysis include strategic needs analysis, structured interviews, surveys, focus groups, and others.

- Sometimes, needs analysis is not an option, but some minimum information is necessary, including who wants the training, how the results will be defined, why the training is being requested now, and what the budget is.

What to Do Next

- If you have the option, carry out a needs analysis to determine if this training is really what your organization requires to succeed. If it isn't, prepare to argue against wasting time, money, and effort on training that will not support the organization's goals.

- If you don't have the option of a needs analysis, make sure that you seek out at least the bare minimum information to conduct effective training.

- Prepare learning objectives that are measurable, clear, and specific.

- If you have little training background, read the next chapter (Chapter 6) to learn about the theories and concepts that are at the root of training design. If you are an experienced trainer, skim Chapter 6 on design theory or go straight to Chapters 7 and 8 for tips on leveraging technology and delivering training, respectively.

Additional Resources

Biech, E., ed. (2008). *ASTD Handbook for Workplace Learning Professionals.* Alexandria, VA: ASTD Press.

Biech, E., ed. (2014). *ASTD Handbook: The Definitive Reference for Training & Development.* Alexandria, VA: ASTD Press.

Russo, C. "Be a Better Needs Analyst." ASTD *Infoline* no. 258502. Alexandria, VA: ASTD Press.

Tobey, D. (2005). *Needs Assessment Basics.* Alexandria, VA: ASTD Press.

Chapter 6

Understanding the Foundations of Training Design

What's in This Chapter

- Introducing adult learning theory
- Exploring multiple intelligences
- Incorporating whole brain learning
- Learning how theory enters into practice

Because this book provides fully designed workshops, you don't need to know all the details of designing a course—the design has already been done for you. However, understanding some of the principle design and learning theories that underpin these workshops is useful and helpful—especially if you are somewhat new to the field of workplace training and development. To effectively deliver training to learners requires a core understanding of how and why people learn. This gives you the flexibility to adapt a course to the unique learners in the room as needed.

Customization is key for all training but even more so with customer service training. To be meaningful, activities need to be practical, immediately applicable, and specific to the work situations the participants encounter when servicing customers.

Although a process or technique may be broadly applicable across industries and positions, the language used to convey it and the examples shared to illustrate it must be immediately recognizable and relatable to the participants. For example, let's say an activity asks participants to apply a program concept to a scenario in which a customer is frustrated because of the inefficiency related to completing paperwork. Simple enough. But if the participants are employees of a local municipality and the scenario describes the customer's annoyance at filling out mortgage application forms, many participants will say "but we don't do this. . . ." In the same way, if bankers are given material in which the customer is trying to get a permit approved, many will focus on the differences, not the similarities. Effective design tailors content to be specific to both the industry and the organization.

Basic Adult Learning Theory

The individual participant addressed in these workshops is typically an adult with learning needs that differ in many (but not all) ways from children. Much has been documented about how adults learn best. A key figure in adult education is Malcolm Knowles, who is often regarded as the father of adult learning. Knowles made several contributions to the field but is best known for popularizing the term *andragogy*, which refers to the art and science of teaching adults. Here are six assumptions about adult learners noted in *The Adult Learner: A Neglected Species* (Knowles 1984):

- Adults need to know why learning something is important before they learn it.
- Adults have a concept of self and do not like others imposing their will on them.
- Adults have a wealth of knowledge and experience and want that knowledge to be recognized.
- Adults open up to learning when they think that the learning will help them with real problems.
- Adults want to know how the learning will help them in their personal lives.
- Adults respond to external motivations, such as the prospect of a promotion or an increase in salary.

Given these principles of adult learning, designing sessions that are highly interactive and engaging is critical (see sidebar on next page for more tips). Forcing anyone to learn anything is impossible, so the goal of effective training design is to provide every opportunity and encouragement to the potential learner. Involvement of the learner is the key. As an old Chinese proverb says, "Tell me and I will forget. Show me and I may remember. Involve me and I will

Tips for Adult Learning

To reach adult learners, incorporate these ideas into your next training session:

- Incorporate self-directed learning activities in the session design.
- Avoid overuse of lectures and "talking to"; emphasize discussion.
- Use interactive methods such as case studies, role playing, and so forth.
- Make the content and materials closely fit assessed needs.
- Allow plenty of time to "process" the learning activities.
- Promote inquiry into problems and affirm the experience of participants.
- Give participants a rationale for becoming involved and provide opportunities for success.
- Promote getting acquainted and interpersonal linkages.
- Diagnose and prioritize learning needs and preferences before and during the session.
- Use learning groups as "home bases" for participants.
- Include interpersonal feedback exercises and opportunities to experiment.
- Use subgroups to provide safety and readiness to engage in open interchange.
- Make all learner assessment self-directed.
- Provide activities that focus on cognitive, affective, and behavioral change.

understand." The designs in this book use several methods to convey information and engage participants. By incorporating varied training media—such as presentation media, discussion sessions, small-group work, structured exercises, and self-assessments—these designs maximize active participant involvement and offer something for every learning style.

In addition to engaging the interest of the learner, interactive training allows you to tap into another source of learning content: the participants themselves. In a group-learning situation, a good learning environment encourages participants to share with others in the group so the entire group's cumulative knowledge can be used.

More Theoretical Ideas Important to Learning

Research on how people learn and how the brain works occurs continuously. A few ideas that come up frequently in training design and delivery are multiple intelligences and whole brain learning.

Multiple Intelligences

Multiple intelligences reflect how people prefer to process information. Howard Gardner, from Harvard University, has been challenging the basic beliefs about intelligence since the early 1980s. Gardner initially described a list of seven intelligences. Later, he added three additional intelligences to his list, and he expects the list to continue to grow (Gardner 2011). The intelligences are

- **interpersonal:** aptitude for working with others
- **logical/mathematical:** aptitude for math, logic, and deduction
- **spatial/visual:** aptitude for picturing, seeing
- **musical:** aptitude for musical expression
- **linguistic/verbal:** aptitude for the written and spoken word
- **intrapersonal:** aptitude for working alone
- **bodily kinesthetic:** aptitude for being physical
- **emotional:** aptitude for identifying emotion
- **naturalist:** aptitude for being with nature
- **existential:** aptitude for understanding one's purpose.

How do multiple intelligences affect your learning? Gardner suggests that most people are comfortable in three or four of these intelligences and avoid the others. For example, if you are not comfortable working with other people, doing group case studies may interfere with your ability to process new material. Video-based instruction will not be good for people with lower spatial/visual aptitudes. People with strong bodily/kinesthetic aptitudes prefer to move around while they are learning.

Allowing your learners to use their own strengths and weaknesses helps them process and learn. Here's an example: Suppose you are debriefing one of the exercises in the material. The exercise has been highly interpersonal (team activity), linguistic (lots of talking), spatial/visual (the participants built an object), musical (music was playing), logical/mathematical (there were rules and structure), and kinesthetic (people moved around). You've honored all the processing styles except intrapersonal, so the people who process information in this manner probably need a return to their strength of working alone. Start the debriefing by asking people to quietly work on their own, writing down five observations of the activity. Then ask them to share as a group.

Whole Brain Learning

Ned Herrmann pioneered the concept of whole brain learning in the 1970s, developing the Herrmann Whole Brain Model, which divides the brain into four distinct types of thinking: analytical, sequential, interpersonal, and imaginative. Each individual tends to favor one type of thinking over another, and this thinking preference evolves continually throughout a person's life. In fact, the brain changes all the time with new input and new ways of thinking—a feature that is known as *plasticity*.

Although each person has a preferred thinking style, he or she may prefer it to varying degrees. To identify a person's thinking preference, Herrmann developed the Herrmann Brain Dominance Instrument in 1979. Learning about your own thinking and learning preferences can motivate you to learn new ways to learn and think. For trainers and facilitators, learning about your own preferences can help you identify where you may be neglecting other styles or preferences in your training design and delivery. As Ann Herrmann-Nehdi, daughter of Ned Herrmann and researcher in her own right, notes in the *ASTD Handbook for Workplace Learning Professionals*, "Effective learning is whole brained—designing, delivering, and evaluating the learning to best meet the varying needs of diverse learners" (2008, p. 215).

Herrmann-Nehdi continues, "Our knowledge of the brain and its inherent uniqueness shows that each individual is a unique learner with learning experiences, preferences, and avoidances that will be different from those of other learners. This means that learning designs must somehow factor in the uniqueness of the individual learner" (2008, p. 221). That is to say that effective facilitation must provide a blend of learning activities that addresses various thinking processes from analytical to sequential to interpersonal to imaginative. Because each individual has a unique combination of varying preferences for different types of learning, such a blend can engage most learners even when they are not directly learning in their preferred style. Engaging varied thinking styles ensures *whole brain learning*, rather than a narrow focus on one or two thinking styles.

Here are some tips for incorporating whole brain learning into your facilitation:

- Identify your own thinking preferences to avoid getting too one-sided in your presentation. Deliberately include styles you don't typically prefer.
- Recognize that your learners have unique brains that have continually changed as a result of a lifetime of experiences, learning, and ways of thinking.

- Address those variations in learning and thinking preferences by learning different ways to deliver learning, including facts, case studies, metaphors, brainstorming, simulations, quizzes, outlines, procedures, group learning, role plays, and so on to engage their whole brains.

- Avoid diminishing learners' motivation to learn.

- Avoid overwhelming the brain or causing stress. Stick to need-to-know rather than nice-to-know.

Theory Into Practice

These theories (and more that are not addressed here) affect the way the content of the workshops are put together. Some examples of training features that derive from these theories include handouts, research references, and presentation media to read; quiet time to write notes and reflect; opportunities for listening and talking; and exercises for practicing skills. The workshop activities and materials for the programs in this book have taken these theories to heart in their design, providing content, activities, and tools that will appeal to and engage many learning and thinking styles. Additional ways to translate learning and design theory into practice include the following:

Establishing a Framework

For learners to understand the goals of training and how material relates to real work situations, a framework can be helpful. When presenting the training in the context of a framework, trainers should provide an overview of why the organization has decided to undertake the training and why it is important. This explanation should also highlight what the trainer hopes to accomplish and how the skills learned in this training will be useful back on the job.

Objectives and goals of the programs and learning activities are described in this workbook; share those objectives with the learners when discussing the purposes of specific exercises. Handouts will also help provide a framework for participants.

Identifying Behaviors

Within any training goal are many behaviors. For example, listening and giving clear directions are necessary behaviors for good customer service. Customer service does not improve simply because employees are told to do so—participants need to understand the reasons and see the relevant parts of the equation. For these reasons, facilitators should identify and discuss relevant behaviors throughout the program.

Training helps people identify the behaviors that are important, so that those behaviors can be targeted for improvement. Learning activities enable participants to analyze different skills and behaviors and to separate the parts from the whole. The learning activities in this book, with their clearly stated objectives, have been carefully crafted to take these considerations into account.

Practicing

Practice is crucial for learning because learning takes place by doing and by seeing. In the training designs included in this workbook, practice occurs in written exercises, verbal exercises, and role playing. Role playing helps participants actually practice the behaviors that are being addressed. Role-play exercises bring skills and behaviors to life for those acting out particular roles and for those observing the scenarios.

Learning a new skill takes a lot of practice. Some participants learn skills more quickly than others. Some people's attitudes might prevent them from being open to trying new behaviors. Your job is to facilitate the session to the best of your ability, taking different learning styles into account. The rest is up to the participants.

Providing Feedback

A key aspect of training is the feedback trainers give to participants. If delivered in a supportive and constructive manner, feedback helps learners develop a deeper understanding of the content you are presenting and the behaviors they are practicing. Feedback in role plays is especially powerful because this is where "the rubber hits the road." In role plays, observers can see if people are able to practice the behaviors that have been discussed, or whether habitual responses will prevail.

Making It Relevant

Throughout the program you will discuss how to use skills and new behaviors on the job. These discussions will help answer the question "So what?" Exercises and action plans help participants bring new skills back to actual work situations. This is also important in addressing the adult need for relevancy in learning.

The Bare Minimum

- **Model it.** As a trainer, the participants in the program are your customers! Use the service behavior skills of the half-day workshop to effectively manage any conflict that arises and mitigate it proactively. Consider your service strategies (covered in the one-day work-shop) and find opportunities to streamline them. Then tell stories of what you did to highlight examples during the training. When you model these skills during training, you can temporarily take off your trainer hat and ask the participants: "What just happened there? How did I use the technique we are working with in *my* customer interaction just then?" In other instances, you might not draw attention to it, but pause subtly, make eye contact with participants, and look for signs that they saw the behavior in action, and saw it work effectively!

- **Keep the focus on self-reflection.** Be purposeful in designing content that encourages participants to analyze their own behaviors instead of what others do wrong.

- **Build practice into the design.** As with many skills, service must be demonstrated. It isn't enough to know how to react or be able to explain it, so provide your participants with hands-on, engaging activities that require them to demonstrate the skills and receive feedback. (What we *think* we are doing often isn't the same as what we *are* doing.)

Key Points

- Adults have specific learning needs that must be addressed in training to make it successful.

- People also have different intelligences; that is, different areas in which they are more comfortable and competent. Addressing different intelligences in the workshop keeps more people engaged in more ways.

- People take in new information in different ways; addressing a variety of different thinking styles can help everyone learn more effectively.

- Bring theory into practice by creating a framework, identifying behaviors, practicing, providing feedback, and making the learning relevant.

What to Do Next

- Look through the training materials to identify how they address the learning theories presented in this book. If you make modifications to the material, consider whether those modifications leave out an intelligence or a thinking style. Can you address more intelligences without making the material cumbersome?

- Read the next chapter to identify how to incorporate technology into the workshop to make it more effective.

Additional Resources

Biech, E., ed. (2008). *ASTD Handbook for Workplace Learning Professionals.* Alexandria, VA: ASTD Press.

Biech, E., ed. (2014). *ASTD Handbook: The Definitive Reference for Training & Development,* 2nd edition. Alexandria, VA: ASTD Press.

Gardner, H. (2006). *Multiple Intelligences: New Horizons in Theory and Practice.* New York: Basic Books.

Gardner, H. (2011). *Frames of Mind: The Theory of Multiple Intelligences.* New York: Basic Books.

Herrmann, N. (1988). *Creative Brain.* Lake Lure, NC: Brain Books.

Herrmann, N. (1996). *Whole Brain Business Book.* San Francisco: McGraw-Hill.

Herrmann-Nehdi, A. (2008). "The Learner: What We Need to Know." In E. Biech, ed., *ASTD Handbook for Workplace Learning Professionals.* Alexandria, VA: ASTD Press.

Jones, J.E., W.L. Bearley, and D.C. Watsabaugh. (1996). *The New Fieldbook for Trainers: Tips, Tools, and Techniques.* Amherst, MA: HRD Press.

Knowles, M.S. (1984). *The Adult Learner: A Neglected Species.* Houston, TX: Gulf Publishing.

Russell, L. (1999). *The Accelerated Learning Fieldbook: Making the Instructional Process Fast, Flexible, and Fun.* San Francisco: Jossey-Bass/Pfeiffer.

Chapter 7

Leveraging Technology to Maximize and Support Design and Delivery

What's in This Chapter

- Recognizing the importance of technology tools
- Determining when to use learning technologies
- Identifying types of learning technologies
- Enhancing learner engagement
- Deepening learner understanding
- Increasing learning application

The workshops offered in this book are designed to be facilitated in person. Even so, learning technologies can and should play a role in adapting workshops to fit your organization, reinforce learning, and measure effectiveness. Technology is an important learning component, but it can also become an expensive distraction. The key is whether and how well technology enhances learners' abilities to understand and apply workshop concepts.

Your use of technology should also align with your organization's culture and readiness. For example, using webinars and wikis in a high-tech environment where employees are familiar with these tools may be logical and welcome, but you might need to introduce these tools more slowly at another company where email is the primary technology used for communication (see Figure 7-1 for some dos and don'ts of recording webinars).

The most important factor to consider when deciding whether to use learning technologies is how they can best support your workshop's learning objectives. This is particularly critical (and not at all straightforward) when delivering these workshops' soft skills training because personal and interpersonal habits and skills tend to require participants to challenge their beliefs and shift their mindsets. This deeper level of self-reflection, though tougher to do in a virtual setting, can be done if you select the right tool and use it at the right time in the learning process.

In the previous chapter, you learned about the adult learning theories and learning styles that underpin the workshops in this volume. Keep these in mind as you assess and weigh opportunities to use learning technologies. In this chapter, you will explore where technology can augment learning transfer and application in your workshop. Please note that the information has been kept general for two reasons. First, each organization has access to specific and limited technologies, and you should learn about them and creatively use what you have. Second, recommendations for specific technologies are likely to become obsolete quickly; so instead, let's focus on the types of learning technologies that might best augment in-person workshops.

Figure 7-1. Dos and Don'ts of Recording Webinars

To increase your chances of a successful webinar, consider and incorporate these tips.

Do
- Introduce yourself and the topic.
- Keep recorded webinars short—ideally 20 minutes or less.
- Use a conversational voice to increase interest.
- Use adequate numbers of slides so that you do not stay on one slide for more than 30 or 45 seconds.
- Address simple, focused topics with five or fewer key points.
- Use pictures and minimal text on slides.

Don't
- Use your computer's microphone to record; instead, invest in a good headset.
- Use a recorded webinar that has poor audio quality; instead, re-record if needed.
- Use too much text or small fonts.
- Assume that participants are just watching the webinar; you have to keep their interest or they will get distracted.
- Try to cover a complex topic using a recorded webinar; the webinar should be focused on one topic with a few main points.

Why Consider Learning Technologies?

You have decided to provide in-person workshops and will use the agendas offered in this book to plan and conduct the training. Learning technologies can be essential tools in your tool kit. Most behavior change does not occur in the classroom. The workshop is important, but it must be supported by strong pre- and post-course reinforcement. To learn something, learners need many points of contact with the new skills and concepts, such as presentation, reflection, discussion, practice, feedback, and exploration. Moreover, most of your participants are very busy and unable to attend multiple in-person pre- or post-course sessions. So to ensure learning

A Word From the Author: Apps, QR Codes, and More

Leveraging technology, when it comes to workplace learning, can mean a lot more than an e-learning solution. In the case of customer service, it can extend to using electronic surveys, social media sites, and your organization's own web presence to gather customer input that feeds into your needs analysis. It can involve creating just-in-time electronic job aids, developing knowledge sharing sites, designing apps to enhance the customer experience (such as one created for a weekend-long music festival with schedules, maps, critical questions, and incentives for sharing your positive experiences and photos).

What existing apps might be useful in enhancing the delivery of service? Some examples that are fair game to consider as a way to leverage technology include apps to convert employees' native language into a customer's first language or a camera app that enables immediate recording of a resource created in class (flip chart list, explanatory graphic, reference chart). You might even start off a session or return from a break by asking participants to share an app they have used to support customer needs; the list of innovative and helpful apps is ever growing.

Another technological option to think about integrating in your overall customer service development strategy is matrix barcodes (commonly referred to as QR or Quick Response Codes). They hold information about the items to which they are attached that can be read by a QR Code reader in a smartphone, for example. Does your environment allow for their use as job aids? Can QR Codes support a customer-centered process improvement (such as those covered in the one-day and two-day workshop agendas)?

Get creative and think beyond the traditional uses of technology for training. Collaborating with the information technology team or internal technology enthusiasts may generate many additional ideas.

transfer, you can augment in-person activities with technology-based engagement. The good news is that you can use technology in many ways to enhance learning, even of soft skills.

Opportunities to Use Learning Technologies

Whether you have many or few technology resources upon which to draw for learning, start by asking yourself this question: For this topic or series, how can I best use technology to increase learner engagement, understanding, and application? You will use these criteria to discover and evaluate potential ways technology might provide value in the learning process, including

- when designing the training
- before the training
- during the training
- after the training
- while building a learner community.

Note that this chapter offers ways to use technology to enhance traditional learning workshops (blended learning). It is important that you consult with a technology partner if you are considering a technology-driven training program—such as a workplace simulation or self-directed online learning. That said, the content found in this training series could be adapted for use in an online learning platform. For more information on how to use the online tools and downloads, see Chapter 14.

When Designing Training

The ATD Workshop Series offers fully designed training you can use with minimal preparation and solid facilitation skills. Even so, you will be creating a learning implementation plan that is an important part of the design process.

To increase engagement: You have to know your audience members to engage them, because engagement is a choice driven by interest, challenge, and relevance of the topic. Use learning technologies to ensure that you understand where your audience is coming from and the learning approaches they will most value. Email groups, online surveys, teleconferencing, and web meetings with polling can help you ascertain their wants and needs before you solidify your training plan. In the two-day workshop agenda, for example, the morning of Day Two begins with a resource review. Participants are asked to find a video, online resource, blog, article, or other resource that supports, furthers, or reinforces the learning and share it with others. This is a simple way to integrate technology, increase learner engagement, and enhance the body of knowledge present in the workshop.

To deepen understanding: When in the planning stage, make sure that you have not tried to cram too much presentation into the learning process and that you have planned sufficient time and attention to engaging participants. Flowcharting or mind-mapping software can help you visualize and communicate your learning plan and ensure that you allow for maximum engagement and practice. Or, you might record a brief video of a key executive commenting on the priority the organization is placing on customer service and the critical role of customer service to the organizational mission.

To increase application: Increasing retention and application requires buy-in from sponsors and managers to ensure that what is learned is welcomed and applied on the job. Use email groups, online surveys, teleconferencing, and web meetings with polling to communicate with sponsors and managers about what they want out of the training and to identify ways to apply the learning back on the job. Having this information is also valuable in developing the training plan.

Before Training

You want to prime your participants' minds for the topic you will be presenting during the workshop. Pre-work does not have to be something arduous and unwelcome. In fact, a great pre-work assignment can help maximize precious time in the classroom and allow you to focus on the topics that require thorough discussion.

To increase engagement: Tap into the most fascinating aspects of the workshop topic and introduce these through video clips, blog posts, and online resources (see Figure 7-2 about the legal use of video clips, images, and so forth). Avoid boring participants with long "how-to" articles or book chapters before the workshop. In fact, do the opposite and ensure that the pre-work is interesting, provocative (even controversial), and brief. You might select a blog post or video clip that offers a counterpoint to the training or something that inspires your participants to think about the topic before attending training.

To deepen understanding: If you know that the workshop topic will be challenging to some of your participants, prepare and share a brief recorded webinar, video clip, or article that introduces the topic. For example, if your managers tend to tell versus coach, try sharing one or two external resources that discuss the value of service-oriented coaching conversations.

To increase application: You can improve the chances that your participants will apply what they learn by ensuring they identify real-world work challenges in which they can apply their new

Figure 7-2. Copyright Beware

Copyright law is a sticky, complex area that is beyond the scope of this book to address in detail. For legal advice, consult your legal department.

However, it's very important to note a few things about copyright, fair use, and intellectual property:

- Just because you found an image, article, music, or video online doesn't mean that you can use it in training without permission. Make sure you obtain permission from the copyright owner before you use it (sometimes the copyright owner is not obvious and you will need to do some research).

- Fair use is pretty limited. Although most fair use allows an educational exception, that does *not* include corporate or organizational training. Other exceptions relate to how much material relative to the original was used, the nature of the original work (creative work generally has more protection), and the effect on the market for the original (Swindling and Partridge 2008). Once again, your best bet is to get written permission.

- Just because something doesn't have a copyright notice on it doesn't mean that it isn't copyright protected. All original material is protected under copyright law as soon as it is published or created.

Don't despair. Plenty of online sources of images, videos, text, and so forth exist that you can use for free or for a minimal fee. Just search on the terms "copyright free" or "open source." Another place to look is Wikimedia Commons, which has millions of freely usable media files. For more information about how copyright law affects your use of materials in this volume, please see Chapter 14 on how to use the online materials and downloads.

skills. Start with a one- or two-question pre-workshop survey (using Survey Monkey or similar) that requires they identify these opportunities and then use the responses to enhance your in-workshop discussions. If your organization has an internal social network or ways to create collaboration groups, use the pre-work questions to begin an online discussion of the topic. The conversations will help your participants think about the topic and will help you prepare for a great workshop (and will give you a beneficial "heads-up" on potential areas of conflict or disagreement).

During Training

Learning technologies can help make your workshops more interesting and can help enhance understanding of the material. Beware, however, that you always want to have a "Plan B" in case of technology glitches or breakdowns. Another critical point to make here is that technology does not change how people learn. Learning and performance drive the technology choice, not the other way around.

To increase engagement: The perennial favorite technology for spicing up a workshop is the use of a great video. Boring videos don't help! If you can find short video clips that reinforce your most important points, please do so. In addition to adding contrast to the workshop flow, having other "experts" say what you want participants to hear is helpful. Another way to increase engagement is to use some kind of audience-response system or electronic polling. Although this might not be practical for small groups (the technology can be a bit pricey), some less expensive alternatives use texting schemas you might want to check out. Your participants will love seeing their collective responses instantly populate your PowerPoint charts. (For more on PowerPoint, see Figure 7-3 and Chapter 8.)

To deepen understanding: Videos can also help improve understanding. If your participants have access to computers during the workshop, consider short technology-based games and short simulations that reinforce the points. You can also ask participants to fill out worksheets and surveys online during the class. Share animated models, flowcharts, or mind maps to help explain key concepts or how they connect together.

To increase application: Learning simulations and practice sessions help prepare participants to apply new skills. You can do these in person, and you can use technology to facilitate practices. This depends a lot on the topic.

After Training

Your participants are busy, and the new skills and concepts they learned in the workshop will become a distant memory without follow-up. Just as you did before the training, you can and should use learning technologies to augment the learning that occurs during the workshop.

To increase engagement: Learners engage when they perceive something as interesting, relevant right now, or challenging. Use tools such as video, blogs, social networks, chat, websites, and email to increase interest in the topic and to provide challenge.

To deepen understanding: Use post-workshop surveys and polling tools to assess understanding so you can address any gap. Add to the participants' understanding of the topic by posting materials on a SharePoint site or through blog posts that you push to their email inboxes using an RSS feed.

To increase application: Provide a just-in-time online resource where participants find quick reference sheets and get application tips using a group site, social network, or SharePoint site. Request or require that participants report how they have used new skills through an online project management collaboration site, wiki, or email group.

While Building a Learning Community

Creating an ongoing network of learners is extremely valuable, especially for soft skills. The in-person workshop is just the beginning of the learning journey and so keeping learners

Figure 7-3. PowerPoint or Prezi or Other?

Although PowerPoint is the most common presentation software, other platforms you might want to consider include Prezi, GoAnimate, Google Docs, mind-mapping programs, or others. Here are a few key considerations that will help you choose:

- Aside from the in-class workshop, where will you want to share the presentation?
- If you will be sharing the presentation with others, consider whether new software will be required.
- Which presentation platform is best for the content you are presenting, or does it matter?
- What are the costs and resources required for each platform?
- Which platform will partner well with technology tools you will use to reinforce the learning?
- What might be the advantage of using two or more platforms throughout the learning process?

engaged is helpful. In addition, you want to create a safe place where learners can discuss challenges, provide encouragement, and share their best practices. Learning technologies are particularly useful for building community among learners and teams.

To increase engagement: Busy people value community but often can't make the time to attend follow-up sessions or network with peers. They might, however, be able to take 10 minutes to check in on an internal social network, group site, or blog to learn from and share with others. If your organization does not have social networking or collaboration software, you might need to get creative. Talk to your technology department about the tools you do have—whether they are SharePoint, blog software, internal messaging, a wiki-type project management collaboration tool, or other. You can even use email groups to connect learners. Look for ways you can create pull (they choose when to engage) and push (they get updates), such as using RSS feeds.

To deepen understanding: After the workshop, use web meetings, teleconferencing, and messaging to connect learning partners or mentors and facilitate their sharing real-time application stories. Periodically facilitate online discussion groups to reinforce the learning and bring participants back together.

To increase application: Use a collaborative online project site or social network to set expectations about post-workshop peer discussions and reinforce engagement. Poll participants and assign sub-teams to lead a portion of each web meeting.

The Bare Minimum

- **Know what resources you have available.** Many organizations have widely varying resources; don't assume that you know everything that is available.

- **Stretch yourself.** Be willing to try something new; develop your skills to use technology in innovative ways to facilitate learning.

- **Know your participants.** They may be far ahead of you in their skills with technology or they may be far behind. If you plan to use learning technologies, do your best to assess their skill level before designing the workshop.

- **Be prepared for challenges.** No matter the skill level of the group, technology glitches are unavoidable. Be sure to cultivate good working relationships with technology support staff.

Key Points

- Most behavior change does not happen in a classroom but through multiple points of reinforcement. Learning technologies are an efficient way to augment learning.

- You can use learning technologies your organization already has if you are creative and partner with your technology team.

- Use learning technologies throughout the learning process to increase engagement, understanding, and application.

What to Do Next

- **Highlight the portions of this chapter that seem most relevant to your learning plan.** Meet with your technology team and get its input on the most applicable tools you might use.

- **Create a plan for how you will use learning technologies to reinforce your workshop.** Ensure that you select only those tools and activities that will enhance the overall learning objectives and be mindful of your organization's culture and comfort level with technology.

- **Test, test, test!** Practice using technology tools to ensure they will deliver what you hope.

- **Read the next chapter to learn ways you can improve your facilitation skills.** Many of these skills will also be useful when using learning technologies, especially collaboration tools.

Additional Resources

Bozarth, J. (2014). "Effective Social Media for Learning." In E. Biech, ed., *ASTD Handbook: The Definitive Reference for Training & Development*, 2nd edition. Alexandria, VA: ASTD Press.

Chen, J. (2012). *50 Digital Team-Building Games: Fast, Fun Meeting Openers, Group Activities and Adventures Using Social Media, Smart Phones, GPS, Tablets, and More.* Hoboken, NJ: Wiley.

Halls, J. (2012). *Rapid Video Development for Trainers: How to Create Learning Videos Fast and Affordably.* Alexandria, VA: ASTD Press.

Kapp, K. (2013). *The Gamification of Learning and Instruction Fieldbook: Ideas Into Practice.* San Francisco: Wiley.

Palloff, R.M., and K. Pratt. (2009). *Building Online Learning Communities: Effective Strategies for the Virtual Classroom.* San Francisco: Jossey-Bass.

Quinn, C. (2014). "M-Thinking: There's an App for That." In E. Biech, ed., *ASTD Handbook: The Definitive Reference for Training & Development,* 2nd edition. Alexandria, VA: ASTD Press.

Swindling, L.B., and M.V.B. Partridge. (2008). "Intellectual Property: Protect What Is Yours and Avoid Taking What Belongs to Someone Else." In E. Biech, *ASTD Handbook for Workplace Learning Professionals.* Alexandria, VA: ASTD Press.

Toth, T. (2006). *Technology for Trainers.* Alexandria, VA: ASTD Press.

Udell, C. (2012). *Learning Everywhere: How Mobile Content Strategies Are Transforming Training.* Nashville, TN: Rockbench Publishing.

Chapter 8

Delivering Your Customer Service Workshop: Be a Great Facilitator

What's in This Chapter

- Defining the facilitator's role
- Creating an effective learning environment
- Preparing participant materials
- Using program preparation checklists
- Starting and ending on a strong note
- Managing participant behaviors

Let's get one thing clear from the get-go: Facilitating a workshop—facilitating learning—is *not* lecturing. The title of ATD's bestselling book says it all: *Telling Ain't Training* (Stolovitch and Keeps 2011). A facilitator is the person who helps learners open themselves to new learning and makes the process easier. The role requires that you avoid projecting yourself as a subject matter expert (SME) and that you prepare activities that foster learning through "hands-on" experience and interaction.

Before you can help someone else learn, you must understand the roles you will embody when you deliver training: trainer, facilitator, and learner. When a workshop begins, you are the trainer, bringing to the learning event a plan, structure, experience, and objectives. This is only possible because you have a strong, repeatable logistics process. As you ask the learners to prioritize the learning objectives, you slowly release control, inviting them to become partners in their own learning. As you move from the trainer role into the facilitator role, the objectives are the contract between the learners and the facilitator. All great facilitators also have a third role in the classroom—the role of learner. If you are open, you can learn many new things when you are in class. If you believe you must be the expert as a learning facilitator, you will not be very effective.

To be most successful as a learning facilitator, consider this checklist:

- ☐ Identify the beliefs that limit your ability to learn and, therefore, to teach.
- ☐ Learning is a gift for you and from you to others.
- ☐ Choose carefully what you call yourself and what you call your outcomes.
- ☐ Clarify your purpose to better honor your roles at a learning event.
- ☐ If you can't teach with passion, don't do it.

This last point is especially important. Not everyone is destined to be a great facilitator and teacher, but you can still have enormous impact if you are passionate about the topic, about the process, and about helping people improve their working lives. If you are serious about becoming a great facilitator, Chapter 12 provides a comprehensive assessment instrument to help you manage your personal development and increase the effectiveness of your training (see Assessment 2). You can use this instrument for self-assessment, end-of-course feedback, observer feedback, or as a professional growth tracker.

With these points firmly in mind—facilitating is not lecturing and passion can get you past many facilitator deficiencies—let's look at some other important aspects of facilitating, starting with how to create an engaging and effective learning environment.

The Learning Environment

Colors, seating, tools, environmental considerations (such as temperature, ventilation, lighting), and your attitude, dress, preparation, and passion all enhance—or detract from—an effective and positive learning environment. This section describes some ways to maximize learning through environmental factors.

Color. Research has shown that bland, neutral environments are so unlike the real world that learning achieved in these "sensory deprivation chambers" cannot be transferred to the job. Color can be a powerful way to engage the limbic part of the brain and create long-term retention. It can align the right and left brains. Ways to incorporate color include artwork, plants, and pictures that help people feel comfortable and visually stimulated. Consider printing your handouts and assessments in color. The training support materials provided in this book are designed in color but can be printed in either color or grayscale (to reduce reproduction costs).

Room Setup. Because much learning requires both individual reflection and role playing, consider seating that promotes personal thought and group sharing. One way to accomplish this is to set up groups of three to five at round or square tables, with each chair positioned so the projection screen can easily be seen. Leave plenty of room for each person so that when he or she does need to reflect, there is a feeling of privacy. Keep in mind that comfortable chairs and places to write help people relax to learn. Figure 8-1 details more room configurations that you can use to accomplish specific tasks or purposes in training.

Tools of the Trade. Lots of flipcharts (one per table is optimal) with brightly colored markers create an interactive environment. Flipcharts are about as basic and low tech as tools get, but they are also low cost and do the trick. Consider putting colorful hard candy on the tables (include sugar-free options), with bright cups of markers, pencils, and pens. Gather pads of colorful sticky notes and "fidgets" (quiet toys such as chenille stems, Koosh balls, and others) to place on the table as well. For the right level of trust to exist, your learners must feel welcome.

Your Secret Weapon. Finally, the key to establishing the optimal learning environment is *you.* You set the tone by your attitude, the way you greet people, the clothes you wear, your passion, and your interest and care for the participants. You set the stage for learning with four conditions that only you as the facilitator can create to maximize learning:

1. **Confidentiality.** Establish the expectation that anything shared during the training program will remain confidential among participants and that as the facilitator you are committed to creating a safe environment. An important step in learning is first admitting ignorance, which has some inherent risk. Adult learners may resist admitting their learning needs because they fear the repercussions of showing their weaknesses. You can alleviate these concerns by assuring participants that the sole purpose of the training is to build their skills, and that no evaluations will take place. Your workshop must be a safe place to learn and take risks.

Figure 8-1. Seating Configurations

Select a room setup that will best support the needs of your learners:

- **Rounds.** Circular tables are particularly useful for small-group work when you have 16 to 24 participants.

- **U-Shaped.** This setup features three long rectangular tables set up to form a U, with you at the open end. It is good for overall group interaction and small-group work (two to three people). This setup also helps you establish rapport with your learners.

- **Classroom.** This setup is a traditional grade-school format characterized by rows of tables with all the participants facing forward toward the trainer. Avoid this setup as much as possible because you become the focal point rather than the learners, and your ability to interact with learners is extremely limited. Problems of visibility also occur when rows in the back are blocked by rows in the front.

- **Chevron.** Chevron setup features rows of tables as in the classroom setup but the tables are angled to form a V-shape. This opens up the room to allow you to interact more with the learners and accommodates a larger group of learners without sacrificing visibility. However, it shares many of the drawbacks of the classroom setup.

- **Hybrid or Fishbone.** This setup combines a U-shaped configuration with that of a chevron. It is useful when there are too many learners to form a good U and there is room enough to broaden the U to allow tables to be set up as chevrons in the center of the U. This hybrid approach allows for interaction and enables the trainer to move around.

Source: Drawn from McCain and Tobey (2004).

2. **Freedom from distractions.** Work and personal demands cannot be ignored during training, but to maximize each participant's learning, and as a courtesy to others, outside demands should be minimized:

   a. Select a training site away from the workplace to help reduce distractions.

   b. Acknowledge that participants probably feel they shouldn't be away from work; remind them that the purpose of the training is to improve their work lives.

   c. Ask that mobile devices be turned off or set to silent alerts.

   d. Emphasize that because they are spending this time in training, trainees should immerse themselves in the learning experience and thereby maximize the value of their time, because far from being time "away from work responsibilities," it *is* a work responsibility.

3. **Personal responsibility for learning.** A facilitator can only create the *opportunity* for learning. Experiential learning requires that participants actively engage with and commit to learning—they cannot sit back and soak up information like sponges.

4. **Group participation.** Each participant brings relevant knowledge to the training program. Through discussion and sharing of information, a successful training session will

tap into the knowledge of each participant. Encourage all participants to accept responsibility for helping others learn.

Program Preparation Checklist

Preparation is power when it comes to facilitating a successful workshop, and a checklist is a powerful tool for effective preparation. This checklist of activities will help you prepare your workshop:

☐ Write down all location and workshop details when scheduling the workshop.

☐ Make travel reservations early (to save money, too), if applicable.

☐ Send a contract to the client to confirm details, or if you are an internal facilitator, develop guidelines and a workshop structure in conjunction with appropriate supervisors and managers.

☐ Specify room and equipment details in writing and then confirm by telephone.

☐ Define goals and expectations for the workshop.

☐ Get a list of participants, titles, roles, and responsibilities.

☐ Send participants a questionnaire that requires them to confirm their goals for the workshop.

☐ Send the client (or the participants, if you are an internal facilitator) an agenda for the workshop, with times for breaks and meals.

☐ Recommend that lunch or dinner be offered in-house, with nutritious food provided.

☐ Make a list of materials that you will need in the room (pads of paper, pens, pencils, markers, flipcharts, and so forth). Make sure to plan for some extras.

☐ Design the room layout (for example, rounds, U-shaped, classroom, chevron, or hybrid).

☐ Confirm whether you or your internal/external client will prepare copies of the workshop handouts. The workshop handouts should include all tools, training instruments, assessments, and worksheets. You may choose also to include copies of the presentation slides as part of the participant guide. All the supplemental materials you need to conduct the workshops in this book are available for download (see Chapter 14 for instructions).

☐ Prepare assessments, tools, training instruments, and workshop materials at least one week before the workshop so that you have time to peruse and check them and assemble any equipment you may need (see the next two sections).

Delivery Tips for Customer Service Training

Once Upon a Time

People remember stories. Stories are relatable. With the right story, participants will make connections in the content, form images in their mind, and store information on the training topic in a way that makes it more easily retrievable when needed. So, start gathering your own customer service stories. Who "got it right"? What, specifically, did they do (whether you were the customer or you observed the interaction)? Conversely, who is "getting it wrong" *and* believes they were right? This combination in a customer service story will help generate meaningful discussion around competing forces in service exchanges. For example, the organization has a policy the employee was following but the *way* he followed it left the customer dissatisfied, or the employee is placing his own "need to be right" over the priority of resolving the situation.

I have shared some of my stories in this book and invite you to make them your own. Eventually, you will begin replacing them with your own stories that will be more meaningful to you—and likely to your participants too.

All Eyes on You

It may seem obvious, but it is worth stating: Participants will be observing (and assessing) the behaviors you model. When you are facilitating customer service training, the participants are your customers; be attentive to their needs, be responsive to their feedback, remain available to them during "down time" (breaks and pre- and post-workshop hours), provide them with options, and seek out their needs. These actions are applicable in any learning event and on any topic. They are critical to your credibility as a service-minded facilitator. In short, walk the talk.

The Gift of a Challenging Participant

This chapter includes a reference for addressing difficult participant behaviors (Figure 8-6). Review it thoroughly and plan for managing the behaviors. I'd also like you to benefit from a revelation I had standing before an especially challenging group in a multi-session training event. It was two weeks into the program and I was beginning to feel battered in response to the large handful of participants who seemed to have it in for me. And then it hit me. They were not a challenge to my credibility, they were a gift enabling me to *demonstrate* the skills of the workshop in real time! I employed the techniques in the workshop to address the challenges. The result? I effectively dealt with the behaviors and was able to show just how powerful the workshop program content could be in action. This insight will be especially true in your customer service workshops.

Participant Materials

Participant materials support participant learning throughout the workshop and provide continuing references after the workshop has ended. There are several kinds of participant materials. Here are some options:

Handouts

The development and "look" of your handouts are vital to help participants understand the information they convey. To compile the handouts properly, first gather all assessments, tools, training instruments, activities, and presentation slides and arrange them in the order they appear in the workshop. Then bind them together in some fashion. There are several options for compiling your material, ranging from inexpensive to deluxe. The kind of binding is your choice—materials can be stapled, spiral bound, or gathered in a ring binder—but remember that a professional look supports success. Your choice of binding will depend on your budget for the project. Because first appearances count, provide a cover with eye-catching colors and appropriate graphics.

Using the agendas in Chapters 1–3, select the presentation slides, learning activities, handouts, tools, and assessments appropriate to your workshop (see Chapter 14: Online Tools and Downloads). If you choose to print out the presentation slides for your participants, consider printing no more than three slides per handout page to keep your content simple with sufficient white space for the participants to write their own notes. Use the learning objectives for each workshop to provide clarity for the participants at the outset. Remember to number the pages, to add graphics for interest (and humor), and to include tabs for easy reference if the packet of materials has multiple sections.

Some participants like to receive the handouts before the workshop begins. You may want to email participants to determine if they would like to receive the handouts electronically.

Presentation Slides

This ATD Workshop Series book includes presentation slides to support the two-day, one-day, and half-day agendas. They have been crafted to adhere to presentation best practices. If you choose to reorder or otherwise modify the slides, keep in mind these important concepts.

When you use PowerPoint software as a teaching tool, be judicious in the number of slides that you prepare. In a scientific lecture, slides are usually a necessity for explaining formulas or results, but a workshop relies on interaction so keep the slide information simple. Also, do not include more than five or six bullet points per slide. See more tips for effective PowerPoint slides in Figure 8-2.

A message can be conveyed quickly through the use of simple graphics. For example, an illustration of two people in conversation may highlight interpersonal communication, whereas a photo of a boardroom-style meeting may illustrate a group engaged in negotiation. Please note that any use of the images in the presentation slides provided with this book other than as part of your presentation is strictly prohibited by law.

When you use presentation slides ask yourself: What will a slide add to my presentation? Ensure that the answer that comes back is "it will enhance the message." If slides are simply used to make the workshop look more sophisticated or technical, the process may not achieve the desired results.

Figure 8-2. Tips for Effective PowerPoint Slides

Presentation slides can enhance your presentation. They can also detract from it by being too cluttered, monotonous, or hard to read. Here are some tips for clear, effective slides:

Fonts

- Use sans-serif fonts such as Arial, Calibri, or Helvetica; other fonts are blurry when viewed from 20 feet or more and are more easily read on LCD screens and in video/web presentations.
- Use the same sans-serif font for most (if not all) of the presentation.
- Use a font size no smaller than 24 points. (This will also help keep the number of bullets per slide down.)
- Consider using a 32-point font—this is the easiest for web/video transmission.
- Limit yourself to one font size per slide.

Colors

- Font colors should be black or dark blue for light backgrounds and white or yellow on dark backgrounds. Think high contrast for clarity and visual impact.
- Avoid using red or green. It doesn't project well, doesn't transfer well when used in a webinar, and causes issues for people who suffer color blindness.

Text and Paragraphs

- Align text left or right, not centered.
- Avoid cluttering a slide—use a single headline and a few bullet points.
- Use no more than six words to a line; avoid long sentences.
- Use sentence case—ALL CAPS ARE DIFFICULT TO READ AND CAN FEEL LIKE YELLING.
- Avoid abbreviations and acronyms.
- Limit use of punctuation marks.

Source: Developed by Cat Russo.

It can be frustrating when a facilitator shows a slide for every page that the participants have in front of them. The dynamics of the class are likely to disconnect. If the information you are teaching is in the handouts or workbook, work from those media alone and keep the workshop personally interactive.

Workbooks and Journals

A participant journal can be included in the binder with your handouts, or it may be a separate entity. Throughout the workshop participants can assess their progress and advance their development by entering details of their personal learning in the journal. The benefit of this journal to participants is that they can separate their personal discoveries and development from the main workshop handouts and use this journal as an action plan if desired.

Videos

If you show a video in your workshop, ensure that the skills it contains are up to date and that the video is less than 20 minutes long. Provide questions that will lead to a discussion of the information viewed. Short video clips can be effective learning tools.

Toys, Noisemakers, and Other Props

Experienced facilitators understand the value of gadgets and games that advance the learning, provide a break from learning, or both.

Adults love to play. When their minds are open they learn quickly and effectively. Something as simple as tossing a rubber ball from person to person as questions are asked about elements studied can liven up the workshop and help people remember what they've learned.

Case studies and lively exercises accelerate learning. Bells and whistles are forms of communication; use them when you pit two teams against each other or to indicate the end of an activity.

Facilitator Equipment and Materials

When all details for the workshop have been confirmed, it is time to prepare for the actual facilitation of the workshop at the site. You may know the site well because you are providing in-house facilitation. If, however, you are traveling off site to facilitate, important elements enter the planning. Here's a checklist of things to consider:

☐ Pack a data-storage device that contains your handouts and all relevant workshop materials. In the event that your printed materials do not reach the workshop location, you will have the electronic files to reprint on site.

- [ ] Pack the proper power cords, a spare battery for the laptop, and a bulb for the LCD or overhead projector in the event that these items are not available at the workshop location. This requires obtaining the make and model of all audiovisual and electronic equipment from the client or the training facility during your planning process.

- [ ] Bring an extension cord.

- [ ] Bring reference materials, books, article reprints, and ancillary content. Take advantage of all technology options, such as tablets or other readers to store reference materials. As a facilitator, you will occasionally need to refer to materials other than your own for additional information. Having the materials with you not only provides correct information about authors and articles, but it also positively reinforces participants' impressions of your knowledge, training, openness to learning, and preparedness.

- [ ] Bring flipcharts, painter's tape, and sticky notes.

- [ ] Pack toys and games for the workshop, a timer or bell, and extra marking pens.

- [ ] Bring duct tape. You may need it to tape extension cords to the floor as a safety precaution. The strength of duct tape also ensures that any flipchart pages hung on walls (with permission) will hold fast.

You can ship these items to the workshop in advance, but recognize that the shipment may not arrive in time, and that even if it does arrive on time, you may have to track it down at the venue. Also, take some time identifying backups or alternatives in case the materials, technology, and so on do not conform to plan. What are the worst-case scenarios? How could you manage such situations? Prepare to be flexible and creative.

A Strong Start: Introduction, Icebreakers, and Openers

The start of a session is a crucial time in the workshop dynamic. How the participants respond to you, the facilitator, can set the mood for the remainder of the workshop. To get things off on the right foot, get to the training room early, at least 30 to 60 minutes before the workshop. This gives you time not only to set up the room if that has not already been done, but also to test the environment, the seating plan, the equipment, and your place in the room. Find out where the restrooms are. When participants begin to arrive (and some of them come very early), be ready to welcome them. Don't be distracted with problems or issues; be free and available to your participants.

While they are settling in, engage them with simple questions:

- How was your commute?
- Have you traveled far for this workshop?

- Was it easy to find this room?

- May I help you with anything?

When a workshop begins, many trainers open with a discussion of their credentials and goals for the workshop. I prefer not to begin that way. Instead I want the participants to become interested, engaged, and immediately see the relevance of the workshop to their job function. Your introduction *will* happen a bit later in the workshop, but you only get one chance to make a first impression, and I have experienced much greater success by placing the focus on the participants first. This can be done with an *intriguing* question, a *meaningful* (to them!) statistic, or an icebreaker that is *relevant* to the workshop.

Because participants sometimes come into a training session feeling inexperienced, skeptical, reluctant, or scared, using an icebreaker activity to open the workshop enables participants to interact in a fun and nonthreatening way and to warm up to the group as well as the topic. Don't limit the time spent on this too much; when designed properly, it isn't a "fluff" exercise but an essential technique to build a safe and comfortable learning environment. Your icebreaker should apply directly to the workshop objectives. The more time participants spend getting to know each other at the beginning of the workshop, the more all of you will benefit as the session proceeds. And, that goes for you too; you will want to participate in the icebreaker as well!

Time your introduction to fall after participants are already interested in the workshop. Remember to talk more about what you want to accomplish in the workshop than about your accomplishments and be sure to connect your experience to the topic—not just list them all. The workshop agendas in Chapters 1-3 include some ideas to include in introducing yourself.

Feedback

Feedback is the quickest, surest way for you, the facilitator, to learn if the messages and instruction are reaching the participants and if the participants are absorbing the content. It is also important for you to evaluate the participants' rate of progress and learning. Answers to the questions you ask throughout the workshop will help you identify much of the progress, but these answers come from only a few of the participants at a time. They're not a global snapshot of the entire group's comprehension and skills mastery.

When you lead a workshop, the participants walk a fine line between retention and deflection of knowledge. Continuing evaluations ensure that learning is taking root. Three levels of questions—learning comprehension, skills mastery, and skills application—help you determine where the training may not be achieving the intended results.

- Learning comprehension checks that the participants understand and grasp the skills being taught (see Figure 8-3).

- Skills mastery means that the participants are able to demonstrate their newly acquired knowledge by some activity, such as teaching a portion of a module to their fellow participants or delivering their interpretation of topic specifics to the class (see Figure 8-4).

- Skills application is the real test. You may choose to substantiate this through role plays or group case studies. When the participants have the opportunity to verbally communicate the skills learned and to reach desired results through such application, then skills application is established (see Figure 8-5).

The questions in Figures 8-3 to 8-5 are designed for written answers so you can incorporate them into the takeaway workbook you create. The questions concerning skills mastery and skills application could be used as a job-based assignment if the workshop is longer than one day. Keep in mind that you will also reevaluate after each day of a multiday session.

Figure 8-3. Learning Comprehension Questions

Here are some questions that can be asked to determine each participant's level of *learning comprehension*:

- Give a brief overview of your learning in this workshop. Begin your phrases with "I have learned. . . ." This will assist you in focusing your responses.
- How/where will you apply this knowledge in your workplace?
- Did you acquire this knowledge through lectures/practice/discussion or a combination of all methods?
- Do you feel sufficiently confident to pass on this knowledge to your colleagues?
- Are there any areas that will require additional learning for you to feel sufficiently confident?

Figure 8-4. Skills Mastery Questions

Now let's look at some questions you can use to evaluate your participants' *skills mastery*:

- If you were asked to teach one skill in this workshop, which skill would it be?
- What would your three key message points be for that skill?
- Describe the steps you would take to instruct each message point (for example, lecture, group discussion, PowerPoint presentation, and so forth).
- What methods would you use to ensure that your participants comprehend your instruction?
- Would feedback from your participants, both positive and negative, affect the development of your skills mastery? If yes, illustrate your response and the changes you would make.

Figure 8-5. Skills Application Questions

And finally, let's consider some questions that identify participants' *ability to apply the skills* they've learned in the workshop:

- Please describe a situation at your workplace where you could employ one specific skill from this workshop.
- How would you introduce this skill to your colleagues?
- How would you set goals to measure the improvement in this skill?
- Describe the input and participation you would expect from your colleagues.
- How would you exemplify mastery of the skill?

Let's now look at other forms of in-class learning assessments: role plays, participant presentations, ball toss, and journaling.

Role Plays

Role plays are an effective tool for assessing learning comprehension. If two or more participants conduct a role play that reveals their understanding of the information, with an outcome that reflects that understanding, then it becomes a "live feed," instantaneous learning for all.

You must set up the role play carefully. It is often wise for you to be a part of the first role-play experience to show participants how it's done and to make them more comfortable with the activity. Ensure that you explain all the steps of the role play and the desired outcome. It is insightful to role-play a negative version first, followed by participant discussion; then role-play a positive aspect the second time. For example, if confrontational communication is the topic and the situation under discussion involves a line manager and his or her supervisor, first enact the role play using the verbal and body language that is causing the negative result. Discuss this as a class to identify the specific language that needs improvement. Then enact the role play again, this time using positive language.

Frequently it is helpful for a participant who has been on the receiving end of negative communication in his or her workplace to adopt the role of deliverer. Walking in the other person's shoes leads to a quicker understanding of the transaction. This positive role play should also be followed by whole-group discussion of the elements that worked. Participants can be invited to write about the process and its results to give them a real-life example to take back to the workplace.

Participant Presentations

You might ask a participant to present a module of learning to the group. This allows you to observe the participants from a different perspective—both as a contributor to the conversation and as a presenter leading the discussion. Be ready to assist or to answer questions. For example, a participant may choose assertive communication as his or her module, and the specific issue on return to the workplace may be a request for promotion. The participant defines and delivers the steps required to ask for the promotion while the facilitator and other participants observe and evaluate the success of the approach and demonstration of confidence and assertiveness.

Ball Toss

A quick method for evaluating a class's knowledge of the material presented is to ask the participants to form a standing circle. The facilitator throws out a soft rubber ball to an individual and asks a question about the previous learning activity. When the catcher gives the right answer, he or she throws the ball to another participant who answers another question. The facilitator can step out of this circle and let the participants ask as well as answer questions to review the skills as a group. Candy for all as a reward for contributions is always enjoyed by the participants (consider keeping some sugar-free treats on hand as well).

Journaling

Keeping a journal is a quiet, introspective way for participants to get a grip on their learning. When you complete an activity, have everyone take five minutes to write a summary of the skill just learned and then ask them to share what they've written with a partner. Invite the partner to correct and improve the material if necessary or appropriate.

Responding to Questions

When participants are asking questions, they are engaged and interested. Your responses to questions will augment the learning atmosphere. The way in which you respond is extremely important. Answers that are evasive can disturb a class because they cast doubts on your credibility. Glib or curt answers are insulting. Lengthy responses break the rhythm of the class and often go off track. When dealing with questions, the value of effective communication is in hearing the question, answering the question asked, and moving on. Repeat questions so that all participants hear them. In addition, this can ensure that you have heard the question correctly.

However, don't rush to answer. Take time to let everyone absorb the information. When time is of the essence, don't be tempted to give long, complicated answers that embrace additional topics. Be courteous and clear. Check that your answer has been understood. When a question comes up that could possibly derail the session or that is beyond the scope of the topic, you can choose to record it on a "parking lot" list and then revisit it later at an assigned time. A parking lot can be as simple as a list on a flipchart. However, whenever possible, answer a question at the time it is asked. Consider answering with analogies when they are appropriate because these often help elucidate challenging concepts.

You are likely aware that effective questions that prompt answers are open ended. Some that you might ask include

- What have you learned so far?
- How do you feel about this concept?
- How would you handle this situation?

Any question that begins with "what" or "how" promotes a more extensive answer. Do you also know, though, that questions that begin with "why"—as in "why do you think that way?"—can promote defensiveness. So what is a facilitator to do when asked a "why" question?

When a participant asks a confrontational or negative question, handle it with dignity and do not become aggressive. It's helpful to ask open-ended questions of the participant to try to clarify the original question. For example, ask, "What do you mean by . . . ?" or "Which part of the activity do you find challenging?" This form of open-ended questioning requires additional accountability from the participant. The reason for the confrontation may have arisen from confusion about the information or the need to hear his or her own thoughts aloud. When you are calm and patient, the altercation is more likely to be resolved. If the participant persists, you may wish to ask him or her to discuss the specifics in a private setting. More ideas for dealing with difficult participants are provided later in this chapter.

Some participants enjoy being questioned because it gives them an opportunity to show their knowledge. Others are reticent for fear of looking foolish if they don't know the answer. Because your participants have unique styles and personalities, always have a purpose for asking questions: Will these questions test the participants' knowledge? Are these questions appropriate? Are you asking them in the style that suits the participant?

Training Room and Participant Management

When everything is in place and ready for the session, it's time to review the "soft skills" portion of your responsibilities—that is, how you conduct the workshop and interact with participants. Here are some things to consider:

- **"Respect and respond" should be a facilitator's mantra.** At all times respect the participants and respond in a timely manner.

- **Learn participants' names at the beginning of the workshop.** Focus on each participant, give a firm handshake, and repeat the name in your greeting. Paying attention to the details they share during your greeting, and thereby getting to know them on a personal level, makes learning names much easier. When you have time, survey the room and write down every name without looking at nametags or name tents on the tables.

- **Manage workshop program time.** This is vital because it ensures that the goals will be met in the time allotted.

- **Read the participants' body language.** This will help you know when to pause and ask questions or to give them a stretch break.

- **Answer questions fully and effectively.** If you don't know an answer, open the question up to the participants or offer to get back to the questioner. Make a note to remind yourself to do so.

- **Add a "parking lot" to the room**—a large sheet of paper taped to one of the walls (use your own artistic prowess to draw a vehicle of some sort). When questions arise that are out of step with the current activity, ask the participant to write the question on a sticky note and put it in the parking lot. When the current activity is completed, you can address the questions parked there.

- **Control unruly participants through assertiveness of vocal tone and message.** When appropriate, invite them to help you with tasks because frequently they just need to be more physically involved. If the unruliness gets out of hand, accompany the person out of the room to discuss the situation.

- **Be sure to monitor a participant who is slower to assimilate the information.** If time permits, give that person some one-on-one time with you.

- **Keep your energy high.** Inject humor wherever possible. Ensure the learning is taking root.

A Word About Dealing With Difficult Participants

Much of the preparation you do before a training session will help you minimize disruptive behavior in your training session. But, sadly, you are still likely at some point to have difficult participants in your training room. Beyond preparation, you may need some specific strategies to help you manage disruptions and keep the learning on track. Figure 8-6, drawn from McCain and Tobey's *Facilitation Basics* (2004), identifies many of these behaviors and gives strategies for nipping them in the bud.

Figure 8-6. Managing Difficult Participants

THE PROBLEM	THE SOLUTION
Carrying on a Side Conversation	• Don't assume the talkers are being disrespectful; depersonalize the behavior by thinking: "Maybe they are unclear about a point in the material, or the material is not relevant to their needs." • Ask the talkers if they don't understand something. • Walk toward the talkers as you continue to make your point; this stops many conversations dead in their tracks.
Monopolizing the Discussion	• Some participants tend to take over the conversation; while the enthusiasm is great, you don't want to leave other learners out. • Tell the monopolizer that her comments are valuable and interesting and that you would like to open up the discussion to others in the group. Then call on another person by name. • Enlist the monopolizer to help you by being a gatekeeper and ensuring that no one monopolizes the conversation.
Complaining	• Don't assume someone who complains doesn't have a valid reason to do so. • Ask the rest of the group if they feel the same way. If they do, try to address the issue as appropriate. If they don't, talk to the individual in the hallway during the break.
Challenging Your Knowledge	• Determine if this person really knows more than you do, or is just trying to act as though he does. • If he does know more, try to enlist his help in the training. If he doesn't, ask him to provide expertise, and he will usually realize he can't and back down.
Daydreaming	• Use the person's name in an example to get her attention. • Switch to something more active. • If behavior affects more than just one person, try to find out if something work related is causing it and have a brief discussion about it.
Heckling	• Don't get upset or start volleying remarks. • Try giving the person learning-oriented attention: "John, you clearly have some background in this area; would you care to share your thoughts with the rest of the group?" • Get the attention off you by switching to a group-oriented activity.
Clowning Around	• Give the person attention in a learning-oriented way by calling on her to answer a question or be a team leader. • If a joke is intended to relieve tension in the room and others seem to be experiencing it, deal with the tension head on by bringing it up. • If it is just a joke, and it's funny and appropriate, laugh!

Continued on next page

Figure 8-6. Managing Difficult Participants, *continued*

THE PROBLEM	THE SOLUTION
Making an Insensitive Remark	• Remember that if the person truly didn't intend offense, you don't want to humiliate him. But you do need to ensure that the person and everyone else in the room know that you will not tolerate bigoted or otherwise inappropriate remarks. • Give the person a chance to retract what he said by asking if that is what he meant to say. If it wasn't, then move on. If it was, you need to let the person know that the comment is not in line with the values of your organization and it can't be allowed to continue. • If the person persists, speak to him in the hallway, or as a last resort, ask him to leave.
Doing Other Work	• Talk to the person at a break to find out if the workshop is meeting her needs. • If the person is truly under too much pressure, offer to have her come to another session.
Not Talking	• If you can tell the person is engaged because he is taking notes, maintaining eye contact, or leaning forward, let him alone. • Give the person opportunities to interact at a greater comfort level by participating in small groups or in pairs.
Withdrawing	• Talk to the person at break to find out if something is going on. Deal with the issue as appropriate. • If the person feels excluded, have her act as a team leader for a turn, or ensure that all members of teams are given opportunities to participate.
Missing the Point	• If someone misses the point, be sensitive in dealing with him or her. Try to find something to agree with in his point. • Try to identify what the person is having trouble grasping and clear up the point with an analogy or an example. • Never laugh at the person or otherwise humiliate him.
Playing With Technology	• Minimize distractions by setting specific ground rules for technology use in the training room. (See Chapter 7 for creative ways to use technology to enhance training.) • Direct a training-related question to the person. • If the behavior persists, talk to the person at break to determine if there is an issue with which you can help.

Source: McCain and Tobey (2004).

When all else fails, you have a few last resorts, although you would clearly rather not get to that point. One option is to simply pull aside the individual who is disrupting the class and talk to her privately. Dick Grote (1998) suggests in "Dealing with Miscreants, Snivelers, and

CUSTOMER SERVICE training

Adversaries" that you can often catch someone off guard by asking: "Is it personal?" The direct question will usually cause the individual to deny that it is personal. Next, you tell the person that the behavior is unacceptable and that you will speak to a supervisor or training sponsor if it continues. This often works.

However, if it does not work, you can ask to have the person removed or cancel the program and speak to the person's supervisor. Clearly, these are not options to be taken lightly, but realize that they are available when you are faced with truly recalcitrant behavior.

Follow up when you have faced a difficult situation. Take some time to reflect on the event and write down the details of what happened. If possible, get perspectives and feedback from participants who witnessed it. If outside perspectives are not an option, think about the event from the points of view of the disruptive individual and other participants and ask yourself: What went wrong? What went well? How could I manage the situation better next time?

An Unforgettable End

In Biech (2008), contributor Mel Silberman explains that

> [m]any training programs run out of steam in the end. In some cases, participants are marking time until the close is near. In other cases, facilitators are valiantly trying to cover what they haven't got to before time runs out. How unfortunate! What happens at the end needs to be "unforgettable." You want participants to remember what they've learned. You also want participants to think what they've learned has been special. (p. 315)

Silberman suggests considering four areas when preparing to end your workshop:

- How will participants review what you've taught them?
- How will participants assess what they have learned?
- What will participants do about what they have learned?
- How will participants celebrate their accomplishments?

For example, consider what you've learned in this chapter. You've developed a well-rounded picture of what it takes to create an optimal, effective learning environment, from creating an inviting and engaging space to preparing and gathering materials that will make you feel like an organizational champ. You're ready to get the training off to a productive start, to manage difficult participants and situations, and to pull it all together in a powerful way. Now review the bullet points below and determine what the next steps are and take pride in the preparation that will enable you to adapt and thrive in the training room.

The Bare Minimum

- **Keep things moving.** Create an engaging, interactive environment.

- **Pay attention to the energy in the room.** Be prepared to adjust the activities as needed. Build in content that can be delivered standing or through networking activities to get participants out of their seats when needed.

- **Have fun!** If you create an upbeat tone and enjoy yourself, the participants are likely to have fun as well.

Key Points

- Facilitation is not lecturing. It's providing learning activities and support to make learning easier for the participant.

- Facilitation is not about the facilitator—it's about the learner.

- An inviting space and a safe, collaborative environment are necessary for learning to occur.

- Good facilitation starts with passion and significant attention to preparation.

- A good start sets the tone for the whole training session.

- A strong ending helps learners to remember the training and carry lessons forward into their work.

What to Do Next

- Choose the appropriate workshop agenda based on the information in the "Which Program Is Best?" section included in the introduction to this book.

- Prepare, modify, and review the training agenda. Use one of the agendas in Section I as a starting point.

- Review the program preparation checklist on page 105 and work through it step by step.

- Make a list of required participant materials and facilitator equipment and begin assembling them.

- Review all learning activities included in the agenda, familiarize yourself with the PowerPoint animations (with customizable materials), and start preparing for your delivery.

Additional Resources

Biech, E. (2006). *90 World-Class Activities by 90 World-Class Trainers.* San Francisco: John Wiley/Pfeiffer.

Biech, E. (2008). *10 Steps to Successful Training.* Alexandria, VA: ASTD Press.

Biech, E., ed. (2008). *ASTD Handbook for Workplace Learning Professionals.* Alexandria, VA: ASTD Press.

Biech, E., ed. (2014). *ASTD Handbook: The Definitive Reference for Training & Development.* Alexandria, VA: ASTD Press.

Duarte, N. (2010). *Resonate: Present Visual Stories That Transform Audiences.* Hoboken, NJ: Wiley.

Grote, D. (1998). "Dealing with Miscreants, Snivelers, and Adversaries," *Training & Development,* 52(10), October.

McCain, D.V., and D. Tobey. (2004). *Facilitation Basics.* Alexandria, VA: ASTD Press.

Stolovitch, H.D., and E.J. Keeps. (2011). *Telling Ain't Training,* 2nd edition. Alexandria, VA: ASTD Press.

Thiagarajan, S. (2005). *Thiagi's Interactive Lectures: Power Up Your Training With Interactive Games and Exercises.* Alexandria, VA: ASTD Press.

Thiagarajan, S. (2006). *Thiagi's 100 Favorite Games.* San Francisco: John Wiley/Pfeiffer.

Chapter 9
Evaluating Workshop Results

What's in This Chapter

- Exploring the reasons to evaluate your program
- Introducing the levels of measurement and what they measure

---

Evaluation represents the last letter of the ADDIE cycle of instructional design (analysis, design, development, implementation, and evaluation). Although evaluation is placed at the end of the model, an argument could be made for including it far earlier, as early as the design and development phase and perhaps even in the analysis phase. Why? Because the goals of the training, or the learning objectives (see Chapter 5), provide insight into what the purpose of the evaluation should be. In fact, business goals, learning goals, and evaluation of those goals are useful subjects to address with organizational leaders or the training sponsor. Trainers often begin a program without thinking about how the program fits into a strategic plan or how it supports and promotes specific business goals, but these are critical to consider before implementing the program.

However, this chapter is not about that upfront evaluation of the program design and materials; it is about evaluating the program after it has been delivered and reporting the results back to the training sponsor. This form of evaluation allows you to determine whether the program objectives were achieved and whether the learning was applied on the job and had an impact on the business. Evaluation can also serve as the basis for future program and budget discussions with training sponsors.

Levels of Measurement

No discussion of measurement would be complete without an introduction to the concepts that underpin the field of evaluation. The following is a brief primer on a very large and detailed subject that can be somewhat overwhelming. If your organization is committed to measuring beyond Level 2, take some time to read the classics of evaluation.

In 1956–57, Donald Kirkpatrick, one of the leading experts in measuring training results, identified four levels of measurement and evaluation. These four levels build successively from the simplest (Level 1) to the most complex (Level 4) and are based on information gathered at previous levels. For that reason, determining upfront at what level to evaluate a program is important. A general rule of thumb is that the more important or fundamental the training is and the greater the investment in it, the higher the level of evaluation to use. The four basic levels of evaluation are

- **Level 1—Reaction:** Measures how participants react to the workshop.
- **Level 2—Learning:** Measures whether participants have learned and understood the content of the workshop.
- **Level 3—Behavior (also referred to as application):** Measures on-the-job changes that have occurred because of the learning.
- **Level 4—Results:** Measures the impact of training on the bottom line.

These four levels correspond with the evaluation methods described below.

Level 1: Measuring Participant Reactions

One of the most common ways trainers measure participants' reactions is by administering end-of-session evaluation forms, often called "smile sheets" when all that they address is participants' enjoyment of the session. But they can be powerful feedback and data collection tools when designed to be. Each of the agendas in this book include evaluation handouts for you to use at the close of the workshop (see Chapter 11). The main benefits of using an evaluation sheet is gaining participant feedback on your delivery and on the workshop design, as well as gathering information to help market the workshop to future participants. If you choose this method, consider the suggestions below, but first decide the purpose of evaluating. Do you want to know if the participants enjoyed the presentation? How they felt about the facilities? Or how they reacted to the content?

Here are a few suggestions for creating evaluation forms:

- Keep the form to one page.

- Make your questions brief.

- Leave adequate space for comments.

- Group types of questions into categories (for example, cluster questions about content, questions about the instructor, and questions about materials).

- Provide variety in types of questions (include multiple-choice, true-false, short-answer, and open-ended items).

- Include relevant decision makers in your questionnaire design.

- Plan how you will use and analyze the data and create a design that will facilitate your analysis.

- Use positively worded items (such as, "I listen to others," instead of "I don't listen to others").

You can find additional tips for creating evaluation sheets and evaluating their results in the *Infoline* "Making Smile Sheets Count" by Nancy S. Kristiansen (2004).

Although evaluation sheets are used frequently, they have some inherent limitations. For example, participants cannot judge the *effectiveness* of training techniques. In addition, results can be overly influenced by the personality of the facilitator or participants' feelings about having to attend training. Be cautious of relying solely on Level 1 evaluations.

Level 2: Measuring the Extent to Which Participants Have Learned

If you want to determine the extent to which participants have understood the content of your workshop, testing is an option. Comparing pre-training and post-training test results indicates the amount of knowledge gained. Or you can give a quiz that tests conceptual information 30 to 60 days after the training to see if people remember the concepts. Because most adult learners do not generally like the idea of tests, you might want to refer to these evaluations as "assessments."

Another model of testing is criterion-referenced testing (CRT), which tests the learner's performance against a given standard, such as "greets the customer and offers assistance within one minute of entering the store" or "initiates the landing gear at the proper time and altitude." Such testing can be important in determining whether a learner can carry out the task, determining the efficacy of the training materials, and providing a foundation for further levels of evaluation. Coscarelli and Shrock (2008) describe a five-step method for developing CRTs that include

1. Determining what to test (analysis)

2. Determining if the test measures what it purports to measure (validity)

3. Writing test items

4. Establishing a cut-off or mastery score

5. Showing that the test provides consistent results (reliability).

Level 3: Measuring the Results of Training Back on the Job

The next level of evaluation identifies whether the learning was actually used back on the job. It is important to recognize that application on the job is where learning begins to have real-world effects and that application is not solely up to the learner. Many elements affect transfer and application, including follow-up, manager support, and so forth. For example, consider a sales training attendee who attends training and learns a new, more efficient way to identify sales leads. However, upon returning to work, the attendee's manager does not allow the time for the attendee to practice applying those new skills in the workplace. Over time, the training is forgotten, and any value it may have had does not accrue.

Methods for collecting data regarding performance back on the job include reports by people who manage participants, reports from staff and peers, observations, quality monitors, and other quality and efficiency measures. In "The Four Levels of Evaluation," Kirkpatrick (2007) provides some guidelines for carrying out Level 3 evaluations:

- Use a control group, if practical.
- Allow time for behavior change to take place.
- Evaluate before and after the program, if possible.
- Interview learners, their immediate managers, and possibly their subordinates and anyone else who observes their work or behavior.
- Repeat the evaluation at appropriate times.

Level 4: Measuring the Organizational Impact of Training

Level 4 identifies how learning affects business measures. Consider an example related to management training. Let's say a manager attends management training and learns several new and valuable techniques to engage employees and help keep them on track. Upon return, the

CUSTOMER SERVICE training

manager gets support in applying the new skills and behaviors. As time passes, the learning starts to have measurable results: Retention has increased, employees are demonstrably more engaged and are producing better-quality goods, and sales increase because the quality has increased. Retention, engagement, quality, and sales are all measurable business results improved as a result of the training.

Measuring such organizational impact requires working with leaders to create and implement a plan to collect the data you need. Possible methods include customer surveys, measurements of sales, studies of customer retention or turnover, employee satisfaction surveys, and other measurements of issues pertinent to the organization.

Robert Brinkerhoff, well-known author and researcher of evaluation methods, has suggested the following method to obtain information relevant to results:

- Send out questionnaires to people who have gone through training, asking: To what extent have you used your training in a way that has made a significant business impact? (This question can elicit information that will point to business benefits and ways to use other data to measure accomplishments.)
- When you get responses back, conduct interviews to get more information.

Return on Investment

Measuring return on investment (ROI)—sometimes referred to as Level 5 evaluation—is useful and can help "sell" training to leaders. ROI measures the monetary value of business benefits such as those noted in the discussion about Level 4 and compares them with the fully loaded costs of training to provide a percentage return on training investment. Hard numbers such as these can be helpful in discussions with organizational executives about conducting further training and raise the profile of training.

ROI was popularized by Jack Phillips. More in-depth information can be found in the *ASTD Handbook of Measuring and Evaluating Training* (Phillips 2010).

Reporting Results

An important and often under-considered component of both ROI and Level 4 evaluations is reporting results. Results from these types of evaluation studies have several different audiences, and it is important to take time to plan the layout of the evaluation report and the method of delivery with the audience in question. Consider the following tasks in preparing communications:

- **Purpose:** The purposes for communicating program results depend on the specific program, the setting, and unique organizational needs.

- **Audience:** For each target audience, understand the audience and find out what information is needed and why. Take into account audience bias, and then tailor the communication to each group.

- **Timing:** Lay the groundwork for communication before program implementation. Avoid delivering a message, particularly a negative message, to an audience unprepared to hear the story and unaware of the methods that generated the results.

- **Reporting format:** The type of formal evaluation report depends on how much detailed information is presented to target audiences. Brief summaries may be sufficient for some communication efforts. In other cases, particularly those programs that require significant funding, more detail may be important.

The Bare Minimum

- If formal measurement techniques are not possible, consider using simple, interactive, informal measurement activities such as a quick pulse-check during the workshop.

- Empower the participants to create an action plan to capture the new skills and ideas they plan to use. Ultimately, the success of any training event will rest on lasting positive change in participants' behavior.

Key Points

- The four basic levels of evaluation cover reaction, learning, application, and organizational impact.

- A fifth level covers return on investment.

- Reporting results is as important as measuring them. Be strategic in crafting your results document, taking into consideration purpose, audience, timing, and format.

What to Do Next

- Identify the purpose and level of evaluation based on the learning objectives and learning goals.

- Prepare a training evaluation form, or use the ones provided in Chapter 11.

- If required, develop plans for follow-up evaluations to determine skills mastery, on-the-job application, and business impact.

Additional Resources

Biech, E., ed. (2014). *ASTD Handbook: The Definitive Reference for Training & Development,* 2nd edition. Alexandria, VA: ASTD Press.

Brinkerhoff, R.O. (2006). *Telling Training's Story: Evaluation Made Simple, Credible, and Effective.* San Francisco: Berrett-Koehler.

Coscarelli, W., and S. Shrock. (2008). "Level 2: Learning—Five Essential Steps for Creating Your Tests and Two Cautionary Tales." In E. Biech, ed., *ASTD Handbook for Workplace Learning Professionals.* Alexandria, VA: ASTD Press.

Kirkpatrick, D.L. (2007). "The Four Levels of Evaluation." *Infoline* No. 0701, Alexandria, VA: ASTD Press.

Kirkpatrick, D., and J.D. Kirkpatrick. (2006). *Evaluating Training Programs: The Four Levels,* 3rd edition. San Francisco: Berrett-Koehler.

Kirkpatrick, D., and J.D. Kirkpatrick. (2007). *Implementing the Four Levels: A Practical Guide for Effective Evaluation of Training Programs.* San Francisco: Berrett-Koehler.

Kristiansen, N.S. (2004). "Making Smile Sheets Count." *Infoline* No. 0402, Alexandria, VA: ASTD Press.

Phillips, P.P., ed. (2010). *ASTD Handbook of Measuring and Evaluating Training.* Alexandria, VA: ASTD Press.

SECTION III
POST-WORKSHOP LEARNING

Chapter 10
The Follow-Up Coach

What's in This Chapter

- Develop a communication plan for the workshop(s)
- Harness managers' critical access to learners
- Connect service standards and organizational metrics
- Focus on action plans created in the workshops
- Align workshops with additional learning opportunities
- Create an environment of encouragement

Although the term *follow-up* seems to imply that it happens after the workshops, it actually needs to be planned and developed *before*. And you may need to recalibrate your definitions of when a workshop starts and ends. To be most effective, a workshop starts well before the participants arrive and continues well after they leave the training room. Don't wait until after the workshop to focus on these activities. Plan for them as you are planning for the workshop itself.

Developing the ability to provide effective customer service is a journey—not an event. Attending workshops can certainly help employees deliver better service; however, as with many skills, it is only with continued practice and sustained follow-up that behaviors are refined and results are improved. It takes time for people to process new information, break old patterns of behavior, and start applying new skills.

To achieve real behavioral change, ideas experienced in a learning environment must continue to be supported. Research on training shows that training with follow-up coaching improves performance dramatically over training alone (Olivero, Bane, and Kopelmann 1997). It is also clear that training is not a once-and-done event. This chapter provides several ideas to help you support learning, improve behavior, and achieve results by creating a communication plan, involving the participants' managers, focusing on action planning, offering continued learning opportunities, and creating an encouraging environment that emphasizes customer service.

Create a Communication Plan

Developing a communication plan that effectively supports customer service training begins with answering a series of key questions:

- Who are the champions and sponsors of the workshop(s)?

- What messages are the participants going to receive from the champions and sponsors, and in what formats? (Email invitation? Video introduction? Personal welcome at the workshop with an explanation of how the training connects to the organization's service focus? Messages after the workshop to encourage skills application?)

- What role will the participants' managers have in establishing learning expectations both before and after the event?

- Will there be a branding campaign to support the customer service training, such as newsletter articles and wall posters with photos of participants and quotes on how they are applying the service skills?

- Can a blog be created expressly for employees to share service successes and challenges they can use assistance with?

- What other communication channels already exist and are available to you, such as weekly staff meetings or daily tailgate meetings? Harness them!

Use the answers to these questions to establish a written communication plan that defines what messages will be distributed, by whom, through what channels, and when. And don't be surprised that you may be the one actually drafting many of the messages.

In short, keep a focus on the topic! Here are some ideas to get you started:

- **Communicate—before.** Ghost-write a pre-workshop email for managers to send to employee participants under their own signature line—not yours. Include the basic logistics of time and location and also establish what they can expect in the workshop. You know best what the workshop addresses, so explain the skills it focuses on, provide the learning objectives, pose a relevant question or challenge, and invite participants to bring work examples to draw from during the workshop. Create enthusiasm for the event. Time the email for delivery seven to 10 days before the workshop begins for maximum impact and effectiveness.

- **Communicate—after.** Don't leave it to the participants' managers to initiate the post-workshop communications. They may have good intentions to do it but too often don't. So ghost-write another message for them. In fact, you can write it before the workshop, but send it to the managers when you want them to distribute it. This time, you will want to establish expectations of what workshop participants should be *doing* with the skills they learned in the workshop. Include specific examples, align the examples with a relevant service standard or performance metric, and write in a supportive tone. You might even pose another relevant question or challenge for the team to discuss in their next staff meeting. Make the workshop part of a continuum of growth and development—not a four-, eight-, or sixteen-hour paid vacation.

- **Keep it up.** There should be an *ongoing* communication plan to support customer service. Touch base with your participants on a daily, weekly, or monthly basis. Plan a special focus during the first week of October, which is National Customer Service Week. Tie messaging to other initiatives in the organization so it becomes part of the culture, not just one more thing to focus on.

Involve Managers in the Transfer of Learning

Who do you believe has the greatest effect on workshop participants' ability to use their new skills in the workplace? The participants themselves? You as the trainer? Or, perhaps, the participants' managers, who directly influence participants' priorities, manage their workload, establish expectations, and incentivize employee behavior (either intentionally or by default)? Certainly, self-directed participants and skilled trainers are important to the transfer of learning. But it may surprise you to learn that research shows that what a manager does *before* training is the single most critical factor in successful application of learning on the job, and what a manager does *after* training is the third most critical factor, according to Broad and Newstrom in their book *Transfer of Training* (Broad and Newstrom 1992). Clearly, managers play a vital role in ensuring that learners develop their customer service skills—both before and after the training event.

Before the Workshop

Here are ideas to implement with managers even before the workshop begins:

- Consult managers (and their appropriate direct reports) during the needs analysis phase of design.

- Invite managers to preview workshop content (possibly even attend a pilot session).

- Ask managers to vet the list of workshop attendees to ensure everyone registered meets the target participant profile.

- Coordinate with managers to provide on-the-job time for participants to complete any pre-work and be sure to draw a direct connection between pre-work you integrate and its value to the learning experience for both the managers and the participants.

- Highlight for managers how workshop content aligns with the organization's performance improvement tools (employee evaluations) and share examples of how they can set performance goals for participants that align with both the tools and the workshop.

- Ask managers to collaborate with participants to establish specific learning goals prior to attending the workshop.

After the Workshop

To help learners integrate the customer service skills developed through training, encourage managers to get involved in these meaningful ways after the workshop:

- Ask managers to schedule a brief conversation with participants about the workshop, what they took away, and their specific plan to implement what they learned and practiced in the workshop.

- Request that managers set aside time in participants' work schedules in the days and weeks following the workshop to focus on implementing their workshop action plans.

- Provide managers with a checklist of behaviors to watch for and samples of appropriate feedback (both encouraging and redirecting) to offer participants.

- Encourage managers to be enthusiastic about new approaches and strategies from the workshop.

- Remind managers that participants will watch their behaviors and make comparisons between what managers say and do. Their modeling of the workshop skills will demonstrate the value they place on the learning.

Connect Service Standards to Organizational Metrics

When it comes to performance, employees usually focus on what gets measured. If organizations don't measure service or if they weight productivity over service, employees won't prioritize service either.

Organizational systems either encourage and reinforce an emphasis on service—or they don't. To make customer service part of the organizational culture, you may need to collaborate internally to integrate service standards into performance evaluation (annual reviews). Work with organizational leaders, human resources staff, and supervisors to determine ways to incentivize employees to prioritize service—give them a reason to *want* to deliver quality service.

I recently encountered an employee incentive that (possibly inadvertently) enhanced the customer service experience. Sitting one row behind the first-class cabin on a Friday evening flight with only two attendants, I overheard the first-class attendant offer his help for beverage service to the main cabin attendant. They began working together swiping credit cards and serving alcoholic beverages. Thinking myself funny, I asked the first-class attendant if he was working on commission now? I wasn't expecting his answer: "Yes. We get credits for every in-flight purchase." Maybe he would have offered his help either way, but the service level for the main cabin certainly benefited from increased speed. How is your organization encouraging or discouraging exceptional service? Is your organization sending a clear message that it values quality customer service?

Focus on Personal Action Planning

Although there is much that you and your organizational partners can do to extend the focus on service outside of the workshop, there is also a lot the participants can do themselves. Two of the workshops (one-day and two-day) have action planning built into them. These action plans help participants set goals and identify specific actions they will take back at their jobs to apply the learning. Don't skip over action planning activities thinking that participants can do them on their own time. Most participants, even those who want to dedicate time to action planning, won't make time to do it after the workshop ends.

Once action plans are created, reinforce the plans by following up with email reminders, requests for specific examples of actions taken that you may share with future workshop participants, or even creating a display area or technology-enabled sharing site where post-workshop accomplishments are posted. The action plan activities in this volume's workshops integrate accountability partners. Encourage participants to support each other as they work to improve their skills and achieve their goals.

Continue to Offer Learning Opportunities

Provide additional workshops that align with both the organization's service standards and participants' skill development needs to enhance service delivery. Skills to consider include active listening, phone etiquette, time management, conflict resolution, product knowledge (specifically, product benefits versus their features), and email effectiveness. Look at your service standards for ideas, ask managers for input on employees' strengths and developmental areas, and review your needs analysis for direction.

Informal lunch-and-learn events can reinforce critical learning points, create opportunities to trouble-shoot additional participant challenges, or even pull select objectives and associated learning activities from other workshop agendas in this volume for a 60-minute event that keeps attention and focus on continuous improvement. An alternative quick-format option is a "bag-and-brag" event in which you ask participants to bring a bagged lunch and brag about how their team is implementing the learning. Follow-up sessions could be done in person or virtually through teleconferencing, webinars, and other online community tools.

Create an Open and Encouraging Environment for Quality Customer Service

Culture change can be a slow and challenging process, but it is well worth the effort because customer service is one of the most impactful aspects of an organization culture. One way to support behavior change is for employees to see and hear actions and messages from executive leadership, managers, and each other that support the ideas communicated during the training program. Consider inviting senior leaders to a lunch-and-learn to convey how critical customer service is to the mission of the organization. Or video their messages and distribute through email or a blog.

The right words at the right time can do a lot to inspire self-reflection and action or to renew a person's focus. Actively collect meaningful messages to share from a variety of sources such as books, blogs, and websites. Here are two I saw on display in an organization recently:

- "Change is never painful; only resistance to change is painful." —Buddha
- "There are no secrets to success. It is the result of preparation, hard work, and learning from failure." —Colin Powell

But don't be limited by the notoriety of who said it; great quotes come from all over. A participant in a recent workshop quoted herself in an email signature line: "Even when you're tired, frustrated, and disappointed, getting back up and starting over is the *best* thing to do. Consistency is required."

Find places to display meaningful messages that will be seen by participants and other employees. Get creative. Hallway whiteboards, conference rooms, the signature line of your email, and the footer of a handout or agenda for a lunch-and-learn can all be opportunities to encourage and affirm people.

Your willingness to remain in contact with participants after the workshop will also send a message of encouragement. Share your email address and invite continued contact. Don't worry about being inundated with messages; in my experience, only some of your participants will reach out for clarification, questions, or feedback. Your sustained support and interest will enhance the learning experience for those who decide to connect and seek your coaching.

Key Points

- Improving customer service skills is a journey—not an event.

- Involve managers early and frequently to derive exponential gain from your investment in training events. They are critical to achieving organizational change.

- Be creative and consistent in promoting customer service as an area of attention. Maintain a focus on the topic to inspire employees to do the same.

What to Do Next

- **Create your communication plan and select specific strategies to engage managers**. To be most efficient, consider these two elements simultaneously. How can one support the other? Streamline efforts and lower the threshold that could otherwise prevent managers from taking action.

- **Select one or two of the remaining follow-up ideas.** Be realistic about what is achievable with the resources available to you, and implement the most meaningful strategies in support of your next workshop.

- **Follow through on your follow-up plan**. Making a plan is one thing. Taking action on it is another. Demonstrate your commitment to your participants' behavior change by continuing on the journey with them long after the workshop is completed.

Additional Resources

Broad, M. L., and J. W. Newstrom. (1992). *Transfer of Training: Action-Packed Strategies to Ensure High Payoff From Training Investment.* New York: Basic Books.

Olivero, G., K. Bane, and R. Kopelmann. (1997). "Executive Coaching As a Transfer of Training Tool: Effects on Productivity in a Public Agency." *Public Personnel Management* 26(4).

SECTION IV

WORKSHOP SUPPORTING DOCUMENTS AND ONLINE SUPPORT

Chapter 11
Learning Activities

What's in This Chapter

- Fifty-one learning activities to use in your workshops
- Complete step-by-step instructions for each activity
- Refer to Chapter 14 for instructions to download full-size learning activities

The learning activities of the three workshops are their essential elements. They will challenge and engage learners, support them in acquiring new knowledge and skills, provide stimulation for different types of learners, and avoid the monotony of ineffective lecturing. Remember that "listening ain't learning," and these activities will cause learning to "stick" by involving the participants in a meaningful, hands-on experience.

Each learning activity provides detailed information about the learning objective(s) it supports, required materials, timeframes, step-by-step instructions, variations, debriefing questions, and transitions. Follow the instructions in each learning activity to prepare for the workshop, identify and gather materials, and successfully guide participants through the activity. See Chapter 14 for complete instructions on how to download the workshop support materials.

The workshops' opening learning activities serve multiple purposes. They engage learners, create interest, establish an interactive and collaborative learning environment, introduce participants, establish expectations, and outline each workshop's learning objectives. Whew! (They are pretty important.)

After each workshop's first three learning activities, subsequent activities are aligned with specific learning objectives. Some learning objectives have multiple learning activities associated with them. As an aid to you, the linkage between learning activities and learning objectives is identified at the top of each learning activity.

Another intentional aid to you is the format of the learning activity instructions. While you certainly want to use your own style and language while facilitating, there are instances where I have shared specific facilitation language. This includes questions that draw knowledge from participants as well as content to explain workshop concepts (such as the HELP process), debriefing questions, and transitions to move smoothly between learning activities. Also included are some sample stories from my experiences. You can take them and use them as yours, or replace them with examples of your own that illustrate the same points. Familiarize yourself with the blend of information provided and bring it all to life in your own way!

Learning Activities Included in *Customer Service Training*

Half-Day Workshop: Service Behaviors That Matter

Learning Activity 1: Intriguing Question or Story

Learning Activity 2: Hello, My Idea Is . . .

Learning Activity 3: Prioritize Learning

Learning Activity 4: I'm Stumped

Learning Activity 5: Keep a Cool Head

Learning Activity 6: Quit Taking It Personally (Q-Tip)

Learning Activity 7: The HELP Process for Customer Interactions

Learning Activity 8: HELP the Customer

Learning Activity 9: Interconnected Service Facets

One-Day Workshop: From the Customer's Perspective

Learning Activity 10: Initial Reactions

Learning Activity 11: Service Heroes

Learning Activity 12: Prioritize Learning

Two-Day Workshop: A Total Approach to Service

Learning Activity 1: Intriguing Question or Story

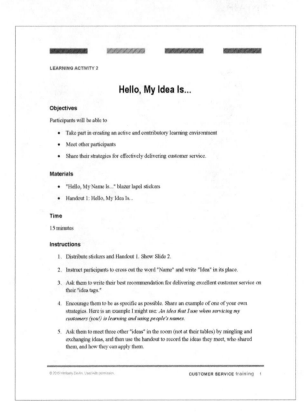

LEARNING ACTIVITY 1

Intriguing Question or Story

Objectives

Participants will become interested and engaged in the training topic.

Time

5 minutes

Instructions

1. Display Slide 1 as participants arrive.

2. Pose an intriguing question to the participants—one that gets them thinking about specific customer service interactions, how they have been treated as customers, or how they respond to service challenges. Here are a few examples:

   • When was the last time a service provider truly impressed you? What did they do?

   • If you could have a service "do over" from the past two weeks, what would you do differently to improve the outcome of that customer interaction?

3. Allow time for them to think. Remain silent and make eye contact with participants.

4. Field responses and follow up with probing questions.

Learning Activity 1: Intriguing Question or Story, *continued*

LEARNING ACTIVITY 1, continued

Variation

• Start with a service experience story instead. Here is one from my experience that I share in workshops:

Getting sick is never fun. It is even worse in a hotel room the night before the start of a multi-day work event. When that happened to me in the middle of the night, I went to the front desk to buy something—anything—to help. The desk clerk informed me they didn't have any remedies for sale, but they had tea available, and she would get some honey packets from the kitchen and might even have some cough drops in her purse. I took my tea with honey and two cough drops back to bed and struggled through my work the next day. What I found in my room that evening wowed me: a bottle of cough syrup, a bag of lozenges, and a handwritten note saying they hoped this helped on what must be a difficult trip. Where do you think I stay every time I am in that town?

Transition

Say: In our time together today, we will focus on practical service skills you can start using immediately: strategies to avoid potential disconnects and disappointments, tools to handle the most difficult interactions, and techniques for you to wow your customers. So let's begin with your experiences, strengths, and ideas.

Learning Activity 2: Hello, My Idea Is . . .

LEARNING ACTIVITY 2

Hello, My Idea Is...

Objectives

Participants will be able to

• Take part in creating an active and contributory learning environment

• Meet other participants

• Share their strategies for effectively delivering customer service.

Materials

• "Hello, My Name Is..." blazer lapel stickers

• Handout 1: Hello, My Idea Is...

Time

15 minutes

Instructions

1. Distribute stickers and Handout 1. Show Slide 2.

2. Instruct participants to cross out the word "Name" and write "Idea" in its place.

3. Ask them to write their best recommendation for delivering excellent customer service on their "idea tags."

4. Encourage them to be as specific as possible. Share an example of one of your own strategies. Here is an example I might use: *An idea that I use when servicing my customers (you!) is learning and using people's names.*

5. Ask them to meet three other "ideas" in the room (not at their tables) by mingling and exchanging ideas, and then use the handout to record the ideas they meet, who shared them, and how they can apply them.

Learning Activity 2: Hello, My Idea Is . . ., *continued*

LEARNING ACTIVITY 2, continued

6. Lead a group discussion to debrief the activity using some of the questions below.

7. After completing the debrief, share your complete introduction. You may want to include the following information:

   • Your experience with customer service (from either the provider side or the customer side)

   • How and why you were selected to lead this session

   • A service delivery challenge you faced and how the concepts in this workshop helped you overcome it

   • What you are looking to get out of this learning event by collaborating with the group.

Variations

• Select a specific aspect of customer service (such as resolving complaints, creating a welcoming environment, or reflective listening) and direct participants to share a strategy ("idea") they use to effectively manage that aspect of the service experience.

• Instruct participants to connect their idea to how it supports one of their organizations' service standards.

Discussion Questions for Debriefing

• Who met an idea they had never thought of before? Whose idea was it?

• Who will share an example of an idea they met that we all can benefit from? Who gave you this idea?

• How many of you learned a new way to satisfy customer needs? Was anyone reminded of things they knew, but don't always remember to do in the service delivery moment?

Learning Activity 3: Prioritize Learning

LEARNING ACTIVITY 3

Prioritize Learning

Objectives

Participants will be able to

- Establish a framework for the goals for the learning event
- See how the program content relates to real work situations
- Prioritize the training topics based on their current needs

Materials

- Handout 2: Learning Objectives (and Personal Progress Tracker)
- Prepared chart of social agreements

Time

5 minutes

Instructions

1. Show Slide 3 and distribute Handout 2.

2. Tell participants: This page shows you where we are headed, identifies how the skills learned here today can benefit you on the job, and provides space for you to journal as we go.

3. Direct participants to read the objectives and their benefits, and then to follow the printed instructions to prioritize the objectives for themselves.

4. Lead a group discussion using the debriefing questions on the next page.

5. Introduce and review social agreements (ground rules) charted for the workshop.

© 2015 by Kimberly Devlin. Used with permission. CUSTOMER SERVICE training 1

Learning Activity 3: Prioritize Learning, *continued*

LEARNING ACTIVITY 3, continued

Discussion Questions for Debriefing

- Which of these objectives resonates most strongly with you today?

- Is anyone struggling to see a connection between these goals and the work you do? (TIP: Those with limited or no direct customer-facing responsibilities often say that they don't have customers, overlook that colleagues are internal customers, don't realize their actions can directly impact external customers' experiences, or don't think that customer service even matters in their jobs. You will want to address this using questioning techniques to draw out how and why customer service skills matter and who their external and internal customers are.)

© 2015 by Kimberly Devlin. Used with permission. CUSTOMER SERVICE training 2

Learning Activity 4: I'm Stumped

LEARNING ACTIVITY 4

I'm Stumped

Objectives

This activity supports Learning Objective 1—develop a personalized set of phrases and actions to increase customer satisfaction.

Participants will be able to

- Develop a toolbox of new strategies to apply to their unique service challenges
- Reflect on the strategies they are using effectively and share them with others.

Materials

- Letter-sized envelopes (one per participant and some extras)
- Index cards (5-10 per table, based on group size and variation selected)
- Handout 3: I'm Stumped Idea Starters (one per participant)

Time

30 minutes

Instructions

1. Engage group in a brief discussion of service delivery barriers they encounter.
2. Distribute envelopes, index cards, and Handout 3. Show Slide 4.
3. Ask participants to think of a service challenge that stumps them. It could be something that, when it happens, they are not sure how to respond, or something that, when it has occurred previously, they were not satisfied with the result of the action they took.

© 2015 by Kimberly Devlin. Used with permission. CUSTOMER SERVICE training 1

Learning Activity 4: I'm Stumped, *continued*

LEARNING ACTIVITY 4, continued

4. Show Slide 5 and instruct them to legibly write their service challenge on the outside of an envelope. (TIP: Be sure they are specific about the service challenge, using industry-specific examples. These challenges are specific enough for our purposes: Customer says "This is ridiculous—this order was confirmed a week ago"; customer says "Let me speak to someone in charge"; I need to tell a customer the product/service/offer they want is no longer available; or the customer's warranty expired and he wants me to make an exception. However, these challenges are too broad or vague: Customer is upset; customer is argumentative; I can't give customers what they want.)

5. Tell participants to create a pile with the table's envelopes and pass the envelope pile to the next table group.

6. With the new pile of envelopes in hand, ask each table group to focus on one envelope at a time, reading aloud each service challenge listed. Tell table teams to discuss potential response behaviors they would take, encouraging them to be as specific as possible (and include the words to say or the actions to take). They should write that action or phrase, legibly, on an index card, place the card back in the envelope, and set it aside. Encourage them to use the handout as a reference tool to spark ideas for phrases and actions they can use to address the service challenge and to capture the group's ideas for future reference.

7. Continue Step 6 until all envelopes have response cards in them.

8. When all envelopes have response cards in them, ask teams to pass their pile of envelopes to the next table. Repeat Steps 6 and 7 until all envelopes are returned to their original table and to the person who wrote the service challenge.

9. Now that they have their service challenges back, ask them to read their peers' suggestions on the index cards and then share their favorite response with their table.

10. To help solidify the learning, lead a large group discussion using the debriefing questions on the next page.

© 2015 by Kimberly Devlin. Used with permission. CUSTOMER SERVICE training 2

Learning Activity 4: I'm Stumped, *continued*

Variations

- This activity works well if participants are sitting at table groups of 5 to 7 people. If another seating arrangement is being used, divide the large group into smaller groups of 5 to 7 people.

- If time is tight, form smaller groups of 4, or consider one of these variations:

  o Instruct each person at the table to pass his or her envelope to person to the right at the table. Working independently, that person writes a response behavior on an index card and places it in the envelope. Continue passing the envelopes to the right for another person's idea to be added until the envelopes return to the person whose challenge is written on the outside. (Potential drawbacks: less exchange of and building upon ideas among tablemates; quiet learning environment.)

  o Provide one envelope and one set of index cards to each table group. Have them select one service challenge as a group and pass envelopes from one table to the next. (Potential drawbacks: not everyone's issue has solutions presented; time might be squandered selecting one challenge for the table's envelope.)

Discussion Questions for Debriefing

- Who will share a new strategy they learned to deal with an ongoing service challenge?

- What might make it difficult for you to implement this strategy?

- What steps do you need to take to have this idea available to you when you need it?

- Is it sometimes easier to think of what to say to someone else's challenge? Why might that be?

Transition

Ask: How many of you found that what has stumped you in the past related to conflict in the customer interaction? Certain words tend to increase conflict, and they might be said by customers or, unintentionally, by us! Let's see how to avoid that.

CUSTOMER SERVICE training 3

Learning Activity 5: Keep a Cool Head

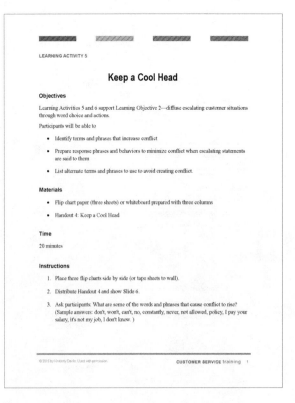

Keep a Cool Head

Objectives

Learning Activities 5 and 6 support Learning Objective 2—diffuse escalating customer situations through word choice and actions.

Participants will be able to

- Identify terms and phrases that increase conflict

- Prepare response phrases and behaviors to minimize conflict when escalating statements are said to them

- List alternate terms and phrases to use to avoid creating conflict.

Materials

- Flip chart paper (three sheets) or whiteboard prepared with three columns

- Handout 4: Keep a Cool Head

Time

20 minutes

Instructions

1. Place three flip charts side by side (or tape sheets to wall).

2. Distribute Handout 4 and show Slide 6.

3. Ask participants: What are some of the words and phrases that cause conflict to rise? (Sample answers: don't, won't, can't, no, constantly, never, not allowed, policy, I pay your salary, it's not my job, I don't know.)

CUSTOMER SERVICE training 1

Learning Activity 5: Keep a Cool Head, *continued*

4. Record responses on left chart, and label it "Conflict Creators."

5. Advance to Slide 7, and ask: When these things (from chart) are said to you, how can you respond to lessen the building tension? For example:

   - What would you say or do in response to an external customer who says (provide an example from the recorded list, such as *You never have a record of my previous order; it is infuriating.*")?

   - And, what would your response be if an internal customer told you (provide an example from the recorded list, such as *I can't do that now...I am just leaving for the night*")?

6. Record responses to Step 5 on middle chart, aligned with appropriate entry on the left chart, and label the middle chart "Ways to Decrease Conflict."

7. Repeat for many of the items on the left chart, asking: Are you ever the one using these (left chart) terms? How can we decrease conflict by avoiding it in the first place? What alternative terms and words can we use in place of these (left chart)? (Provide an example from the left chart, such as: Instead of saying "*I can't do what you are asking,*" say "*Here is what I can do for you...*" to an internal customer.)

8. Record responses to Step 7 on right chart, aligned with appropriate term on left chart. Label the right chart: "Ways to Avoid Conflict."

9. Repeat for many of the items on the left chart.

10. Advance to Slide 8, and ask: How many of our terms are listed here? In which column do you think they belong? If you are using the customizable PowerPoint version of the presentation slides, advance the slide animation to show positioning of the terms and again to show their alignment. If you are using the free, pdf-version of the presentation slides, you will automatically display the aligned positioning.

11. Lead a group debrief using some of the debriefing questions on the next page.

CUSTOMER SERVICE training 2

Learning Activity 5: Keep a Cool Head, *continued*

Variations

- Instead of a facilitated discussion, invite participants to record ideas for middle and right charts on sticky notes and display them in alignment with the entries on the left chart. Ask volunteers to read out ideas and invite the group to "vote" by standing if they agree with the strategy that has been read aloud. The ideas with the most votes can be typed up and shared as a post-workshop resource.

- Record responses to "What are some of the words and phrases that cause conflict to rise?" Invite table groups to brainstorm their "Ways to Decrease Conflict" and "Ways to Avoid Conflict" for 3-5 of the recorded items. Have a volunteer from each table share their top two ideas (no repeats from table to table).

- Have extra time? Following this activity, distribute a list of customer scenarios you have prepared, and direct learners to role play the situations using the language and phrases recorded in this activity.

Discussion Questions for Debriefing

- What conclusions can we draw from this activity?

- How will your service behaviors differ going forward based on this activity?

- Who has changed their opinion about the cause of conflict in service interactions and their own ability to decrease the conflict?

- What is one action you plan to take to avoid creating conflict in customer communications going forward?

Transition

Say: When we return from break, we will put some of these ideas we have recorded into action. So, be ready to apply the ideas from the last two activities to some real-world scenarios and receive instant feedback from the group.

Show break Slide 9.

CUSTOMER SERVICE training 3

Learning Activity 6: Quit Taking It Personally (Q-Tip)

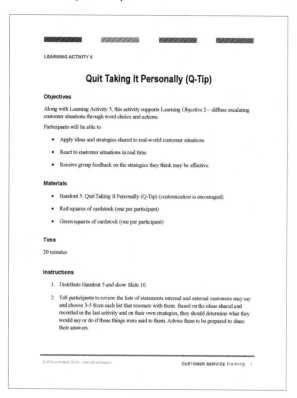

LEARNING ACTIVITY 6

Quit Taking It Personally (Q-Tip)

Objectives

Along with Learning Activity 5, this activity supports Learning Objective 2—diffuse escalating customer situations through word choice and actions.

Participants will be able to

- Apply ideas and strategies shared to real-world customer situations

- React to customer situations in real time

- Receive group feedback on the strategies they think may be effective.

Materials

- Handout 5: Quit Taking It Personally (Q-Tip) (customization is encouraged)

- Red squares of cardstock (one per participant)

- Green squares of cardstock (one per participant)

Time

20 minutes

Instructions

1. Distribute Handout 5 and show Slide 10.

2. Tell participants to review the lists of statements internal and external customers may say and choose 3-5 from each list that resonate with them. Based on the ideas shared and recorded in the last activity and on their own strategies, they should determine what they would say or do if these things were said to them. Advise them to be prepared to share their answers.

© 2015 by Kimberly Devlin. Used with permission.   **CUSTOMER SERVICE** training   1

Learning Activity 6: Quit Taking It Personally (Q-Tip), *continued*

LEARNING ACTIVITY 6, continued

3. As participants work, give each person one red and one green card.

4. Once participants have had time to work with the list, show Slide 11 and explain the pop-up process:

    a. You will read out an item from the handout.

    b. When a participant has a response idea to share and receive feedback on, he or she pops up and shares it (in 10-12 seconds) loudly enough for all to hear.

    c. Everyone "votes" (by holding up a red or green card) to indicate if the response would satisfy *them* if they were the customer: red indicates they would not be satisfied; green indicates they would.

5. Read out entries. Allow multiple pop-ups.

6. Lead a brief discussion to debrief the activity, referring to the questions on the next page.

Variations

- Print each statement on an index card. Invite volunteers to pull a card and play the role of that customer by reading the statement aloud as you moderate the pop-up responses.

- Instead of "voting" with a colored card, use a text-polling software tool to allow the group to give each idea shared a thumbs up or thumbs down.

- Create your own challenging statements and situations based on your pre-training interviews with service providers. (TIP: Make them specific and applicable to all attending.)

- Add other internal or external customer characteristics to the list (confused, hesitant, lacking a clear understanding of the need, and so on).

© 2015 by Kimberly Devlin. Used with permission.   **CUSTOMER SERVICE** training   2

Learning Activity 6: Quit Taking It Personally (Q-Tip), *continued*

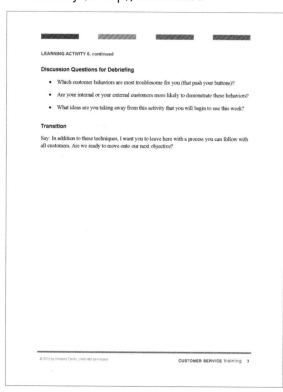

LEARNING ACTIVITY 6, continued

Discussion Questions for Debriefing

- Which customer behaviors are most troublesome for you (that push your buttons)?

- Are your internal or your external customers more likely to demonstrate these behaviors?

- What ideas are you taking away from this activity that you will begin to use this week?

Transition

Say: In addition to these techniques, I want you to leave here with a process you can follow with all customers. Are we ready to move onto our next objective?

© 2015 by Kimberly Devlin. Used with permission.   **CUSTOMER SERVICE** training   3

Learning Activity 7: The HELP Process for Customer Interactions

LEARNING ACTIVITY 7

The HELP Process for Customer Interactions

Objectives

Learning Activities 7 and 8 are interrelated and support Learning Objective 3—follow the four-step HELP process for customer interactions.

Participants will

- Participate in a discussion that presents a structured process for achieving successful customer outcomes

- Refer to sample statements and sentence stems to use in customer interactions.

Materials

- Handout 6: The HELP Process for Customer Interactions

Time

15 minutes

Instructions

1. Distribute Handout 6.

2. Using Slides 12 through 19 and the content that follows, facilitate a large group discussion of the HELP process. HELP is an acronym built on the first letters of four key actions: **H**ear their concerns, **E**xpand your view to see other sides, **L**et the customer participate in choosing the solution, and **P**erform the actions committed to. (TIP: Familiarize yourself with the animated slide builds to complement the discussion.)

© 2015 by Kimberly Devlin. Used with permission.   **CUSTOMER SERVICE** training   1

Learning Activity 7: The HELP Process for Customer Interactions, *continued*

a. Slide 12: HELP—Instruct participants to complete the Handout as you share a high-level explanation of HELP.

b. Slide 13: Hear Their Concerns

- Ask: What does it mean to listen reflectively? *(paraphrase/restate message)*

- Ask: What are the two components of a customer's message we want to reflect when demonstrating we are hearing them? *(content and feelings)*

c. Slide 14: Hear Their Concerns

- Ask: What are some common emotions your customers demonstrate they are feeling?

- Ask: Are there varying degrees of intensity in those feelings? For example, are an annoyed customer and a furious customer feeling the same degree of anger?

- Explain: This table shows multiple levels of intensity across four emotions (mad, glad, sad, afraid). These words can be helpful when constructing a reflective statement.

d. Slide 15: Hear Their Concerns

- Ask: Who will share an example of how one of the feelings words can be added into one of these reflective sentence stems? (Possible responses may include *Is it correct that you are disappointed with how your request was handled? I hear in your voice that you are upset.*)

- Ask: What other stems do you use in customer interactions?

e. Slide 16: Expand Your View to See Other Sides

- Ask: How can probing questions be helpful in resolving situations? *(They draw out information that is unknown, they can demonstrate empathy, answers to them often provide the customer's context.)*

- Ask: What are some characteristics of probing questions? *(asked in response to information already shared, commonly open-ended questions)*

- Ask: In what way do open, probing questions differ from closed questions? *(require more than a one- or two-word response)*

Learning Activity 7: The HELP Process for Customer Interactions, *continued*

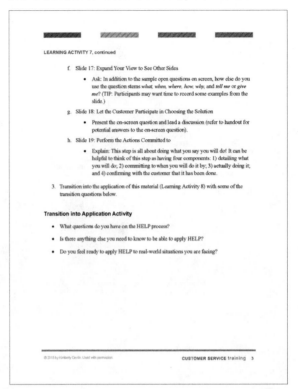

f. Slide 17: Expand Your View to See Other Sides

- Ask: In addition to the sample open questions on screen, how else do you use the question stems *what, when, where, how, why,* and *tell me or give me?* (TIP: Participants may want time to record some examples from the slide.)

g. Slide 18: Let the Customer Participate in Choosing the Solution

- Present the on-screen question and lead a discussion (refer to handout for potential answers to the on-screen question).

h. Slide 19: Perform the Actions Committed to

- Explain: This step is all about doing what you say you will do! It can be helpful to think of this step as having four components: 1) detailing what you will do; 2) committing to when you will do it by; 3) actually doing it; and 4) confirming with the customer that it has been done.

3. Transition into the application of this material (Learning Activity 8) with some of the transition questions below.

Transition into Application Activity

- What questions do you have on the HELP process?

- Is there anything else you need to know to be able to apply HELP?

- Do you feel ready to apply HELP to real-world situations you are facing?

Learning Activity 8: HELP the Customer

HELP the Customer

Objectives

Learning Activity 8 provides application practice for the content in Learning Activity 7. Together, they support Learning Objective 3—follow the four-step HELP process for customer interactions.

Participants will be able to

- Record the elements of service interactions that challenge them

- Apply the HELP process to challenging interactions to achieve positive customer outcomes.

Materials

- Handout 7: HELP the Customer—Interview Tool (one per participant)

- Handout 8: HELP the Customer—Planning Worksheet (one per participant)

- Handout 9: HELP the Customer—Observer Worksheet (two per participant)

Time

40 minutes

Instructions

PART 1

1. Have participants partner with a person they do not know well.

2. Distribute Handout 7 and show Slide 20.

Learning Activity 8: HELP the Customer, *continued*

a. Slide 12: HELP—Instruct participants to complete the Handout as you share a high-level explanation of HELP.

b. Slide 13: Hear Their Concerns

- Ask: What does it mean to listen reflectively? *(paraphrase/restate message)*

- Ask: What are the two components of a customer's message we want to reflect when demonstrating we are hearing them? *(content and feelings)*

c. Slide 14: Hear Their Concerns

- Ask: What are some common emotions your customers demonstrate they are feeling?

- Ask: Are there varying degrees of intensity in those feelings? For example, are an annoyed customer and a furious customer feeling the same degree of anger?

- Explain: This table shows multiple levels of intensity across four emotions (mad, glad, sad, afraid). These words can be helpful when constructing a reflective statement.

d. Slide 15: Hear Their Concerns

- Ask: Who will share an example of how one of the feelings words can be added into one of these reflective sentence stems? (Possible responses may include *Is it correct that you are disappointed with how your request was handled? I hear in your voice that you are upset.*)

- Ask: What other stems do you use in customer interactions?

e. Slide 16: Expand Your View to See Other Sides

- Ask: How can probing questions be helpful in resolving situations? *(They draw out information that is unknown, they can demonstrate empathy, answers to them often provide the customer's context.)*

- Ask: What are some characteristics of probing questions? *(asked in response to information already shared, commonly open-ended questions)*

- Ask: In what way do open, probing questions differ from closed questions? *(require more than a one- or two-word response)*

Learning Activity 8: HELP the Customer, *continued*

16. The feedback time built into the learning activity will debrief each role play; use any remaining time to lead a large group debrief discussion using some of the questions below.

Variations

- Have each pair select one of their two situations to role play in front of the observers. (A drawback with this variation is that only half of the participants are applying HELP.)
- Skip the interviewing portion and provide prepared customer scenarios for them to work with in the role plays. In this case, opt for trios: customer, service provider, and observer. Provide at least three scenarios so that each participant rotates through each role with a new situation. During planning, service provider and observer will create a plan together, and all of the customers will form one group to plan how they will behave in the role play. (TIP: Update slides accordingly.)

Discussion Questions for Debriefing

- What part(s) of HELP were easiest to apply? Hardest?
- How many of us found we were thinking about the actions we'd take at the last step (P, Perform the actions committed to), but forgot to tell the customer the details, timelines, and so on? Why do you think that is?
- How will the HELP process assist you in identifying customers' true needs in and resolving them?

Transition

Ask: How are you feeling about the skills we have been working on today? Are you taking away new techniques to better service your customers? Will these techniques address *all* customer concerns?

Say: Because these service *behavior* techniques will not address all customer concerns, before we bring today to a close, I'd like to share one last chunk of information that can help you take a bigger-picture approach to customer service to supplement your excellent efforts at demonstrating positive service behaviors.

Learning Activity 9: Interconnected Service Facets

Interconnected Service Facets

Objectives

This activity supports Learning Objective 4—distinguish service behaviors from service strategies and service systems.

Participants will be able to

- Participate in a discussion of the differences in the three aspects of service delivery
- Raise their awareness that all three facets contribute to the overall customer experience

Materials

- Handout 10: Interconnected Service Facets

Time

10 minutes

Instructions

1. Distribute Handout 10. Invite participants to refer to and add to it during the discussion.
2. Using Slide 23 and the content below, facilitate a discussion and supplement it with lecturette on the interconnected service facets (behaviors, strategies, and systems).
   a. **Service Behaviors**—Person-to-person skills
      - Explain: We have spent today focusing on this aspect of service.
      - Ask: What are some examples of service behaviors? (*active listening, being respectful, conflict management, eye-contact*)

Learning Activity 9: Interconnected Service Facets, *continued*

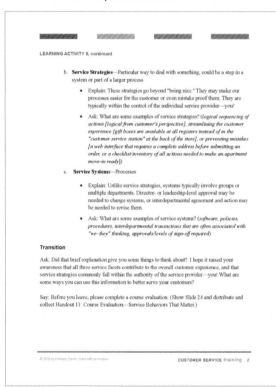

   b. **Service Strategies**—Particular way to deal with something, could be a step in a system or part of a larger process
      - Explain: These strategies go beyond "being nice." They may make our processes easier for the customer or even mistake proof them. They are typically within the control of the individual service provider—you!
      - Ask: What are some examples of service strategies? (*logical sequencing of actions [logical from customer's perspective], streamlining the customer experience [gift boxes are available at all registers instead of in the "customer service station" at the back of the store], or preventing mistakes [a web interface that requires a complete address before submitting an order; or a checklist/inventory of all actions needed to make an apartment move-in ready]*)
   c. **Service Systems**—Processes
      - Explain: Unlike service strategies, systems typically involve groups or multiple departments. Director- or leadership-level approval may be needed to change systems, or interdepartmental agreement and action may be needed to revise them.
      - Ask: What are some examples of service systems? (*software, policies, procedures, interdepartmental transactions that are often associated with "we-they" thinking, approvals/levels of sign-off required*)

Transition

Ask: Did that brief explanation give you some things to think about? I hope it raised your awareness that all three service facets contribute to the overall customer experience, and that service strategies commonly fall within the authority of the service provider—you! What are some ways you can use this information to better serve your customers?

Say: Before you leave, please complete a course evaluation. (Show Slide 24 and distribute and collect Handout 11: Course Evaluation—Service Behaviors That Matter.)

Learning Activity 10: Initial Reactions

Initial Reactions

Objectives

Participants will become interested and engaged in the training topic and be encouraged to take a big-picture approach to customer service.

Materials

- Text polling application

Time

15 minutes

Instructions

1. Display Slide 1 as participants arrive.
2. Use a polling via texting application to display participants' responses to this question: When you think of customer service, what words come to mind? (Common responses will be behavior-related and may include: *friendly, use their name, resolve issues, smile, eye-contact.*)
3. Lead a discussion around the words shared. For example, ask: "Friendly...what does that look like?" or "Use customers' name...why does that matter?"
4. Use the polling via texting application to display participants' responses to a second question: "In two or three words, when you are not able to satisfy a customer, what is the cause of their dissatisfaction?" (Responses are commonly industry-specific service strategy or service system issues, and not behavior related. For example, *reservation system won't release the rooms/seats/tickets; complex series of required steps in a process; error in advertised promotion; policy won't allow; and others.*)

Learning Activity 10: Initial Reactions, *continued*

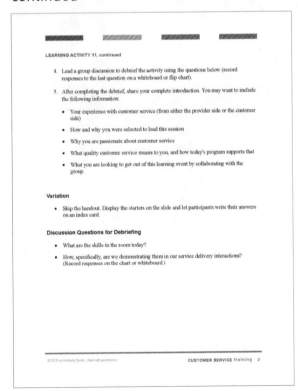

LEARNING ACTIVITY 10, continued

5. Lead a discussion around the responses. Ask, for example: "If you can't provide the desired product, will using the customer's name while smiling make up for that?...Are there service disconnects that occur repeatedly, even predictably?...What can be done to change the strategy or system to improve the customer experience?"

Variations

- Instead of using a text polling tool, generate ideas to the first question through table brainstorming and a round-robin shout-out. Record words or phrases on flip chart. Facilitate discussion, as above, and repeat with second question.
- Alternate Opener: Display the first statistic (below) and ask the group what it means to them. Repeat with the second. Reveal the third, and ask if this statistic influences their earlier comments and thoughts.
  - Seventy percent of buying experiences are based on how the customer feels they are being treated. (Source: Cited on https://fonolo.com/blog/2014/02/20-important-customer-experience-statistics-for-2014/.)
  - Eighty-two percent of consumers say the number one factor that leads to a great customer service experience is having their issues resolved quickly. (Source: Cited on https://fonolo.com/blog/2014/02/20-important-customer-experience-statistics-for-2014/.)
  - Forty-two percent of service agents are unable to efficiently resolve customer issues due to disconnected systems, archaic user interfaces, and multiple applications. (Source: Cited on http://blogs.salesforce.com/company/2013/08/customer-service-stats.html.)

Transition

Say: Clearly, we can demonstrate positive service behaviors and still have dissatisfied customers because of bigger-picture issues. Equally true, if customers receive what they wanted but still feel they were treated poorly, that is not a winning experience either. Both are critical. Therefore, today, we will be working with tools and techniques to support service behaviors as well as service strategies and systems.

© 2015 by Kimberly Devlin. Used with permission.   CUSTOMER SERVICE training   2

Learning Activity 11: Service Heroes

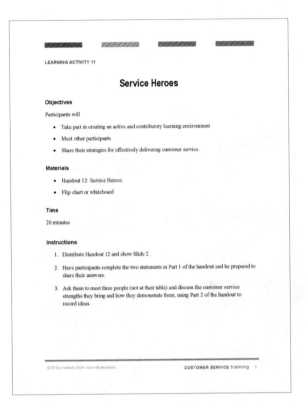

LEARNING ACTIVITY 11

Service Heroes

Objectives

Participants will

- Take part in creating an active and contributory learning environment
- Meet other participants
- Share their strategies for effectively delivering customer service.

Materials

- Handout 12: Service Heroes
- Flip chart or whiteboard

Time

20 minutes

Instructions

1. Distribute Handout 12 and show Slide 2.
2. Have participants complete the two statements in Part 1 of the handout and be prepared to share their answers.
3. Ask them to meet three people (not at their table) and discuss the customer service strengths they bring and how they demonstrate them, using Part 2 of the handout to record ideas.

© 2015 by Kimberly Devlin. Used with permission.   CUSTOMER SERVICE training   1

Learning Activity 11: Service Heroes, *continued*

LEARNING ACTIVITY 11, continued

4. Lead a group discussion to debrief the activity using the questions below (record responses to the last question on a whiteboard or flip chart).
5. After completing the debrief, share your complete introduction. You may want to include the following information:
   - Your experience with customer service (from either the provider side or the customer side)
   - How and why you were selected to lead this session
   - Why you are passionate about customer service
   - What quality customer service means to you, and how today's program supports that
   - What you are looking to get out of this learning event by collaborating with the group.

Variation

- Skip the handout. Display the starters on the slide and let participants write their answers on an index card.

Discussion Questions for Debriefing

- What are the skills in the room today?
- How, specifically, are we demonstrating them in our service delivery interactions? (Record responses on the chart or whiteboard.)

© 2015 by Kimberly Devlin. Used with permission.   CUSTOMER SERVICE training   2

Learning Activity 12: Prioritize Learning

LEARNING ACTIVITY 12

Prioritize Learning

Objectives

Participants will

- Establish a framework for the goals for the learning event
- See how the program content relates to real work situations
- Prioritize the training topics based on their current needs.

Materials

- Handout 13: Learning Objectives
- Handout 14: Participant Journal
- Prepared chart of social agreements

Time

5 minutes

Instructions

1. Review content of Slides 3 and 4.
2. Distribute Handout 13.
3. Tell participants: This one page serves three purposes. First, it shows where we are headed by listing our learning objectives (first column). Second, it indicates how the skills learned here can benefit you on the job (second column). And, third, it allows you to rate each of our objectives relative to how critical it is to you right, now...today...at this moment (third column).

© 2015 by Kimberly Devlin. Used with permission.   CUSTOMER SERVICE training   1

Learning Activity 12: Prioritize Learning, *continued*

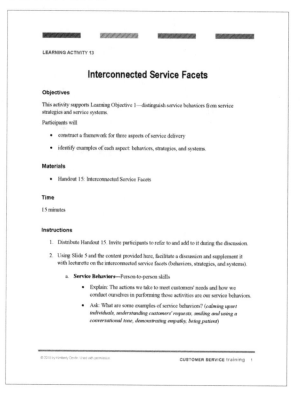

LEARNING ACTIVITY 12, continued

4. Ask them to read the objectives and their benefits, and then follow the printed instructions to individually prioritize the objectives.

5. As they work, distribute Handout 14.

6. Lead a group discussion using the debriefing questions below.

7. Introduce and review social agreements (ground rules) charted for the session.

Discussion Questions for Debriefing

- Which of these objectives resonates most strongly with you today?
- Is there anything we should be adding to our goals for the day?
- Are there needs you have that don't seem to be addressed in these objectives?

Transition

Explain: Handout 14 is included here as a place for you to record details associated with your personal learning. When you hear a great idea, write it down. When a follow-up action comes to mind for you, record it here. This page is provided as a tool for you; use it as best meets your needs.

© 2015 by Kimberly Devlin. Used with permission.   CUSTOMER SERVICE training   2

Learning Activity 13: Interconnected Service Facets

LEARNING ACTIVITY 13

Interconnected Service Facets

Objectives

This activity supports Learning Objective 1—distinguish service behaviors from service strategies and service systems.

Participants will

- construct a framework for three aspects of service delivery
- identify examples of each aspect: behaviors, strategies, and systems.

Materials

- Handout 15: Interconnected Service Facets

Time

15 minutes

Instructions

1. Distribute Handout 15. Invite participants to refer to and add to it during the discussion.

2. Using Slide 5 and the content provided here, facilitate a discussion and supplement it with lecturette on the interconnected service facets (behaviors, strategies, and systems).

    a. **Service Behaviors**—Person-to-person skills
      - Explain: The actions we take to meet customers' needs and how we conduct ourselves in performing those activities are our service behaviors.
      - Ask: What are some examples of service behaviors? (*calming upset individuals, understanding customers' requests, smiling and using a conversational tone, demonstrating empathy, being patient*)

© 2015 by Kimberly Devlin. Used with permission.   CUSTOMER SERVICE training   1

Learning Activity 13: Interconnected Service Facets, *continued*

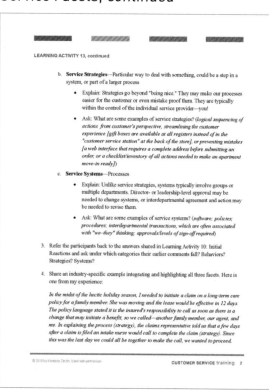

LEARNING ACTIVITY 13, continued

    b. **Service Strategies**—Particular way to deal with something, could be a step in a system, or part of a larger process
      - Explain: Strategies go beyond "being nice." They may make our processes easier for the customer or even mistake proof them. They are typically within the control of the individual service provider—you!
      - Ask: What are some examples of service strategies? (*logical sequencing of actions from customer's perspective, streamlining the customer experience [gift boxes are available at all registers instead of in the "customer service station" at the back of the store], or preventing mistakes [a web interface that requires a complete address before submitting an order, or a checklist/inventory of all actions needed to make an apartment move-in ready]*)

    c. **Service Systems**—Processes
      - Explain: Unlike service strategies, systems typically involve groups or multiple departments. Director- or leadership-level approval may be needed to change systems, or interdepartmental agreement and action may be needed to revise them.
      - Ask: What are some examples of service systems? (*software; policies; procedures; interdepartmental transactions, which are often associated with "we–they" thinking; approvals/levels of sign-off required*)

3. Refer the participants back to the answers shared in Learning Activity 10: Initial Reactions and ask under which categories their earlier comments fall? Behaviors? Strategies? Systems?

4. Share an industry-specific example integrating and highlighting all three facets. Here is one from my experience:

    In the midst of the hectic holiday season, I needed to initiate a claim on a long-term care policy for a family member. She was moving and the lease would be effective in 12 days. The policy language stated it is the insured's responsibility to call as soon as there is a change that may initiate a benefit, so we called—another family member, our agent, and me. In explaining the process (strategy), the claims representative told us that a few days after a claim is filed an intake nurse would call to complete the claim (strategy). Since this was the last day we could all be together to make the call, we wanted to proceed.

© 2015 by Kimberly Devlin. Used with permission.   CUSTOMER SERVICE training   2

Learning Activity 13: Interconnected Service Facets, *continued*

LEARNING ACTIVITY 13, continued

The representative stopped us and said their policy (system) is to wait until the insured has moved or is within 10 days of moving...because things change and they don't want to have to do rework (strategy/behavior). By our math, with mom moving in 12 days and it taking "a few days" for the intake nurse to call, we'd be at 10 days or less! Add onto that the holidays and our agent's vacation plans, and we were clearly eager to proceed. Only then, did she say "Well, if you want me to, I can open the claim" (strategy), with a tone that implied we were inconveniencing her (behavior).

Transition

(TIP: Ensure all are clear on the distinctions of the three categories before moving into the application activity.)

Ask: What questions do you have on the differences among behaviors, strategies, and systems? We are about to apply these concepts in a group activity.

© 2015 by Kimberly Devlin. Used with permission.   CUSTOMER SERVICE training   3

Learning Activity 14: Do They Agree?

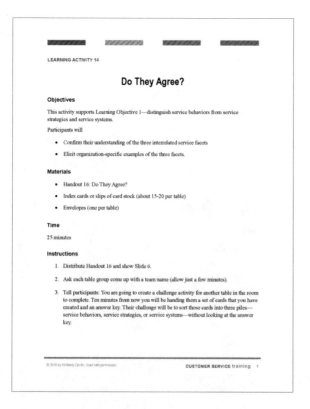

LEARNING ACTIVITY 14

Do They Agree?

Objectives

This activity supports Learning Objective 1—distinguish service behaviors from service strategies and service systems.

Participants will

- Confirm their understanding of the three interrelated service facets
- Elicit organization-specific examples of the three facets.

Materials

- Handout 16: Do They Agree?
- Index cards or slips of card stock (about 15-20 per table)
- Envelopes (one per table)

Time

25 minutes

Instructions

1. Distribute Handout 16 and show Slide 6.

2. Ask each table group come up with a team name (allow just a few minutes).

3. Tell participants: You are going to create a challenge activity for another table in the room to complete. Ten minutes from now you will be handing them a set of cards that you have created and an answer key. Their challenge will be to sort those cards into three piles—service behaviors, service strategies, or service systems—without looking at the answer key.

Learning Activity 14: Do They Agree?, *continued*

LEARNING ACTIVITY 14, continued

4. Have groups brainstorm examples of all three service facets, encouraging them to focus on behaviors, strategies, and systems that are specific to the organization and that go beyond the obvious so that the activity is a bit of a challenge.

5. As they brainstorm, visit tables and offer direction as needed (guide them to select examples from their lists that are different from other tables' selections).

6. After brainstorming, show Slide 7 and direct them to select 5-7 items for each category and write them on the answer key handout.

7. Distribute index cards and envelopes and ask them to write each term or phrase from the answer key on its own index card, shuffle the cards, and place the cards and the answer key in the envelope. (TIP: Provide, or have them write cards, that say: Service behaviors, service strategies, and service systems to include in the envelope and to serve as "labels" during the grouping part of the activity.)

8. Instruct them to pass their stuffed envelope to the next table.

9. Show Slide 8 and ask groups to remove the cards, but not the answer key, and work together to sort the cards into three piles: service behaviors, service strategies, or service systems. Tell them to place the cards face up.

10. See debrief (below) for remaining steps.

Discussion Questions for Debriefing

Note: No cards should be moved (until Step 4, below, if desired by the group).

1. Have table groups rotate to the next table (where the cards they created were sorted) to see if the group who sorted the cards agrees with the group who wrote the cards.

2. Rotate groups again to the next table to see if the rotating group agrees with how the table group sorted the cards.

3. Repeat Step 2 of debriefing until all groups are back at their tables.

4. Ask them to review their own groupings and consider if any should be re-grouped.

Learning Activity 14: Do They Agree?, *continued*

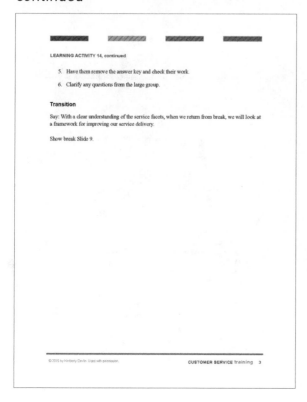

LEARNING ACTIVITY 14, continued

5. Have them remove the answer key and check their work.

6. Clarify any questions from the large group.

Transition

Say: With a clear understanding of the service facets, when we return from break, we will look at a framework for improving our service delivery.

Show break Slide 9.

Learning Activity 15: Performance Improvement Service Levels

LEARNING ACTIVITY 15

Performance Improvement Service Levels

Objectives

This activity supports Learning Objective 2—assess your service environment to target improvement opportunities.

Participants will

- Share their interpretations of the three performance improvement levels (As Is, Should Be, Could Be)
- Establish a baseline consensus of these terms for all to work from moving forward.

Materials

- Handout 17: Performance Improvement

Time

20 minutes

Instructions

1. Show Slide 10.

2. Ask participants to partner with another person and share what the terms *As Is, Should Be,* and *Could Be* mean to them. Encourage them to think in terms of service delivery and performance improvement, explaining that there aren't right and wrong answers, just individual interpretations.

3. As they work, move through the room and listen to conversations.

Learning Activity 15: Performance Improvement Service Levels, *continued*

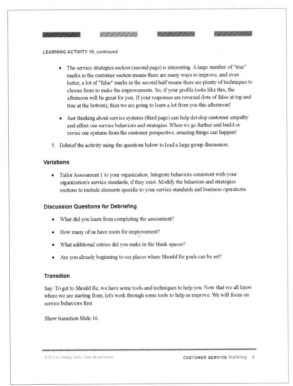

4. Acknowledge that you are hearing many interesting comments in the room—some that are similar to one another and others that are different. Invite participants to share some of their thoughts to get the group on the same page with these terms and share a common definition of each.

5. Distribute Handout 17 and show Slide 11.

6. Ask if this additional information either reinforces or shifts initial interpretations.

7. Using Slides 12 to 14, facilitate a large group discussion to include the following concepts. Encourage participants to capture insights from the discussion on the lines provided on the handout.

    a. **As Is**—Our current state; a snapshot in time.

      • When we assess the As Is, we want to measure where we truly are: not the best we have ever done, not what we are capable of, not what we would do if the situation were different but rather what we currently are doing.

    b. **Should Be**—What we are capable of with what we have.

      • Our short-term goals should be set here.

      • We ought to be performing at this level.

      • It is the prime target for our efforts here today!

    c. **Could Be**—Without constraining our goals or limiting our thinking by circumstances, these are future possibilities.

      • The Could Be level might be longer range.

      • Some of these things may be outside our control. Or maybe they are things we can influence, but not fully control.

Transition

Say: Because the first step in determining our As Is involves objective evaluation, let's assess ourselves.

© 2015 by Kimberly Devlin. Used with permission.   **CUSTOMER SERVICE** training 2

Learning Activity 16: Where Are We Now?

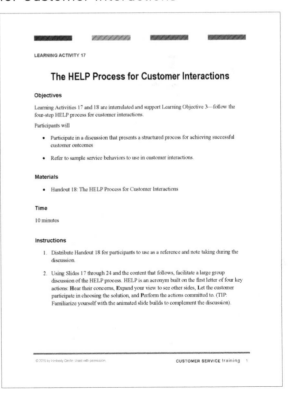

Where Are We Now?

Objectives

This activity supports Learning Objective 2—assess your service environment to target improvement opportunities.

Participants will objectively assess their As Is state.

Materials

• Assessment 1: Where Are We Now?

Time

15 minutes

Instructions

1. Distribute Assessment 1 and show Slide 15.

2. Ask participants to complete the assessment, keeping in mind what was said earlier about the need to objectively assess where we truly are. Explain that in each section there is space or a question allowing them to personalize the assessment.

3. Allow 10 minutes.

4. Share the following:

    • Most of us, when we are truly objective, will have a range of ratings for the service behaviors (first page). The higher ratings may be strengths we can leverage to improve our lower rankings.

© 2015 by Kimberly Devlin. Used with permission.   **CUSTOMER SERVICE** training 1

Learning Activity 16: Where Are We Now?, *continued*

• The service strategies section (second page) is interesting. A large number of "true" marks in the customer section means there are many ways to improve, and even better, a lot of "false" marks in the second half means there are plenty of techniques to choose from to make the improvements. So, if your profile looks like this, the afternoon will be great for you. If your responses are reversed (lots of false at top and true at the bottom), then we are going to learn a lot from you this afternoon!

• Just thinking about service systems (third page) can help develop customer empathy and affect our service behaviors and strategies. When we go further and build or revise our systems from the customer perspective, amazing things can happen!

5. Debrief the activity using the questions below to lead a large group discussion.

Variations

• Tailor Assessment 1 to your organization. Integrate behaviors consistent with your organization's service standards, if they exist. Modify the behaviors and strategies sections to include elements specific to your service standards and business operations.

Discussion Questions for Debriefing

• What did you learn from completing the assessment?

• How many of us have room for improvement?

• What additional entries did you make in the blank spaces?

• Are you already beginning to see places where Should Be goals can be set?

Transition

Say: To get to Should Be, we have some tools and techniques to help you. Now that we all know where we are starting from, let's work through some tools to help us improve. We will focus on service behaviors first.

Show transition Slide 16.

© 2015 by Kimberly Devlin. Used with permission.   **CUSTOMER SERVICE** training 2

Learning Activity 17: The HELP Process for Customer Interactions

The HELP Process for Customer Interactions

Objectives

Learning Activities 17 and 18 are interrelated and support Learning Objective 3—follow the four-step HELP process for customer interactions.

Participants will

• Participate in a discussion that presents a structured process for achieving successful customer outcomes

• Refer to sample service behaviors to use in customer interactions.

Materials

• Handout 18: The HELP Process for Customer Interactions

Time

10 minutes

Instructions

1. Distribute Handout 18 for participants to use as a reference and note taking during the discussion.

2. Using Slides 17 through 24 and the content that follows, facilitate a large group discussion of the HELP process. HELP is an acronym built on the first letter of four key actions: **H**ear their concerns, **E**xpand your view to see other sides, **L**et the customer participate in choosing the solution, and **P**erform the actions committed to. (TIP: Familiarize yourself with the animated slide builds to complement the discussion).

© 2015 by Kimberly Devlin. Used with permission.   **CUSTOMER SERVICE** training 1

Learning Activity 17: The HELP Process for Customer Interactions, *continued*

LEARNING ACTIVITY 17, continued

   a. Slide 17: The HELP process—Instruct participants to complete the handout as you share a high-level explanation of HELP.

   b. Slide 18: Hear Their Concerns

- Ask: What does it mean to listen reflectively? (*paraphrase/restate message*)
- Ask: What are the two components of a customer's message we want to reflect when demonstrating we are hearing them? (*content and feelings*)

   c. Slide 19: Hear Their Concerns

- Ask: What are some common emotions your customers demonstrate they are feeling?
- Ask: Are there varying degrees of intensity in those feelings? For example, are an annoyed customer and a furious customer feeling the same degree of anger?
- Explain: This table shows multiple levels of intensity across four emotions (mad, glad, sad, afraid). These words can be helpful when constructing a reflective statement.

   d. Slide 20: Hear Their Concerns

- Ask: Who will share an example of how one of the feelings words can be added into one of these reflective sentence stems? (Possible responses could include *Is it correct that you are disappointed with how your request was handled? I hear in your voice that you are upset.*)
- Ask: What other stems do you use in customer interactions?

   e. Slide 21: Expand Your View to See Other Sides

- Ask: How can probing questions be helpful in resolving situations? (*They draw out information that is unknown, they can demonstrate empathy, answers to them often provide the customer's context.*)
- Ask: What are some characteristics of probing questions? (*asked in response to information already shared, commonly open-ended questions*)
- Ask: In what way do open, probing questions differ from closed questions? (*require more than a one- or two-word response*)

© 2015 by Kimberly Devlin. Used with permission.   CUSTOMER SERVICE training 2

Learning Activity 17: The HELP Process for Customer Interactions, *continued*

LEARNING ACTIVITY 17, continued

   f. Slide 22: Expand Your View to See Other Sides

- Ask: In addition to the sample open questions on screen, how else do you use the question stems *what, when, where, how, why,* and *tell me* or *give me*? (TIP: Participants may want time to record some examples from the slide.)

   g. Slide 23: Let the Customer Participate in Choosing the Solution

- Present the on-screen question and lead a discussion (refer to handout for potential answers to the on-screen question).

   h. Slide 24: Perform the Actions Committed to

- Explain: This step is all about doing what you say you will do! It can be helpful to think of this step as having four components: 1) detailing *what* you will do; 2) committing to *when* you will do it; 3) *doing it*, and 4) *confirming* with the customer that it has been done.

3. Transition into the application of this material (Learning Activity 18) with some of the transition questions below.

Transition into Application Activity

- What questions do you have on the HELP process?
- Is there anything else you need to know to be able to apply HELP?
- Do you feel ready to apply HELP to real-world situations we are facing?

© 2015 by Kimberly Devlin. Used with permission.   CUSTOMER SERVICE training 3

Learning Activity 18: HELP the Customer: Interviews and Role Plays

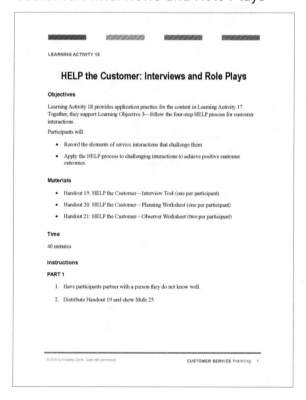

LEARNING ACTIVITY 18

HELP the Customer: Interviews and Role Plays

Objectives

Learning Activity 18 provides application practice for the content in Learning Activity 17. Together, they support Learning Objective 3—follow the four-step HELP process for customer interactions.

Participants will

- Record the elements of service interactions that challenge them
- Apply the HELP process to challenging interactions to achieve positive customer outcomes.

Materials

- Handout 19: HELP the Customer—Interview Tool (one per participant)
- Handout 20: HELP the Customer—Planning Worksheet (one per participant)
- Handout 21: HELP the Customer—Observer Worksheet (two per participant)

Time

40 minutes

Instructions

PART 1

1. Have participants partner with a person they do not know well.

2. Distribute Handout 19 and show Slide 25.

© 2015 by Kimberly Devlin. Used with permission.   CUSTOMER SERVICE training 1

Learning Activity 18: HELP the Customer: Interviews and Role Plays, *continued*

LEARNING ACTIVITY 18, continued

3. Explain: You will be interviewing a partner using this interview tool worksheet. Ask the worksheet questions and record your partner's answers beneath each one because the answers will form the basis of the role plays (Part 2 of this activity).

4. After the first interview, ask partners to switch roles so that both individuals have been interviewed.

PART 2

5. Using the situations just recorded and the HELP process, partners will role play the interactions with another team observing them.

6. Instruct interview pairs to partner with another pair, forming quads.

7. Tell quads to switch partners (one person from Pair A partners with one person from Pair B). The remaining two people also partner.

8. Distribute Handout 20 and show Slide 26.

9. Explain: Working with this new partner, plan your HELP role plays for the situations Pair A recorded in the interviews and then the situation Pair B recorded. Use the planning worksheet to help you map out what you will say and do as the service partner during the role play. CRITICAL: During the role play, each person will "act out" their original partner's role in the situation. That means, the person interviewed on a service interaction in Part 1 will be the customer during the role play of that situation. The planning will be done for the situations each person took interview notes on.

10. Allow planning time and assist groups in clarifying the roles they will play.

11. Explain: So that you receive feedback on your use of HELP, each role play will have two observers who will use the observer worksheet (Handout 21) to record notes for feedback.

12. Distribute Handout 21 (two per participant).

13. Have quads begin the first role play and show Slide 27 (as a reference during the role plays).

14. Ask the observing team to share feedback to the service provider in the role play. (Encourage them to capture their feedback insights on the observer worksheet.)

© 2015 by Kimberly Devlin. Used with permission.   CUSTOMER SERVICE training 2

Learning Activity 18: HELP the Customer: Interviews and Role Plays, *continued*

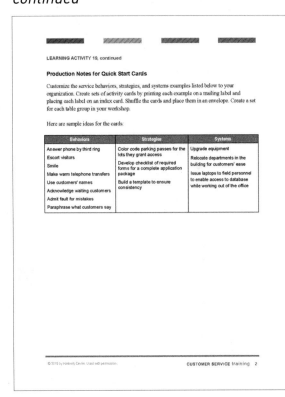

15. Repeat Steps 13 and 14 until all four quad members have applied HELP.

16. The feedback time built into the learning activity will debrief each role play; however, use any remaining time to lead a large group debrief discussion using some of the questions below.

Variations

- Have each pair select one of their two situations to role play in front of the observers (The drawback is that only half of the participants are applying HELP.)

- Skip the interviewing portion and provide prepared scenarios for them to work with in the role plays. In this case, opt for trios: customer, service provider, and observer. Provide at least three scenarios so that each participant rotates through each role with a new situation. During planning, service provider and observer will create a plan together, and all of the customers will form one group to plan how they will behave. (TIP: Update slides accordingly.)

Discussion Questions for Debriefing

- How will the HELP process take you from As Is to Should Be in your service behaviors?

- What part(s) of HELP were easiest to apply? Hardest?

- How many of us found we were thinking about the actions we'd take, but forget to tell the customer the details and timelines? Why do you think that is?

- How will the HELP process assist you in identifying customers' true needs and in resolving them?

Transition

Ask: What questions do you have about HELP? How do you see it helping you? Will HELP address and resolve all customer concerns? We can get the behaviors right and still have disconnects.

Say: Therefore, when we return from lunch, we will be working with service strategies and end our day with a look at service systems—the two other service facets that supplement your efforts at demonstrating positive service behaviors.

Show lunch Slide 28.

© 2015 by Kimberly Devlin. Used with permission.   CUSTOMER SERVICE training   3

Learning Activity 19: Quick Start

Quick Start

Objectives

Participants will be able to

- Reconnect to the morning content and ease back into the afternoon

- Confirm their ability to distinguish among service behaviors, strategies, and systems.

Materials

- Envelopes filled with sets of prepared cards (one set per table)

Time

10 minutes

Instructions

1. During lunch break, place a quick start envelope on each table (see production notes on next page).

2. Display Slide 29 as participants return from lunch.

3. As groups return, invite them to complete the on-screen activity.

© 2015 by Kimberly Devlin. Used with permission.   CUSTOMER SERVICE training   1

Learning Activity 19: Quick Start, *continued*

Production Notes for Quick Start Cards

Customize the service behaviors, strategies, and systems examples listed below to your organization. Create sets of activity cards by printing each example on a mailing label and placing each label on an index card. Shuffle the cards and place them in an envelope. Create a set for each table group in your workshop.

Here are sample ideas for the cards:

Behaviors	Strategies	Systems
Answer phone by third ring	Color code parking passes for the lots they grant access	Upgrade equipment
Escort visitors		Relocate departments in the building for customers' ease
Smile	Develop checklist of required forms for a complete application package	Issue laptops to field personnel to enable access to database while working out of the office
Make warm telephone transfers		
Use customers' names	Build a template to ensure consistency	
Acknowledge waiting customers		
Admit fault for mistakes		
Paraphrase what customers say		

© 2015 by Kimberly Devlin. Used with permission.   CUSTOMER SERVICE training   2

Learning Activity 20: Mistake Proofing

Mistake Proofing

Objectives

This activity supports Learning Objective 4—improve existing service strategies from the customer's perspective.

Participants will

- Develop a framework of what mistake proofing is

- Identify how mistake proofing can benefit customer service outcomes

- Record how they are currently using mistake-proofing techniques.

Materials

- Handout 22: Mistake Proofing to Improve Customer Service

Time

20 minutes

Instructions

1. Show transition Slide 30.

2. Show Slide 31 and draw out the group's knowledge of mistake proofing by asking:

   - Who has experience working with mistake proofing?

   - What does mistake proofing mean?

   - How do you go about mistake proofing?

   - What are some characteristics of the best mistake-proofing techniques? (*simple, inexpensive, easy to implement, effective, creative*)

© 2015 by Kimberly Devlin. Used with permission.   CUSTOMER SERVICE training   1

Learning Activity 20: Mistake Proofing, *continued*

LEARNING ACTIVITY 20, continued

3. Make a connection between the technique and the workshop by asking:

    • What does mistake proofing have to do with customer service?

4. Distribute Handout 22 and show Slide 32.

5. Share key concepts of mistake proofing and provide examples of mistake-proofing techniques at use in the organization using Slides 33 to 35. (TIP: Some sample images are included in slides. Replacing them with organization-specific examples may be beneficial.) Invite participants to record additional ideas mentioned in the discussion in the right-hand column of the handout.

6. Share examples of mistake proofing you have encountered recently. Here are some recent examples from my experiences:

    • *In my state, a trip to the DMV (Division of Motor Vehicles) can be a lengthy experience. I recently went to purchase a parking pass and saved myself hours because of a mistake-proofing technique. Right there, on the front door of the DMV was a sign that read: "This location only accepts cash and checks"; because I had neither, I never even walked in. Imagine my annoyance if I took a number and a seat and then learned this at the counter.*

    • *Another DMV-related example is the orientation of driver's licenses. Drivers under the legal drinking age have a vertical license instead of a horizontal one.*

    • *A plumber came to my home to install a cast-iron tub and drain. This involved entering a very low crawl space at one end of my house and crawling under it to the other end to connect the drain. For the finished job to be correct, the fittings under the house and inside the bathroom needed to be aligned perfectly. Rather than crawl under and set it, crawl out and check it, (repeating until right), and then crawling under to connect it, we devised a mistake-proof technique. Using cell phones, I snapped photos of the tub from above and sent them to the plumber. Perfect job in one trip!*

7. Ask participants for examples of mistake-proofing techniques they have recently encountered.

© 2015 by Kimberly Devlin. Used with permission.   CUSTOMER SERVICE training   2

Learning Activity 20: Mistake Proofing, *continued*

LEARNING ACTIVITY 20, continued

8. Share at least one example of how mistake proofing can go wrong. Here is one from my experience:

    When a municipality undertook on a service initiative, one librarian decided to use a baiting technique as an exception for a customer. A woman had tried to return her books on time, but the branch closed early due to a power outage. She was annoyed to now be asked to pay a late fine, and the librarian waived the fee and said he was doing it in support of excellent service. Good, right? Well, all of the librarians began waiving all of the late fees—in support of the municipalities' focus on service. It wasn't long before the leadership (and accountants!) imposed a new rule that librarians were no longer allowed to waive any fees.

9. Instruct participants to complete page 2 of the handout, recording how they are already using some of these techniques. Then have them pair with a partner and compare notes.

Variation

• Instead of using the handout in Step 4 (above), create a hands-on manipulative activity. Print card-sized pictures of mistake-proofing techniques in use in the organization. Cut them into individual cards. After facilitated discussion, distribute a set to each table group and instruct them to sort them by techniques type (that is, layout, color coding, checklists, templates, grouping, and so on). Then instruct them to identify three ways they can apply these ideas to any aspect of their own work.

Transition

Say: To build on how you are already using these techniques, we are going to spend time finding more service strategies to mistake proof and design or plan more mistake-proof techniques.

© 2015 by Kimberly Devlin. Used with permission.   CUSTOMER SERVICE training   3

Learning Activity 21: Creating Mistake-Proof Techniques

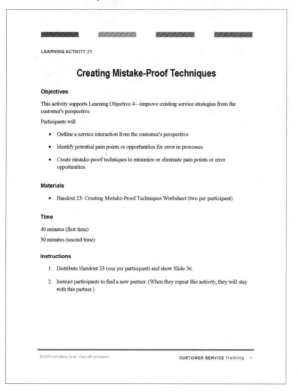

LEARNING ACTIVITY 21

Creating Mistake-Proof Techniques

Objectives

This activity supports Learning Objective 4—improve existing service strategies from the customer's perspective.

Participants will

• Outline a service interaction from the customer's perspective

• Identify potential pain points or opportunities for error in processes

• Create mistake-proof techniques to minimize or eliminate pain points or error opportunities.

Materials

• Handout 23: Creating Mistake-Proof Techniques Worksheet (two per participant)

Time

40 minutes (first time)

30 minutes (second time)

Instructions

1. Distribute Handout 23 (one per participant) and show Slide 36.

2. Instruct participants to find a new partner. (When they repeat this activity, they will stay with this partner.)

© 2015 by Kimberly Devlin. Used with permission.   CUSTOMER SERVICE training   1

Learning Activity 21: Creating Mistake-Proof Techniques, *continued*

LEARNING ACTIVITY 21, continued

3. Explain: To know where to implement a mistake-proof technique, tool, or device, we need to begin by locating pain points where customers encounter a frustration or make a mistake, or where we are not as effective or efficient as we should be.

    a. So, we begin by outlining the process as it is.

    b. Then we look at it objectively to find those pain points.

    c. Next, we get creative and match up the tools such as color coding, streamlining, sequencing, checklists, grouping, and others to design a mistake-proof technique.

    d. So, to reiterate, implementing mistake-proof techniques involve three steps: outline the process, identify potential pain points, and devise mistake-proof solutions.

4. OPTION: If the group is unfamiliar with process mapping, walk through an organization-specific example or relate this generic example:

    A customer wants to return ship a damaged item and receive an alternate item free of charge. The first step might be to locate a phone number. Other steps in the process may be to locate order number on bill of lading, complete return slip properly with reason code to justify free shipping, qualify for return by meeting return deadline, include all original packaging to qualify, ship to a different address, and so on.

5. Point out that the customer does not need to have direct interaction with the mistake-proof techniques to benefit from them. For example, a technique that enables a field technician to complete a repair more quickly will not necessarily involve the customer but can lead to greater customer satisfaction.

6. Ask participants to complete the worksheet. (TIP: They may find it useful to look back at their self-assessment results from Learning Activity 16: Where Are We Now? Refer specifically to the service strategies page where they indicated Yes/No to many common customer challenges and Yes/No to their current use of mistake-proof techniques.)

7. Lead a group discussion to debrief the activity with the questions on the following page.

© 2015 by Kimberly Devlin. Used with permission.   CUSTOMER SERVICE training   2

Learning Activity 21: Creating Mistake-Proof Techniques, *continued*

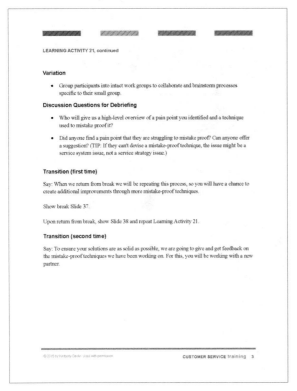

LEARNING ACTIVITY 21, continued

Variation

- Group participants into intact work groups to collaborate and brainstorm processes specific to their small group.

Discussion Questions for Debriefing

- Who will give us a high-level overview of a pain point you identified and a technique used to mistake proof it?
- Did anyone find a pain point that they are struggling to mistake proof? Can anyone offer a suggestion? (TIP: If they can't devise a mistake-proof technique, the issue might be a service system issue, not a service strategy issue.)

Transition (first time)

Say: When we return from break we will be repeating this process, so you will have a chance to create additional improvements through more mistake-proof techniques.

Show break Slide 37.

Upon return from break, show Slide 38 and repeat Learning Activity 21.

Transition (second time)

Say: To ensure your solutions are as solid as possible, we are going to give and get feedback on the mistake-proof techniques we have been working on. For this, you will be working with a new partner.

Learning Activity 22: Critiquing Mistake-Proof Techniques

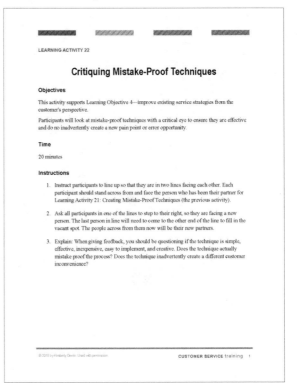

LEARNING ACTIVITY 22

Critiquing Mistake-Proof Techniques

Objectives

This activity supports Learning Objective 4—improve existing service strategies from the customer's perspective.

Participants will look at mistake-proof techniques with a critical eye to ensure they are effective and do no inadvertently create a new pain point or error opportunity.

Time

20 minutes

Instructions

1. Instruct participants to line up so that they are in two lines facing each other. Each participant should stand across from and face the person who has been their partner for Learning Activity 21: Creating Mistake-Proof Techniques (the previous activity).

2. Ask all participants in one of the lines to step to their right, so they are facing a new person. The last person in line will need to come to the other end of the line to fill in the vacant spot. The people across from them now will be their new partners.

3. Explain: When giving feedback, you should be questioning if the technique is simple, effective, inexpensive, easy to implement, and creative. Does the technique actually mistake proof the process? Does the technique inadvertently create a different customer inconvenience?

Learning Activity 22: Critiquing Mistake-Proof Techniques, *continued*

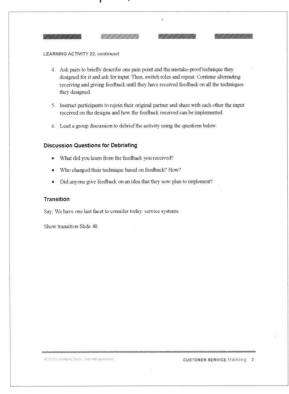

LEARNING ACTIVITY 22, continued

4. Ask pairs to briefly describe one pain point and the mistake-proof technique they designed for it and ask for input. Then, switch roles and repeat. Continue alternating receiving and giving feedback until they have received feedback on all the techniques they designed.

5. Instruct participants to rejoin their original partner and share with each other the input received on the designs and how the feedback received can be implemented.

6. Lead a group discussion to debrief the activity using the questions below.

Discussion Questions for Debriefing

- What did you learn from the feedback you received?
- Who changed their technique based on feedback? How?
- Did anyone give feedback on an idea that they now plan to implement?

Transition

Say: We have one last facet to consider today: service systems.

Show transition Slide 40.

Learning Activity 23: Our Service Systems

LEARNING ACTIVITY 23

Our Service Systems

Objectives

This activity supports Learning Objective 5—examine the organization's service systems for breakdowns from the customer's perspective.

Participants will

- Participate in process mapping an organization-specific service system
- Locate potential service system breakdowns.

Materials

- Previously prepared reference copy of a cross-functional map of an organization-specific service system in which the participants play a direct role (this is for you to reference, not distribute).
- Repositionable work surface (TIP: Create your own with craft paper, plastic sheeting, or lightweight fabric. Spray the surface with temporary spray adhesive so that the index cards will adhere but can still be repositioned as needed.)
- Temporary spray adhesive
- Index cards in multiple colors
- Markers

Time

30 minutes

Learning Activity 23: Our Service Systems, *continued*

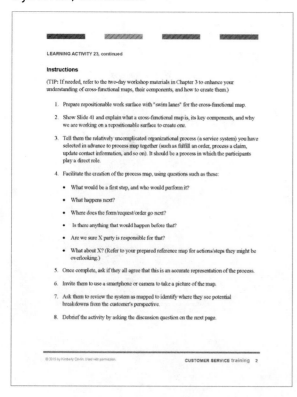

LEARNING ACTIVITY 23, continued

Instructions

(TIP: If needed, refer to the two-day workshop materials in Chapter 3 to enhance your understanding of cross-functional maps, their components, and how to create them.)

1. Prepare repositionable work surface with "swim lanes" for the cross-functional map.

2. Show Slide 41 and explain what a cross-functional map is, its key components, and why we are working on a repositionable surface to create one.

3. Tell them the relatively uncomplicated organizational process (a service system) you have selected in advance to process map together (such as fulfill an order, process a claim, update contact information, and so on). It should be a process in which the participants play a direct role.

4. Facilitate the creation of the process map, using questions such as these:

   • What would be a first step, and who would perform it?

   • What happens next?

   • Where does the form/request/order go next?

   • Is there anything that would happen before that?

   • Are we sure X party is responsible for that?

   • What about X? (Refer to your prepared reference map for actions/steps they might be overlooking.)

5. Once complete, ask if they all agree that this is an accurate representation of the process.

6. Invite them to use a smartphone or camera to take a picture of the map.

7. Ask them to review the system as mapped to identify where they see potential breakdowns from the customer's perspective.

8. Debrief the activity by asking the discussion question on the next page.

Learning Activity 23: Our Service Systems, *continued*

LEARNING ACTIVITY 23, continued

Variations

• Use process mapping software instead of the repositionable work surface.

• If tight on time, or if participants would not all be involved in one selected service system, skip this activity. Instead, distribute copies of the previously prepared process map(s), invite participants to review them and note questions. Lead a discussion to clarify questions on the processes and to identify potential breakdowns from the customer's perspective in preparation for the next activity.

Discussion Question for Debriefing

• Now that you see the As Is state of this service system, what might you do next to improve the customer experience?

Transition

Say: Very nice work! It isn't easy to process map, is it?

Learning Activity 24: Where and How Can I Help?

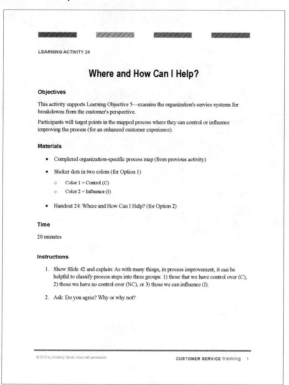

LEARNING ACTIVITY 24

Where and How Can I Help?

Objectives

This activity supports Learning Objective 5—examine the organization's service systems for breakdowns from the customer's perspective.

Participants will target points in the mapped process where they can control or influence improving the process (for an enhanced customer experience).

Materials

• Completed organization-specific process map (from previous activity)

• Sticker dots in two colors (for Option 1)

   o Color 1 = Control (C)

   o Color 2 = Influence (I)

• Handout 24: Where and How Can I Help? (for Option 2)

Time

20 minutes

Instructions

1. Show Slide 42 and explain: As with many things, in process improvement, it can be helpful to classify process steps into three groups: 1) those that we have control over (C), 2) those we have no control over (NC), or 3) those we can influence (I).

2. Ask: Do you agree? Why or why not?

Learning Activity 24: Where and How Can I Help?, *continued*

LEARNING ACTIVITY 24, continued

3. Lead a discussion with these questions:

   • What would be an indication that we do have control over a process step?

   • How might we know that we have influence over a step?

   • What would be characteristic of steps we have no control over?

4. Tell participants to review the group-created cross-functional map and identify potential breakdowns with C–NC–I in mind. Ask: Where can you improve this process? Where can you exert influence over improving this process?

5. Option 1—Tell participants to write their initials on colored stickers and place them on the map at the relevant points.

   • Color 1 = Control (C)

   • Color 2 = Influence (I)

6. Option 2—Tell participants to complete Handout 24 by referring to the map with an emphasis on columns one and three (Control and Influence, respectively).

7. Use the debriefing process that corresponds to the option you chose above.

Discussion Questions for Debriefing

Option 1 Debrief:

• What conclusions can we draw from this activity?

• How will your service behaviors differ from now on based on this activity?

• Who has changed their opinion about the cause of conflict in service interactions and their own ability to decrease the conflict?

• What is one action you plan to take to avoid creating conflict in customer communications going forward?

Learning Activity 24: Where and How Can I Help?, *continued*

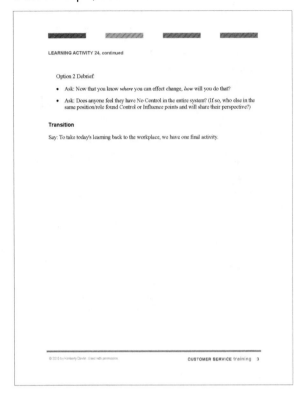

Option 2 Debrief:

- Ask: Now that you know *where* you can effect change, *how* will you do that?
- Ask: Does anyone feel they have No Control in the entire system? (If so, who else in the same position/role found Control or Influence points and will share their perspective?)

Transition

Say: To take today's learning back to the workplace, we have one final activity.

Learning Activity 25: Where We Go From Here

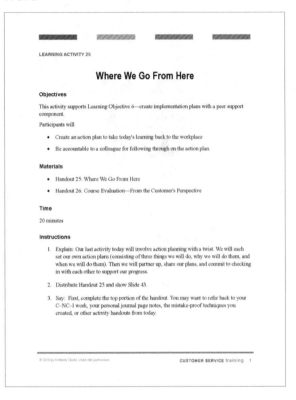

Where We Go From Here

Objectives

This activity supports Learning Objective 6—create implementation plans with a peer support component.

Participants will

- Create an action plan to take today's learning back to the workplace
- Be accountable to a colleague for following through on the action plan.

Materials

- Handout 25: Where We Go From Here
- Handout 26: Course Evaluation—From the Customer's Perspective

Time

20 minutes

Instructions

1. Explain: Our last activity today will involve action planning with a twist. We will each set our own action plans (consisting of three things we will do, why we will do them, and when we will do them). Then we will partner up, share our plans, and commit to checking in with each other to support our progress.

2. Distribute Handout 25 and show Slide 43.

3. Say: First, complete the top portion of the handout. You may want to refer back to your C-NC-I work, your personal journal page notes, the mistake-proof techniques you created, or other activity handouts from today.

Learning Activity 25: Where We Go From Here, *continued*

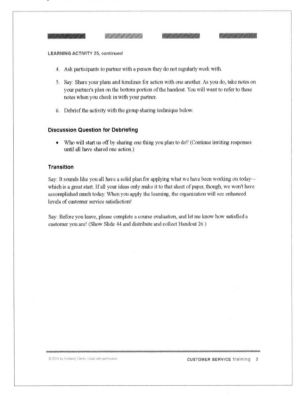

4. Ask participants to partner with a person they do not regularly work with.

5. Say: Share your plans and timelines for action with one another. As you do, take notes on your partner's plan on the bottom portion of the handout. You will want to refer to these notes when you check in with your partner.

6. Debrief the activity with the group sharing technique below.

Discussion Question for Debriefing

- Who will start us off by sharing one thing you plan to do? (Continue inviting responses until all have shared one action.)

Transition

Say: It sounds like you all have a solid plan for applying what we have been working on today—which is a great start. If all your ideas only make it to that sheet of paper, though, we won't have accomplished much today. When you apply the learning, the organization will see enhanced levels of customer service satisfaction!

Say: Before you leave, please complete a course evaluation, and let me know how satisfied a customer you are! (Show Slide 44 and distribute and collect Handout 26.)

Learning Activity 26: Wall Graffiti

Wall Graffiti

Objective

Participants will become engaged in the training topic.

Materials

- Flip chart paper
- Markers

Time

10 minutes

Instructions

1. Tape five sheets of chart paper to the walls around the room. Label the charts as follows:

   - What customers want
   - What customers get
   - If customers only knew…
   - Our service strengths
   - One change I can make to benefit customers

2. Show Slide 2 and explain we are going to begin with their observations on five concepts.

3. Divide participants evenly among the wall charts and direct them to graffiti the charts based on the headings. Encourage them to use pictures, color, words, even stick figures to make this graffiti. Allow 2-3 minutes at their chart. (After all, graffiti artists have to work quickly!).

Learning Activity 26: Wall Graffiti, *continued*

LEARNING ACTIVITY 26, continued

4. Ask each group to rotate to the next chart, review what is on it and add to it for another few minutes.

5. Repeat Step 3 until all charts have been visited by each group.

Variations

1. Cover table rounds in butcher block paper for Table Graffiti. Label them in the same way as above. Consider having each table group "own" a concept, followed by a rotating table review, or rotate groups to each station, adding to each table as described above.

2. If Table Graffiti is used, at relevant points during the workshop, ask a spokesperson from the relevant table to report out the graffiti elements on the butcher block.

3. Skip dividing into groups and rotating; instead, allow participants 10 minutes to "tag" as many charts as they can, moving at their own pace and interest.

Transition

Say: During this workshop we will be focusing on the systems, strategies, and behaviors behind the graffiti notes we just recorded. This active, practical learning will serve as a starting point. There will also be work to do after the workshop, and my goal is to position you to do that work by being efficient and effective here. I'd like to share our planned activities and ask you to prioritize them.

CUSTOMER SERVICE training   2

Learning Activity 27: Prioritize Learning

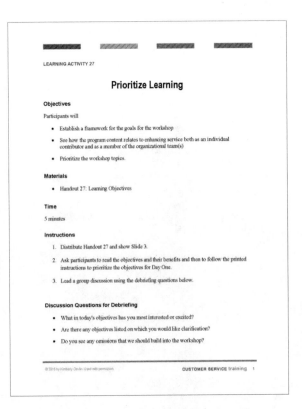

LEARNING ACTIVITY 27

Prioritize Learning

Objectives

Participants will

- Establish a framework for the goals for the workshop
- See how the program content relates to enhancing service both as an individual contributor and as a member of the organizational team(s)
- Prioritize the workshop topics.

Materials

- Handout 27: Learning Objectives

Time

5 minutes

Instructions

1. Distribute Handout 27 and show Slide 3.

2. Ask participants to read the objectives and their benefits and then to follow the printed instructions to prioritize the objectives for Day One.

3. Lead a group discussion using the debriefing questions below.

Discussion Questions for Debriefing

- What in today's objectives has you most interested or excited?
- Are there any objectives listed on which you would like clarification?
- Do you see any omissions that we should build into the workshop?

CUSTOMER SERVICE training   1

Learning Activity 27: Prioritize Learning, *continued*

LEARNING ACTIVITY 27, continued

Transition

Explain: As you can see, we have a lot to cover. Setting up some guidelines for our time together will keep us on track and proactively avoid many potential pitfalls. You might know them as ground rules, I like the term *social agreements*.

CUSTOMER SERVICE training   2

Learning Activity 28: Social Agreements

LEARNING ACTIVITY 28

Social Agreements

Objective

Participants will develop a set of behavior guidelines for the workshop.

Materials

- Flip chart

Time

10 minutes

Instructions

1. Show Slide 4 and ask for an explanation of "social agreements" (that is, ground rules, workshop guidelines, and so on).

2. Explain the benefits of proactively establishing a set of guidelines to dictate how the group will interact and manage potentially disruptive behavior or off-topic tangents.

3. Facilitate a round-robin shout-out of, and record on a flip chart, the ground rules the group proposes. Here are common items to include: *adhere to start and end times, bring sidebars to the large group, encourage and allow all to participate, mobile device protocols,* and *provide advance notice of scheduling conflicts.* Based on your needs assessment findings, there may be special needs of the group to include here as well, such as *relinquish silo thinking, no hidden agendas,* or *remain open-minded to new approaches.* Based on your scheduling of the two days and expected participants actions between and after workshop days, you might also consider adding: *timely follow up on commitments made during the workshop.*

4. Review the list and agree to its role in the workshop with the debriefing questions on the next page.

CUSTOMER SERVICE training   1

Learning Activity 28: Social Agreements, *continued*

LEARNING ACTIVITY 28, continued

Discussion Questions for Debriefing

- Is there anything we have overlooked that should be added?
- Can we all agree to adhere to these guidelines?
- How do we, as a group, want to address behaviors that are not in keeping with these guidelines?

Transition

Explain: Keeping our social agreements in mind will benefit all of us as we focus on our first learning objective.

Learning Activity 29: Now You Know

LEARNING ACTIVITY 29

Now You Know

Objectives

This activity supports Learning Objective 1—strengthen internal relationships and your awareness of lateral service challenges.

Participants will prepare and share answers to a series of questions aimed at revealing unknown aspects of their job function and themselves.

Materials

- Handout 28: Now You Know

Time

35 minutes

Instructions

1. Explain that even when we work alongside others for a long time, there is often a lot about their jobs that we know very little about. This is even truer with colleagues working in other departments or sections of the organization. This activity will minimize what we don't know about each other, increase what we do know, and also shed light on how our work affects and is affected by others' work.

2. Distribute Handout 28 and show Slide 5.

3. Ask participants to complete the first and last four statements on the handout with information they are willing to share with others in the room and then to select four additional questions to answer.

Learning Activity 29: Now You Know, *continued*

LEARNING ACTIVITY 29, continued

4. Share an example of how you would complete the statements (or use the examples provided below). Allow 5-7 minutes to complete page 1 of the worksheet.

- My job title is... *training specialist*.
- In five words or less, what I do is... *help employees improve their effectiveness*.
- Basically, that means that I: *design and lead classes that are targeted to employees' needs, are practical, and that provide for immediate application and feedback*.
- What I like about my job is: *helping others improve while also learning from them*.
- My least favorite part of my job is... *paperwork*.
- Something most people do not know about my job is... *the preparation involved*.
- External customers come to me for (or expect me to)... *be relevant to their work situations and create a fun environment for learning to happen*.
- Internal customers come to me for (or expect me to)... *offer balanced feedback and specific recommendations on their designs and facilitation techniques*.
- Three big challenges I face in providing excellent service to every customer are
    a. *deadlines competing for my time*
    b. *attention to detail*
    c. *becoming too task-focused*.
- One "go-to" strategy I use with customers that reliably provides a positive result is... *realize that without this customer, my job wouldn't be needed*.
- It would greatly improve my ability to serve our customers if *participants* would *complete pre-work*!
- I am passionate about *dancing* (either personally or professionally).
- A professional goal I have (or a professional challenge I'd like to take on) is... *master a second language well enough to facilitate bilingually*.
- A personal goal I have (or a personal challenge I'd like to take on) is... *through-hike the Appalachian Trail*.

Learning Activity 29: Now You Know, *continued*

LEARNING ACTIVITY 29, continued

5. Ask participants to form two concentric circles. Have each person partner with a participant across from them in the other circle to share their answers to the worksheet items.

6. Tell pairs to share their answers to the worksheet items and record notes from each conversation on page 2 of the handout. (TIP: Ensure all pairs answer the question at the top of page 2 and write down the actions they commit to.)

7. Allow 10 minutes for the two exchanges. (TIP: The 10 minutes goes quickly and participants commonly want more time. Therefore, announce the 5-minute mark to aid time management.)

8. Have participants in the outer circle rotate two to three positions (TIP: by moving more than one position, there is unexpected variety in the pairings and less likelihood of redundancy based on overhearing neighboring pairs' conversations).

9. Allow 10 more minutes.

10. Repeat Steps 8 and 9 one more time. (TIP: Participants typically enjoy these exchanges and want to continue. Either modify the timing for the workshop and allow for more exchanges, or remind them they can continue these discussions post-workshop. See variations below for an idea on building this into pre-work.)

11. Close the activity with some of the debriefing questions on the next page.

12. After completing the debrief, share your complete introduction. You may want to include the following information:

- Your experience with customer service (from either the provider side or the customer side)
- How and why you were selected to lead this session
- Why you are passionate about customer service
- What quality customer service means to you, and how this workshop supports that
- What you are looking to get out of this learning event by collaborating with the group.

Learning Activity 29: Now You Know, *continued*

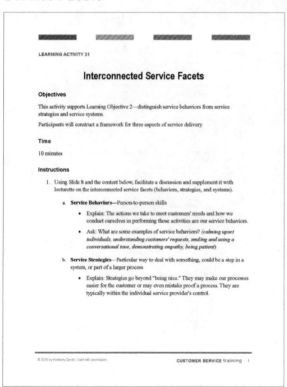

LEARNING ACTIVITY 29, continued

Variations

- If time is tight, send Handout 28 to participants as pre-work. Have them follow the instructions on page one and bring the completed handout to the workshop. Facilitate Steps 5 to 11 as described above.
- If space is not conducive to forming two large, concentric circles, consider the merits and drawbacks of the following pairing techniques:
  - **Pre-planned.** Collaborate with your subject matter expert (SME) or project sponsor to strategically match pairs based on their positions and interpersonal relationship dynamics.
  - **Random.** Have each person write their name on an index card and place the card in a box. Shuffle the cards and have each participant draw a name to partner off.
  - **Set parameters.** Provide up to 30 seconds for participants to partner with anyone in the room who isn't at their table, in their work group, or a close acquaintance. (Vary the three criteria to create the desired pairing diversity.)
- Repeat Steps 8 and 9 (above) more than three times to allow for more exchanges and sharing. This variation will require you to adjust workshop timing.

Discussion Questions for Debriefing

- Who learned that others in the room are facing similar challenges to those you face?
- Did anyone discover that your job affects or is affected by the job of someone else you spoke with? How? What are you planning to do with that information?
- How many of us have had conversations such as this with colleagues in our departments? Outside of our departments? If not, why not? If so, how and when do you structure the discussions?
- What about the final question? How have you committed to help one another? What assistance did you ask for? What actions did you commit to?

Transition

Say: Now you know more about three of your colleagues. We are going to continue building on what you know about the other participants too and record the strengths and skills we have in the room.

© 2015 by Kimberly Devlin. Used with permission.   CUSTOMER SERVICE training   4

Learning Activity 30: Group Résumé

LEARNING ACTIVITY 30

Group Résumé

Objectives

This activity supports Learning Objective 1—strengthen internal relationships and your awareness of lateral service challenges.

Participants will document the collective skill set in the room that can be tapped into to improve service delivery.

Materials

- Flip chart paper

Time

25 minutes

Instructions

1. Divide participants into small groups of 4 to 7 individuals and show Slide 6.
2. Provide each group with a sheet of chart paper and markers.
3. Ask each small group to create a collective résumé of their skills, strengths, and talents associated with customer service, process improvement, streamlining procedures for enhanced performance, business reengineering, and so on. Encourage them to go beyond years of experience and delve into accomplishments, responsibilities, certifications, organizational savvy, and other strengths.
4. Each group should document its résumé on the chart paper and be prepared to summarize it for the group.
5. Conduct a round-robin debrief, asking each group to assign a spokesperson to present a two-minute overview of their collective strengths.

Transition

Say: When we return from break, we will move on to our second learning objective. Please be back and ready to start in 15 minutes.

Show break Slide 7.

© 2015 by Kimberly Devlin. Used with permission.   CUSTOMER SERVICE training

Learning Activity 31: Interconnected Service Facets

LEARNING ACTIVITY 31

Interconnected Service Facets

Objectives

This activity supports Learning Objective 2—distinguish service behaviors from service strategies and service systems.

Participants will construct a framework for three aspects of service delivery.

Time

10 minutes

Instructions

1. Using Slide 8 and the content below, facilitate a discussion and supplement it with lecturette on the interconnected service facets (behaviors, strategies, and systems).

   a. **Service Behaviors**—Person-to-person skills
      - Explain: The actions we take to meet customers' needs and how we conduct ourselves in performing those activities are our service behaviors.
      - Ask: What are some examples of service behaviors? *(calming upset individuals, understanding customers' requests, smiling and using a conversational tone, demonstrating empathy, being patient)*

   b. **Service Strategies**—Particular way to deal with something, could be a step in a system, or part of a larger process
      - Explain: Strategies go beyond "being nice." They may make our processes easier for the customer or may even mistake proof a process. They are typically within the individual service provider's control.

© 2015 by Kimberly Devlin. Used with permission.   CUSTOMER SERVICE training   1

Learning Activity 31: Interconnected Service Facets, *continued*

LEARNING ACTIVITY 31, continued

- Ask: What are some examples of service strategies? *(logical sequencing of actions from the customer's perspective, streamlining the customer experience [for example, gift boxes are available at all registers instead of in the customer service station at the back of the store], or preventing mistakes [a web interface that requires a complete address before submitting an order, or a checklist/inventory of all actions needed to make an apartment move-in ready])*

   c. **Service Systems**—Processes
      - Explain: Unlike service strategies, systems typically involve groups or multiple departments. Director- or leadership-level approval may be needed to change systems, or interdepartmental agreement and action may be needed to revise them.
      - Ask: What are some examples of service systems? *(software, policies, procedures, interdepartmental transactions [often associated with "we-they" thinking], approvals/levels of sign-off required)*

2. Ask for examples of service interactions performed by the participants in which they can highlight where and how all three facets come into play. (See Learning Activity 13 for a sample story.)
3. Request feedback from the large group on their agreement or disagreement with the examples.

Transition

(TIP: Ensure all are clear on the distinctions of the three categories of service facets before moving into the application activity.)

Ask: What questions do you have on the differences among behaviors, strategies, and systems? We are about to apply these concepts in an activity.

© 2015 by Kimberly Devlin. Used with permission.   CUSTOMER SERVICE training   2

Learning Activity 32: The Root Issue Is?

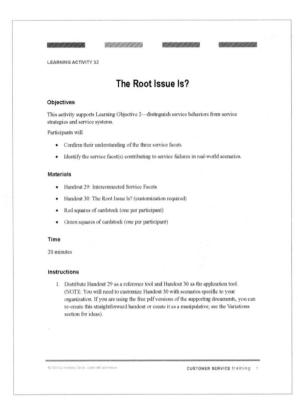

Learning Activity 32: The Root Issue Is?, *continued*

Learning Activity 33: Performance Improvement Service Levels

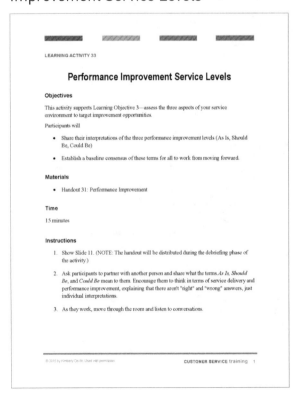

Learning Activity 33: Performance Improvement Service Levels, *continued*

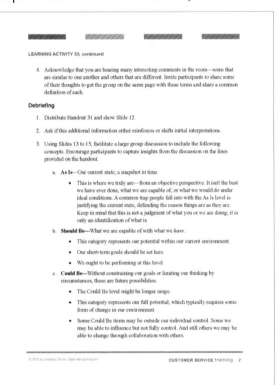

Learning Activity 33: Performance Improvement Service Levels, *continued*

LEARNING ACTIVITY 33, continued

Transition

Ask: Do you think we can get so used to looking at something that we no longer see it as it truly is? That we lose our objectivity? Do you think that our customers see things that we might be missing?

Say: With our next exercise, we are going to work to flip that. I'll challenge you to step into the customer's shoes and experience service delivery as they do. So, we are going to go on field trips!

Show transition Slide 16.

© 2015 by Kimberly Devlin. Used with permission.   CUSTOMER SERVICE training   3

Learning Activity 34: Field Trip

LEARNING ACTIVITY 34

Field Trip

Objectives

This activity supports Learning Objective 3—assess the three aspects of your service environment to target improvement opportunities.

Participants will objectively assess their As Is state by experiencing their service interactions as customers do.

Materials

- Handout 32: Field Trip Log
- Handout 32B: Virtual Field Trip Map (optional, if variation 1 is used)
- Assessment 1: Where Are We Now? (optional)
- Flip chart or whiteboard

Time

65 minutes

Instructions

1. Introduce the concept of points of contact through a facilitated discussion using these questions:
   - When thinking of a service interaction, what does point of contact (POC) mean to you? (*A POC is a place where the customer touches the organization during the delivery of service. Obvious POCs are engaging with an employee, arriving at a location, and physically receiving the desired service. Less obvious POCs can include using the organization's website to locate hours, phone numbers, or an address; following instructions on how to complete a form; following signage to arrive at the intended location.*)

© 2015 by Kimberly Devlin. Used with permission.   CUSTOMER SERVICE training   1

Learning Activity 34: Field Trip, *continued*

LEARNING ACTIVITY 34, continued

   - How many individual POCs do you think a customer experiences in a single transaction?
   - Let's create a list of POCs to order a sandwich to be delivered for lunch. (Record responses on a flip chart or whiteboard in chronological order from the customer's perspective, which may require leaving blank space as the group shouts out POCs. Encourage them to step further and further back in time to the start of the customer's experience to include all POCs.

2. Show Slide 17 and explain the field trip. (NOTE: Based on roles of workshop participants within the organization, you may choose to set this up as an individual, pair, trio, or small group activity—or some combination. The guidance given here is written assuming an individual activity.)

3. Tell participants:
   - Each of you will visit your own work site as a customer.
   - You will want to step outside of what you know. Do not walk directly to the office using your access pass, rather approach the building as if for the first time. Stop at the security desk to sign in and ask for directions (you may need to explain that you are participating in this activity), rely on signage to direct you, consider asking a passerby for assistance, and so on.
   - During your field trip, record and rate each POC on the handout. Remember, a POC can be with a person, the facility, a support tool, a sign, a step in the process, or other—not only people.

4. Distribute Handout 32 and explain how to complete it. Answer any questions.

5. Ask participants what skills and strengths from their group résumés would be helpful to draw on.

6. Explain that the field trip activity and the lunch break will be considered one block of time. Clarify the return time and the expectation for participants to have conducted the field trip and have eaten lunch by then. (The field trip is scheduled for 45 minutes and lunch for 60 minutes.)

© 2015 by Kimberly Devlin. Used with permission.   CUSTOMER SERVICE training   2

Learning Activity 34: Field Trip, *continued*

LEARNING ACTIVITY 34, continued

7. Show lunch Slide 18.

8. The debrief of the activity will happen after lunch using the quick start activity (Learning Activity 35) and the debriefing questions included with it.

Variations

- If a physical field trip is unrealistic (for example, remote training location or job functions that occur in the field), convert activity into a virtual field trip. Have participants pair off to talk through and document the customer experience using Handout 32B. The partner's role is to listen critically and interject with questions that represent the customer's unfamiliarity with the process such as: *Where would I have found the address? Do GPS programs reliably direct to the actual location? Is there signage I will or won't see? How do I find the office once in the building?* The answers may identify additional POCs. Each POC offers a potential threat to a positive customer experience. Ensure participants are clear that the customer interaction typically begins many steps before actually interacting with an individual service provider.

- Consider using the three-page assessment instrument from the One-Day Workshop materials (Assessment 1: Where Are We Now?) in Chapter 12.

© 2015 by Kimberly Devlin. Used with permission.   CUSTOMER SERVICE training   3

Learning Activity 35: Quick Start—Field Trip Debrief

LEARNING ACTIVITY 35

Quick Start—Field Trip Debrief

Objectives

This activity supports Learning Objective 3—assess the three aspects of your service environment to target improvement opportunities.

Participants will

- Reconnect to the field trip experience and ease back into the afternoon
- Share their field trip findings and reflect on them.

Materials

- Flip chart paper

Time

15 minutes

Instructions

1. During lunch break, prepare five flip charts and post them on a wall. Label them as follows:
   a. What I never realized but learned on the field trip is...
   b. Our customers are fortunate that...
   c. We are doing our customers a disservice by...
   d. If I were the customer, after the field trip, I'd feel...
   e. I identified _____ (#) POCs on my field trip.

2. Display Slide 19 as participants return from lunch.

Learning Activity 35: Quick Start—Field Trip Debrief, *continued*

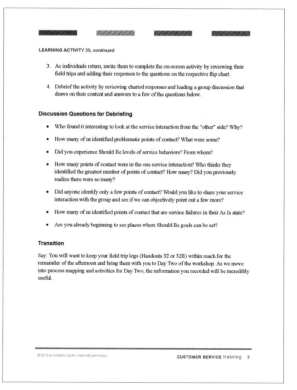

LEARNING ACTIVITY 35, continued

3. As individuals return, invite them to complete the on-screen activity by reviewing their field trips and adding their responses to the questions on the respective flip chart.

4. Debrief the activity by reviewing charted responses and leading a group discussion that draws on their content and answers to a few of the questions below.

Discussion Questions for Debriefing

- Who found it interesting to look at the service interaction from the "other" side? Why?
- How many of us identified problematic points of contact? What were some?
- Did you experience Should Be levels of service behaviors? From whom?
- How many points of contact were in the one service interaction? Who thinks they identified the greatest number of points of contact? How many? Did you previously realize there were so many?
- Did anyone identify only a few points of contact? Would you like to share your service interaction with the group and see if we can objectively point out a few more?
- How many of us identified points of contact that are service failures in their As Is state?
- Are you already beginning to see places where Should Be goals can be set?

Transition

Say: You will want to keep your field trip logs (Handouts 32 or 32B) within reach for the remainder of the afternoon and bring them with you to Day Two of the workshop. As we move into process mapping and activities for Day Two, the information you recorded will be incredibly useful.

Learning Activity 36: Working With Cross-Functional Process Mapping

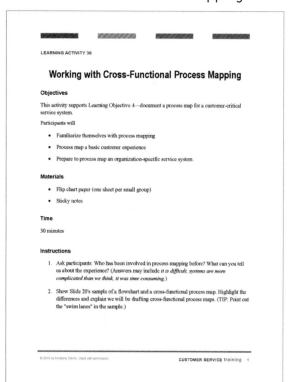

LEARNING ACTIVITY 36

Working with Cross-Functional Process Mapping

Objectives

This activity supports Learning Objective 4—document a process map for a customer-critical service system.

Participants will

- Familiarize themselves with process mapping
- Process map a basic customer experience
- Prepare to process map an organization-specific service system.

Materials

- Flip chart paper (one sheet per small group)
- Sticky notes

Time

30 minutes

Instructions

1. Ask participants: Who has been involved in process mapping before? What can you tell us about the experience? (Answers may include *it is difficult, systems are more complicated than we think, it was time consuming.*)

2. Show Slide 20's sample of a flowchart and a cross-functional process map. Highlight the differences and explain we will be drafting cross-functional process maps. (TIP: Point out the "swim lanes" in the sample.)

Learning Activity 36: Working With Cross-Functional Process Mapping, *continued*

LEARNING ACTIVITY 36, continued

3. Answer any questions.

4. Explain that often when we start to map something out, we miss steps, put steps in the wrong spot, or assign actions to the wrong individuals. This is why we want to be able to reposition them as we work.

5. Tell them: To get our feet wet with cross-functional process mapping, we will start with a process we should all be able to relate to on some level.

6. Ask participants to create a process map on a flip chart for "Going to dinner at a restaurant with your spouse and two children." Explain each action should be recorded on its own sticky note. Show Slide 21 to model how their process map should be set up.

7. Conduct a large group discussion debrief using the questions below.

Variations

- Facilitate the process mapping as one group, drawing input from the entire group.
- Use the repositionable work surface from the next activity instead of flip chart paper and sticky notes.

Discussion Questions for Debriefing

- What was your experience working on this as a team?
- Who found that the process behind going to dinner was more complex than expected?
- Which aspects of process mapping were most challenging?
- How will the lessons learned from this activity help you in process mapping one of our organizational systems next? (Record responses to this question on a whiteboard or flip chart. Draw participants' attention back to this list as they work, especially if they encounter challenges.)

Learning Activity 37: Cross-Functional Process Mapping Our Processes

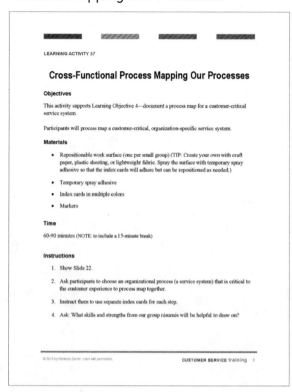

LEARNING ACTIVITY 37

Cross-Functional Process Mapping Our Processes

Objectives

This activity supports Learning Objective 4—document a process map for a customer-critical service system.

Participants will process map a customer-critical, organization-specific service system.

Materials

- Repositionable work surface (one per small group) (TIP: Create your own with craft paper, plastic sheeting, or lightweight fabric. Spray the surface with temporary spray adhesive so that the index cards will adhere but can be repositioned as needed.)
- Temporary spray adhesive
- Index cards in multiple colors
- Markers

Time

60-90 minutes (NOTE: to include a 15-minute break)

Instructions

1. Show Slide 22.

2. Ask participants to choose an organizational process (a service system) that is critical to the customer experience to process map together.

3. Instruct them to use separate index cards for each step.

4. Ask: What skills and strengths from our group résumés will be helpful to draw on?

© 2015 by Kimberly Devlin. Used with permission.   CUSTOMER SERVICE training   1

Learning Activity 37: Cross-Functional Process Mapping Our Processes, *continued*

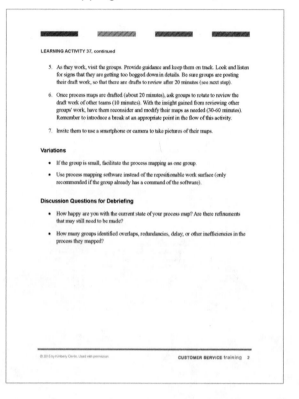

LEARNING ACTIVITY 37, continued

5. As they work, visit the groups. Provide guidance and keep them on track. Look and listen for signs that they are getting too bogged down in details. Be sure groups are posting their draft work, so that there are drafts to review after 20 minutes (see next step).

6. Once process maps are drafted (about 20 minutes), ask groups to rotate to review the draft work of other teams (10 minutes). With the insight gained from reviewing other groups' work, have them reconsider and modify their maps as needed (30-60 minutes). Remember to introduce a break at an appropriate point in the flow of this activity.

7. Invite them to use a smartphone or camera to take pictures of their maps.

Variations

- If the group is small, facilitate the process mapping as one group.
- Use process mapping software instead of the repositionable work surface (only recommended if the group already has a command of the software).

Discussion Questions for Debriefing

- How happy are you with the current state of your process map? Are there refinements that may still need to be made?
- How many groups identified overlaps, redundancies, delay, or other inefficiencies in the process they mapped?

© 2015 by Kimberly Devlin. Used with permission.   CUSTOMER SERVICE training   2

Learning Activity 38: Cross-Functional Process Map Reviews

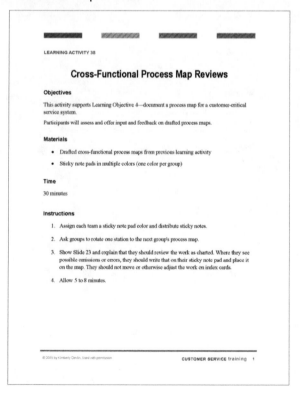

LEARNING ACTIVITY 38

Cross-Functional Process Map Reviews

Objectives

This activity supports Learning Objective 4—document a process map for a customer-critical service system.

Participants will assess and offer input and feedback on drafted process maps.

Materials

- Drafted cross-functional process maps from previous learning activity
- Sticky note pads in multiple colors (one color per group)

Time

30 minutes

Instructions

1. Assign each team a sticky note pad color and distribute sticky notes.

2. Ask groups to rotate one station to the next group's process map.

3. Show Slide 23 and explain that they should review the work as charted. Where they see possible omissions or errors, they should write that on their sticky note pad and place it on the map. They should not move or otherwise adjust the work on index cards.

4. Allow 5 to 8 minutes.

© 2015 by Kimberly Devlin. Used with permission.   CUSTOMER SERVICE training   1

Learning Activity 38: Cross-Functional Process Map Reviews, *continued*

LEARNING ACTIVITY 38, continued

5. Repeat Steps 2 and 3 until each group has had an opportunity to provide feedback on each process map.

6. Ask each group to return to their process map, review the feedback on sticky notes, make any quick adjustments noted, and work to internalize the comments. If a piece of feedback is unclear, the color coding of the sticky notes will alert them to which group to ask for clarification. (NOTE: More time may be needed to process and integrate the feedback. Time may be dedicated to this early in Day Two of the workshop, or between workshop days.)

7. Invite them to use a smartphone or camera to take pictures of their annotated maps.

Discussion Questions for Debriefing

- What do you think of the feedback received?
- Now that you see the As Is state of this process, what do you think needs to happen to improve the customer experience?

© 2015 by Kimberly Devlin. Used with permission.   CUSTOMER SERVICE training   2

Learning Activity 39: Day-One Workshop Closure

Day-One Workshop Closure

Objectives

Participants will

- Receive direction for a brief assignment to bring to Day Two
- Provide feedback on the content and process of Day One
- Give input on the agenda for Day Two
- Receive direction on any additional action to take between workshop days.

Materials

- Flip chart

Time

15 minutes

Instructions

1. Show Slide 24 and explain workshop assignment. For Day Two, each participant will research, locate, and bring with them a resource to share with others that adds to, expands on, or exemplifies customer service excellence. It might be a video, blog post, article, job aid, social media site dedicated to service, or other resource.

2. Draw a T-chart on a flip chart. Facilitate a discussion of, and record on the T-chart, what participants liked about Day One and then their suggestions to include for Day Two of the workshop. (NOTE: A T-chart is used for listing two separate viewpoints of a topic. Simply draw a horizontal line at the top of the page and a vertical line dividing the page in two, making a big letter *T*. Label one side "What's Working" and the other "Changes to Consider.")

Learning Activity 39: Day-One Workshop Closure, *continued*

3. Share an overview of the intended agenda for Day Two.

4. Solicit input on agenda and modify as needed. (For example, do they want additional time built in for a second round of Learning Activity 29: Now You Know or will they need additional time on Day Two to refine the process maps? While the maps do not need to be perfect, participants' time will be undervalued on Day Two if the process maps are wrong or of marginal quality.)

5. Determine date of Day Two (if not previously set).

6. Agree on strategy for having the wall charts (social agreements, wall graffiti, group résumés, quick start charts) and process maps available in the room for Day Two. Can they remain in place? Will you take them? Will a volunteer from each group take theirs and bring it back? Should they be left in the room but set aside?

7. Remind participants to bring back their assignment and Handouts 27 and 32 (or 32B or Assessment 1, if used).

Variations

- Create and distribute a feedback form to assess Day One.
- Based on quality and completeness of process maps, you might have groups work together before next meeting to refine them.
- If field trips did not happen for some or all participants, direct them to complete the activity before Day Two.

Learning Activity 40: Welcome Back!—Quick Start

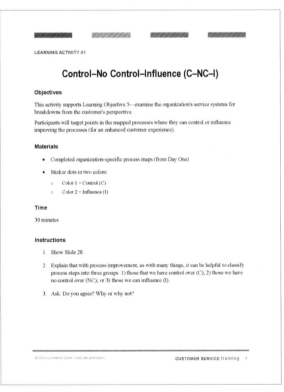

Welcome Back!—Quick Start

Objectives

Participants will

- Reconnect with one another and the topic
- Share with others the customer service resources they identified for their assignments from Day One.

Time

20 minutes

Instructions

1. Display Slide 26 on screen as participants arrive for Day Two.

2. As individuals arrive, invite them to form trios and begin the on-screen activity. (TIP: Late arrivals will have less time to complete the activity. Your priority should be ending this activity on time regardless of each trio's progress; there is enough time to complete it for all that arrive on time.)

3. Show Slide 27 and review learning objectives for Day Two.

Transition

Ask: Are our process maps as we need them to be? Have you integrated the feedback received and improved them sufficiently?

Say: Next we will be looking at where we have control, influence, or no control over process.

Learning Activity 41: Control–No Control–Influence (C–NC–I)

Control–No Control–Influence (C–NC–I)

Objectives

This activity supports Learning Objective 5—examine the organization's service systems for breakdowns from the customer's perspective.

Participants will target points in the mapped processes where they can control or influence improving the processes (for an enhanced customer experience).

Materials

- Completed organization-specific process maps (from Day One)
- Sticker dots in two colors:
  - Color 1 = Control (C)
  - Color 2 = Influence (I)

Time

30 minutes

Instructions

1. Show Slide 28.

2. Explain that with process improvement, as with many things, it can be helpful to classify process steps into three groups: 1) those that we have control over (C); 2) those we have no control over (NC); or 3) those we can influence (I).

3. Ask: Do you agree? Why or why not?

Learning Activity 41: Control–No Control–Influence (C–NC–I), *continued*

Learning Activity 41: Control–No Control–Influence (C–NC–I), *continued*

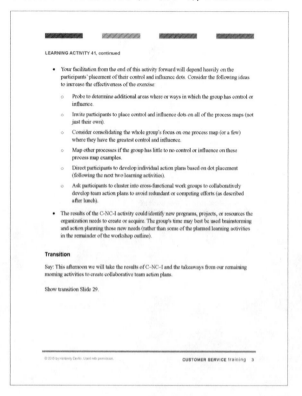

LEARNING ACTIVITY 41, continued

4. Lead a discussion with these questions:
   - What would be an indication we *do* have control over a process step?
   - How might we know that we have influence over a step?
   - What would be characteristic of steps we have no control over?

5. Have participants review the group-created cross-functional maps with C–NC–I in mind. Ask: Where can we improve these processes? Where can we exert influence over improving these processes?

6. Tell participants to write their initials on colored stickers and place them on their map at the relevant points.
   - Color 1 = Control (C)
   - Color 2 = Influence (I)

7. Lead a discussion based on results.

8. Debrief the activity using the questions below, and refer to the variations section for additional information on how you might proceed.

Discussion Questions for Debriefing
- Now that you know where you can effect change or encourage it through your influence, how will you do that?
- How many of you see your initials at a process step where others also placed theirs? How will you collaborate? How will you decide on responsibilities and accountability?

Variations
- Consider (as previously described in Learning Activity 39: Day-One Workshop Closure) allowing time to refine the process maps before beginning this activity if the maps have significant errors or omissions, require integration of feedback, or are too rough a sketch of the service systems.

© 2016 by Kimberly Devlin. Used with permission.   CUSTOMER SERVICE training   2

LEARNING ACTIVITY 41, continued

- Your facilitation from the end of this activity forward will depend heavily on the participants' placement of their control and influence dots. Consider the following ideas to increase the effectiveness of the exercise:
  - Probe to determine additional areas where or ways in which the group has control or influence.
  - Invite participants to place control and influence dots on all of the process maps (not just their own).
  - Consider consolidating the whole group's focus on one process map (or a few) where they have the greatest control and influence.
  - Map other processes if the group has little to no control or influence on these process map examples.
  - Direct participants to develop individual action plans based on dot placement (following the next two learning activities).
  - Ask participants to cluster into cross-functional work groups to collaboratively develop team action plans to avoid redundant or competing efforts (as described after lunch).
- The results of the C-NC-I activity could identify new programs, projects, or resources the organization needs to create or acquire. The group's time may best be used brainstorming and action planning those new needs (rather than some of the planned learning activities in the remainder of the workshop outline).

Transition

Say: This afternoon we will take the results of C-NC-I and the takeaways from our remaining morning activities to create collaborative team action plans.

Show transition Slide 29.

© 2016 by Kimberly Devlin. Used with permission.   CUSTOMER SERVICE training   3

Learning Activity 42: Mistake Proofing

Learning Activity 42: Mistake Proofing, *continued*

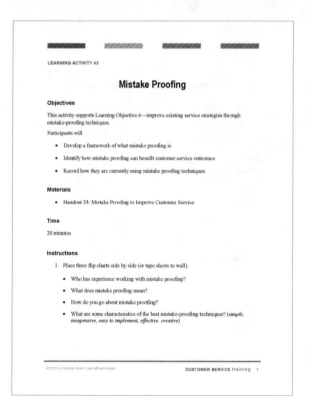

LEARNING ACTIVITY 42

Mistake Proofing

Objectives

This activity supports Learning Objective 6—improve existing service strategies through mistake-proofing techniques.

Participants will

- Develop a framework of what mistake proofing is
- Identify how mistake proofing can benefit customer service outcomes
- Record how they are currently using mistake proofing techniques.

Materials

- Handout 33: Mistake Proofing to Improve Customer Service

Time

20 minutes

Instructions

1. Place three flip charts side by side (or tape sheets to wall).
   - Who has experience working with mistake proofing?
   - What does mistake proofing mean?
   - How do you go about mistake proofing?
   - What are some characteristics of the best mistake-proofing techniques? (*simple, inexpensive, easy to implement, effective, creative*)

© 2016 by Kimberly Devlin. Used with permission.   CUSTOMER SERVICE training   1

LEARNING ACTIVITY 42, continued

2. Make a connection between the technique and the workshop by asking:
   - How does mistake proofing fit in with our process maps and customer service?

3. Distribute Handout 33 and show Slide 31.

4. Share key concepts of mistake proofing and provide examples of mistake-proofing techniques at use in the organization using Slides 32 to 34. (TIP: Some sample images are included in slides. Replacing them with organization-specific examples may be beneficial.) Invite participants to record additional ideas mentioned in the discussion in the right-hand column of the handout.

5. Share examples of mistake proofing you have encountered recently. Here are some recent examples from my experiences:
   - *In my state, a trip to the DMV (Division of Motor Vehicles) can be a lengthy experience. I recently went to purchase a parking pass and saved myself hours because of a mistake-proofing technique. Right there, on the front door of the DMV was a sign that read: "This location only accepts cash and checks"; because I had neither, I never even walked in. Imagine my annoyance if I took a number and a seat and then learned this at the counter.*
   - *Another DMV-related example is the orientation of driver's licenses. Drivers under the legal drinking age have a vertical license instead of a horizontal one.*
   - *A plumber came to my home to install a cast iron tub and drain. This involved entering a very low crawl space at one end of my house and crawling under it to the other end to connect the drain. For the finished job to be correct, the fittings under the house and inside the bathroom needed to be aligned perfectly. Rather than crawl under and set it, crawl out and check it, (repeating until right), and then crawling under to connect it, we devised a mistake-proof technique. Using cell phones, I snapped photos of the tub from above and sent them to the plumber. Perfect job in one trip!*

6. Ask participants for examples of mistake-proofing techniques they have encountered recently.

© 2016 by Kimberly Devlin. Used with permission.   CUSTOMER SERVICE training   2

Learning Activity 42: Mistake Proofing, *continued*

7. Share at least one example of how mistake proofing can go wrong. Here is one from my experience:

   When a municipality undertook a service initiative, one librarian decided to use a baiting technique as an exception for a customer. A woman had tried to return her books on time, but the branch closed early due to a power outage. She was annoyed to now be asked to pay a late fine, and the librarian waived the fee and said he was doing it in support of excellent service. Good, right? Well, all of the librarians began waiving all of the late fees—in support of the municipalities' focus on service. It wasn't long before the leadership (and accountants) imposed a new rule that librarians were no longer allowed to waive any fees.

8. Instruct participants to complete page 2 of the handout, recording how they are already using some of these techniques. Then have them pair with a partner and compare notes.

Transition

Say: When we return from break, armed with the knowledge of what mistake proofing is and the examples you identified where you are already using it, we are going to look for opportunities to integrate more mistake-proofing techniques in our process maps and further develop them.

Show break: Slide 35.

Learning Activity 43: Mistake-Proofing Process Map Elements

Mistake-Proofing Process Map Elements

Objectives

This activity supports Learning Objective 6—improve existing service strategies through mistake-proofing techniques.

Participants will

- Identify potential pain points or error opportunities in their process maps
- Create mistake-proof techniques to minimize or eliminate pain points and error opportunities.

Materials

- Handout 34: Mistake-Proofing Process Map Elements

Time

30 minutes

Instructions

1. Distribute Handout 34 and show Slide 36.

2. Direct participants to find a partner who also exerts Control or Influence in an area of a process map that they do. (Or, a partner with whom they have not yet worked.)

3. Explain that pain points are places where customers encounter a frustration or make a mistake, or where we are not as effective or efficient as we should be. It can be a place where we make mistakes too.

Learning Activity 43: Mistake-Proofing Process Map Elements, *continued*

4. Provide the following directions:

   a. Now that we have outlined a few processes as they are, we will look at them objectively to find their pain points.

   b. Then, you'll get creative and match up the tools such as color coding, streamlining, sequencing, checklists, grouping, and others to design mistake-proof techniques.

   c. So, we are focusing on two steps right now: identifying potential pain points and devising mistake-proof solutions for them.

5. Point out that the customer does not need to have direct interaction with the mistake-proof techniques to benefit from them. A technique that enables a field technician to complete a repair more quickly, for example, will not necessarily involve the customer but can lead to greater customer satisfaction.

6. Lead a group discussion to debrief the activity with the questions below.

Discussion Questions for Debriefing

- Who will share a pain point you identified and a technique you designed to mistake proof it?

- Did anyone else develop a different technique for the same issue? Is one easier, more reliable, less expensive? Do they complement one another? Are they redundant?

- Did anyone find a pain point that they are struggling to mistake proof? Who can offer a suggestion?

Transition

Say: It is important to vet your mistake-proof techniques. You want to ensure that they are effective and do not create an unintended negative consequence somewhere else in the process. So, in our next activity, we are going to critique one another's ideas and plans.

Learning Activity 44: Critiquing Mistake-Proof Techniques

Critiquing Mistake-Proof Techniques

Objectives

This activity supports Learning Objective 6—improve existing service strategies through mistake-proofing techniques.

Participants will look at mistake-proof techniques with a critical eye to ensure they are effective and do not inadvertently create a new pain point or error opportunity.

Time

30 minutes

Instructions

1. Ask participants to line up so that they are in two lines facing each other. Each participant should be standing across from and facing the person who has been their partner for Learning Activity 43: Mistake-Proofing Process Map Elements (the previous activity).

2. Instruct all participants in one of the lines to step to their right, so they are facing a new person. The last person in line will need to come to the other end of the line to fill in the vacant spot. The person across from them now will be their new partner.

3. Show Slide 37 and explain: When giving feedback, you should be questioning if the technique is simple, effective, inexpensive, easy to implement, or creative. Does the technique actually mistake proof the process? Does the technique inadvertently create a different customer inconvenience?

4. Have pairs briefly describe one pain point and the mistake-proof technique they designed for it and ask for input. Then, ask them to switch roles and repeat. Continue alternating receiving and giving feedback until they have received feedback on all the techniques they designed.

Learning Activity 44: Critiquing Mistake-Proof Techniques, *continued*

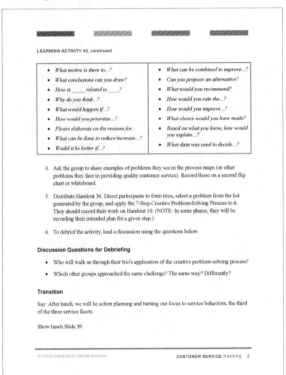

LEARNING ACTIVITY 44, continued

5. Instruct participants to rejoin their original partner. Tell them to share with each other the input received on the designs and how the feedback received can be implemented.

6. Lead a group discussion to debrief the activity using the questions below.

Discussion Questions for Debriefing

- What did you learn from the feedback you received?

- Who changed their technique based on feedback? How?

- Did anyone give feedback on an idea that you will also be implementing now that you have heard it?

Transition

Ask: Now that we have devised a number of effective ways to minimize error in these service systems, we are in a better position to see what aspect could benefit from business reengineering—making changes to how these systems operate. A creative problem-solving process can help with that, so I'd like to introduce a model for it to you. Chances are it will have some of the same components you already use. Let's build on your strengths!

Learning Activity 45: Creative Problem-Solving

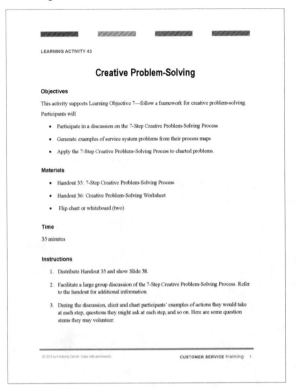

LEARNING ACTIVITY 45

Creative Problem-Solving

Objectives

This activity supports Learning Objective 7—follow a framework for creative problem-solving. Participants will

- Participate in a discussion on the 7-Step Creative Problem-Solving Process

- Generate examples of service system problems from their process maps

- Apply the 7-Step Creative Problem-Solving Process to charted problems.

Materials

- Handout 35: 7-Step Creative Problem-Solving Process

- Handout 36: Creative Problem-Solving Worksheet

- Flip chart or whiteboard (two)

Time

35 minutes

Instructions

1. Distribute Handout 35 and show Slide 38.

2. Facilitate a large group discussion of the 7-Step Creative Problem-Solving Process. Refer to the handout for additional information.

3. During the discussion, elicit and chart participants' examples of actions they would take at each step, questions they might ask at each step, and so on. Here are some question stems they may volunteer:

Learning Activity 45: Creative Problem-Solving, *continued*

LEARNING ACTIVITY 45, continued

• What motive is there to...?	• What can be combined to improve...?
• What conclusions can you draw?	• Can you propose an alternative?
• How is _____ related to _____?	• What would you recommend?
• Why do you think...?	• How would you rate the...?
• What would happen if...?	• How would you improve...?
• How would you prioritize...?	• What choice would you have made?
• Please elaborate on the reasons for...	• Based on what you know, how would you explain...?
• What can be done to reduce/increase...?	• What data was used to decide...?
• Would it be better if...?	

4. Ask the group to share examples of problems they see in the process maps (or other problems they face in providing quality customer service). Record these on a second flip chart or whiteboard.

5. Distribute Handout 36. Direct participants to form trios, select a problem from the list generated by the group, and apply the 7-Step Creative Problem-Solving Process to it. They should record their work on Handout 10. (NOTE: In some places, they will be recording their intended plan for a given step.)

6. To debrief the activity, lead a discussion using the questions below.

Discussion Questions for Debriefing

- Who will walk us through their trio's application of the creative problem-solving process?

- Which other groups approached the same challenge? The same way? Differently?

Transition

Say: After lunch, we will be action planning and turning our focus to service behaviors, the third of the three service facets.

Show lunch Slide 39.

Learning Activity 46: Quick Start

LEARNING ACTIVITY 46

Quick Start

Objectives

Participants will reconnect to the earlier workshop content and ease back into the afternoon.

Materials

- Prepared index cards (one set per table)

Time

15 minutes

Instructions

1. During lunch break, place a set of Quick Start cards on each table (see production notes below).

2. Display Slide 40 on screen as participants return from lunch.

3. As individuals return, invite them to complete the on-screen activity with their tablemates with a focus on the workshop content.

Production Notes for Quick Start Cards

Write the following sentence stems (or your own) on each set of index cards:

- Something I have been doing I need to *stop* doing is...

- Something I have been doing that I need to *change* is...

- Something I want to *remember* is...

Learning Activity 46: Quick Start, *continued*

- Assistance I will need to implement the workshop concepts is...
- A question I still have is...
- I am feeling...
- Something I have noticed is...
- A follow up action I need to take is...
- What is still missing for me is...

Transition

Ask: Based on your responses to the Quick Start, are there questions you want to ask? Things you'd like me to clarify? Anything I should know, or that I can assist you with?

Say: It is important that we all be on the same page before moving on to action planning.

Learning Activity 47: Next Steps to Improve Our Systems

Next Steps to Improve Our Systems

Objectives

This activity supports Learning Objective 8—create team action plans to enhance the service systems documented on Day One.

Participants will be able to

- Create action plans to implement post-workshop
- Be accountable to their colleagues for following through on the action plan.

Materials

- Handout 37: Next Steps to Improve Our Systems
- Previously completed copies of Handout 36: Creative Problem-Solving Worksheet

Time

45 minutes

Instructions

1. Distribute Handout 37 and show Slide 41.
2. Divide participants into collaboration teams. Division might be based on work groups, C–NC–I dot placement, direct involvement with a specific process map, or other method.
3. Tell participants to refer to their Creative Problem-Solving Worksheet and their C–NC–I dot placement and then identify and document on Handout 37 key actions to take to streamline, reengineer, or fill gaps in the service system they process mapped.

Learning Activity 47: Next Steps to Improve Our Systems, *continued*

4. Explain the importance and purpose of each column heading on the handout. Point out that the fifth column is only a start to a communication plan. Once they know who needs to know about an action, they will want to develop a full communication plan, including timing of the communication, medium, source (who will communicate it), content, and so on.
5. Debrief the activity with the questions below.

Discussion Questions for Debriefing

- Who will start us off by sharing one thing you plan to do? (Repeat multiple times.)
- Who identified a critical communication need and will be developing a comprehensive communication plan related to it?
- Why are designated individuals and deadlines so critical to action planning?
- How do you plan to track the team's progress on these plans?

Transition

Say: Clearly, these two days together are our starting point. As I mentioned at the start of Day One, there will be a lot to do following the workshop to implement improvements, communicate them effectively, check on their effectiveness, and potentially rework some of them. I'd say you have earned a break! Let's take 15 minutes and look at our service behaviors when we return.

Show break Slide 42.

Learning Activity 48: Keep a Cool Head

Keep a Cool Head

Objectives

Learning Activities 48 and 49 support Learning Objective 9—identify strategies for managing conflict.

Participants will be able to

- Identify terms and phrases that increase conflict
- Prepare response phrases and behaviors to minimize conflict when escalating statements are said to them
- List alternate terms and phrases to use to avoid creating conflict.

Materials

- Flip chart paper (three sheets) or whiteboard prepared with three columns
- Handout 38: Keep a Cool Head

Time

30 minutes

Instructions

1. Show transition Slide 43.
2. Place three flip charts side by side (or tape sheets to wall).
3. Distribute Handout 38 for note taking and show Slide 44.
4. Ask participants: What are some of the words and phrases that cause conflict to rise? (Sample answers: *don't, won't, can't, no, constantly, never, not allowed, policy, I pay your salary, it's not my job, I don't know.*) NOTE: They should only be focused on words, not actions, now.

Learning Activity 48: Keep a Cool Head, *continued*

5. Record responses on left chart, and label it "Conflict Creators."

6. Advance to Slide 45, and ask: When these things (from chart) are said to you, how can you respond to lessen the building tension? For example:

   • What would you say or do in response to an external customer who says (provide an example using a word or phrase identified in Conflict Creators chart, such as *"You never have a record of my previous order; it is infuriating."*)?

   • And, what would your response be if an internal customer told you (provide an example using a word or phrase identified in Conflict Creators chart, such as *"I can't do that now...I am just leaving for the night"*)?

7. Record responses to Step 6 on middle chart, aligned with appropriate entry on the left chart, and label the middle chart "Ways to Decrease Conflict."

8. Repeat for many of the items on the left chart, asking: Are you ever the one using these (left chart) terms? How can we decrease conflict by avoiding it in the first place? What alternative terms and words can we use in place of these (left chart)? (Provide an example from the left chart, such as: "Instead of saying *'I can't do what you are asking', say 'Here is what I can do for you...'* to an internal customer.")

9. Record responses to Step 8 on right chart, aligned with appropriate term on left chart. Label the right chart: "Ways to Avoid Conflict."

10. Repeat for many of the items on the left chart.

11. Advance to Slide 46, and ask: How many of our terms are listed here? In which column do you think they belong? (If you are using the customizable PowerPoint version of the presentation slides, advance the slide animation to show positioning of the terms and again to show their alignment. If you are using the free, pdf-version of the presentation slides, you will automatically display the aligned positioning.)

12. Ask table groups to brainstorm actions that fall into the three categories and record them on their handout too (middle of the page).

13. Lead a round-robin review of their ideas.

Learning Activity 48: Keep a Cool Head, *continued*

14. Facilitate a group debrief using some of the debriefing questions below.

15. Have participants answer the final two questions under "My Triggers" on the handout.

Variations

• Instead of a facilitated discussion, invite participants to record ideas for middle and right charts on sticky notes and display them in alignment with the entries on the left chart. Ask volunteers to read out ideas and invite the group to "vote" by standing if they agree with the strategy that has been read aloud. The ideas with the most votes can be typed up and shared as a post-workshop resource.

• Record responses to "What are some of the words and phrases that cause conflict to rise?" Invite table groups to brainstorm their "Ways to Decrease Conflict" and "Ways to Avoid Conflict" for 3-5 of the recorded items. Have a volunteer from each table share their top two ideas (no repeats from table to table).

• Have extra time? Following this activity, distribute a list of customer scenarios you have prepared, and direct learners to role play the situations using the language and actions recorded in this activity.

Discussion Questions for Debriefing

• What conclusions can we draw from this activity?

• How will your service behaviors differ from now on based on this activity?

• Who has changed their opinion about the cause of conflict in service interactions and their own ability to decrease the conflict?

• What is one action you plan to take to avoid creating conflict in customer communications going forward?

Transition

Ask: Ready to put some of these ideas we have recorded into action? We are going to apply these ideas to some real-world scenarios and receive instant feedback from the group.

Learning Activity 49: Quit Taking It Personally (Q-Tip)

Quit Taking It Personally (Q-Tip)

Objectives

Along with Learning Activity 48, this activity supports Learning Objective 9—identify strategies for managing conflict.

Participants will

• Apply ideas and strategies shared to real-world customer situations

• React to customer situations in real time

• Receive group feedback on the strategies they think may be effective.

Materials

• Handout 39: Quit Taking It Personally (Q-Tip) (customization is encouraged)

• Red squares of cardstock (one per participant)

• Green squares of cardstock (one per participant)

Time

30 minutes

Instructions

1. Distribute Handout 39 and show Slide 47.

2. Tell participants to review the lists of statements that internal and external customers may say and choose 3-5 from each list on the handout that resonate with them. Based on the ideas shared and recorded in the last activity and their own strategies, they should determine what they would say or do if these things were said to them. Advise them to be prepared to share their answers.

Learning Activity 49: Quit Taking It Personally (Q-Tip), *continued*

3. As participants work, give each person a red and a green card (if collected earlier).

4. Once participants have had time to work with the list, show Slide 48 and explain the pop-up process.

   a. Read out an item from the handout.

   b. When a participant has a response idea to share and receive feedback on, he or she pops up and shares it (in 10-12 seconds) loudly enough for all to hear.

   c. Everyone "votes" (by holding up a red or green card) to indicate if the response would satisfy *them* if they were the customer. Red indicates *not satisfied* and green indicates *satisfied*.

5. Read out entries. Allow multiple pop-ups.

6. Lead a brief discussion to debrief the activity, referring to the questions on the next page.

Variations

• Print each statement on an index card. Invite volunteers to pull a card and play the role of that customer by reading the statement aloud as you moderate the pop-up responses.

• Instead of "voting" with a colored card, use a text-polling software tool to allow the group to give each idea shared a thumbs up or thumbs down.

• Create your own challenging statements and situations based on your pre-training interviews with service providers. (TIP: Make them specific and applicable to all attending.)

• Add other internal or external customer characteristics to the list (confused, hesitant, lacking a clear understanding of the need, and so on.)

Learning Activity 49: Quit Taking It Personally (Q-Tip), *continued*

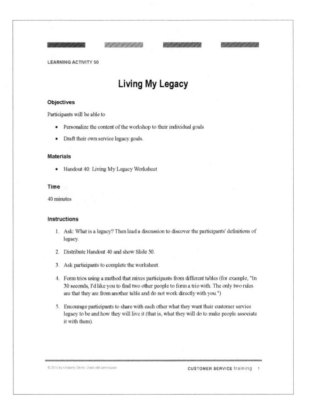

LEARNING ACTIVITY 49, continued

Discussion Questions for Debriefing

- Which customer behaviors are most troublesome for you (that push your buttons)?
- Are your internal or external customers more likely to demonstrate these behaviors?
- What ideas are you taking away from this activity that you will begin to use this week?

Transition

Say: Our next activity combines all that we have covered and allows you to take it to a very personal level. With our remaining time, we will be deciding on what we want our individual service legacies to be—that is, what we want to be known for.

(OPTION: Lead group through an in-room stretch break before winding down with Learning Activities 50 and 51. Show stretch break Slide 49.)

© 2015 by Kimberly Devlin. Used with permission.   CUSTOMER SERVICE training   3

Learning Activity 50: Living My Legacy

LEARNING ACTIVITY 50

Living My Legacy

Objectives

Participants will be able to

- Personalize the content of the workshop to their individual goals
- Draft their own service legacy goals.

Materials

- Handout 40: Living My Legacy Worksheet

Time

40 minutes

Instructions

1. Ask: What is a legacy? Then lead a discussion to discover the participants' definitions of legacy.
2. Distribute Handout 40 and show Slide 50.
3. Ask participants to complete the worksheet.
4. Form trios using a method that mixes participants from different tables (for example, "In 30 seconds, I'd like you to find two other people to form a trio with. The only two rules are that they are from another table and do not work directly with you.")
5. Encourage participants to share with each other what they want their customer service legacy to be and how they will live it (that is, what they will do to make people associate it with them).

© 2015 by Kimberly Devlin. Used with permission.   CUSTOMER SERVICE training   1

Learning Activity 50: Living My Legacy, *continued*

LEARNING ACTIVITY 50, continued

Variation

- An activity as personal and introspective as defining and writing a legacy plan may require shifting the tone and energy in the room. Playing soft music after you set the stage for this activity will help drown out the deafening silence and may help some participants tap into their internal thoughts.

Discussion Questions for Debriefing

- Was it challenging to define your legacy? Why?
- What opportunity did you have yesterday to live this legacy?
- What action will you take when you return to work tomorrow to live this legacy?

© 2015 by Kimberly Devlin. Used with permission.   CUSTOMER SERVICE training   2

Learning Activity 51: Day-Two Workshop Closure

LEARNING ACTIVITY 51

Day-Two Workshop Closure

Objectives

Participants will be able to

- Receive still-needed answers and information for effective implementation
- Receive direction on expectations for next steps
- Provide feedback on the workshop.

Materials

- Handout 41: Course Evaluation—A Total Approach to Service

Time

25 minutes

Instructions

1. Show Slide 51.
2. Tell participants: We are quickly coming to the end of our in-room workshop time together. Before you head out, there are just a few critical actions for us.
3. Share a high-level recap of all that has been covered and achieved in the two days, allowing participants to review what they have learned.
4. To give participants an opportunity to assess what they have learned and to provide them with needed support and clarification, ask: What do we need to do, what do you need to know, to leave here confident in your plans to improve customer service?

© 2015 by Kimberly Devlin. Used with permission.   CUSTOMER SERVICE training   1

Learning Activity 51: Day-Two Workshop Closure, *continued*

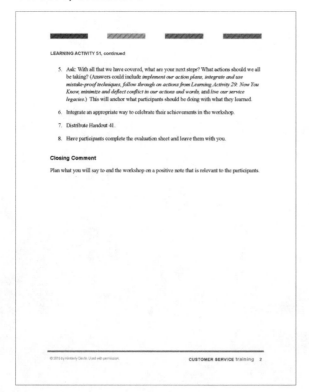

5. Ask: With all that we have covered, what are your next steps? What actions should we all be taking? (Answers could include *implement our action plans, integrate and use mistake-proof techniques, follow through on actions from Learning Activity 29: Now You Know, minimize and deflect conflict in our actions and words,* and *live our service legacies.*) This will anchor what participants should be doing with what they learned.

6. Integrate an appropriate way to celebrate their achievements in the workshop.

7. Distribute Handout 41.

8. Have participants complete the evaluation sheet and leave them with you.

Closing Comment

Plan what you will say to end the workshop on a positive note that is relevant to the participants.

CUSTOMER SERVICE training   2

Chapter 12

Assessments

What's in This Chapter

- Two assessments to use in the workshop sessions or as professional development

- Instructions on how and when to use the assessments

Assessments and evaluations can be critical to a workshop. Using assessments during the workshop helps participants identify areas of strength and weakness, enabling them to capitalize on their strengths and improve their weaknesses to become more effective in the workplace and beyond. You may choose to have participants refer back to their self-assessments during subsequent workshop activities to check in on participants' learning so that both of you can make needed adjustments as you go.

In addition, Assessment 2: Facilitator Competencies provides an instrument to help you manage your professional development and increase the effectiveness of your workshops. You can use this tool in a number of ways: self-assessment, end-of-course feedback, or peer-to-peer observer feedback.

Assessments Included in *Customer Service Training*

Assessment 1: Where Are We Now?

Assessment 2: Facilitator Competencies

Assessment 1: Where Are We Now?

Assessment 1: Where Are We Now?, *continued*

Assessment 1: Where Are We Now?, *continued*

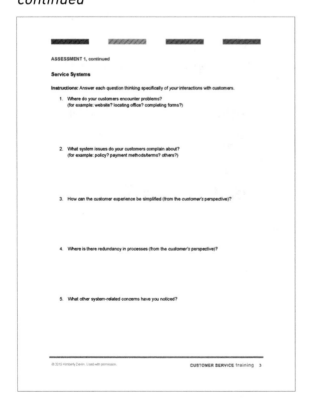

Assessment 2: Facilitator Competencies

Assessment 2: Facilitator Competencies, *continued*

Assessment 2: Facilitator Competencies, *continued*

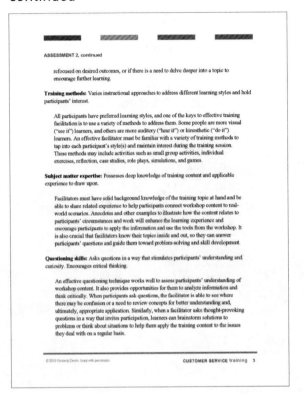

ASSESSMENT 2, continued

Presentation skills: Conveys content clearly to achieve the desired outcomes of the workshop. Encourages learners to generate their own answers by effectively leading group discussions.

The facilitator's ability to convey content effectively and in an engaging way is one of the first things participants notice and is a significant driver of a successful workshop. The nature of adult learning makes it equally important that the facilitator is not a talking head but excels at initiating, drawing out, guiding, and summarizing information gleaned from large group discussions. The facilitator's role is not to feed information to participants as if they are empty vessels waiting to be filled. Rather, it is the facilitator's primary task to generate learning on the part of the participants through their own process of discovery.

Communication skills: Expresses self well, both verbally and in writing. Understands nonverbal communication and listens effectively.

Beyond conveying information and leading discussions, it is vital for a facilitator to be highly skilled in all aspects of communication. He or she should use language that participants understand; give clear directions for activities; involve participants through appropriate humor, anecdotes, and examples; and build on the ideas of others. This will lead to workshops that are engaging and highly valued by the participants. Facilitators must also be able to listen well and attend to participants' nonverbal communication to create common meaning and mutual understanding.

Emotional intelligence: Respects participants' viewpoints, knowledge, and experience. Recognizes and responds appropriately to others' feelings, attitudes, and concerns.

Because participants may have many different backgrounds, experience levels, and opinions in the same workshops, facilitators must be able to handle a variety of situations and conversations well and be sensitive to others' emotions. They must pay close attention to the dynamics in the room, be flexible enough to make immediate changes to activities during training to meet the needs of learners, and create an open and trusting learning environment. Participants should feel comfortable expressing their opinions, asking questions, and participating in activities without fear of repercussion or disapproval. Monitoring their emotions during a workshop also helps the facilitator gauge when it may be time to change gears if conflict arises, if a discussion needs to be

© 2015 Kimberly Devlin. Used with permission. **CUSTOMER SERVICE** training 2

refocused on desired outcomes, or if there is a need to delve deeper into a topic to encourage further learning.

Training methods: Varies instructional approaches to address different learning styles and hold participants' interest.

All participants have preferred learning styles, and one of the keys to effective training facilitation is to use a variety of methods to address them. Some people are more visual ("see it") learners, and others are more auditory ("hear it") or kinesthetic ("do it") learners. An effective facilitator must be familiar with a variety of training methods to tap into each participant's style(s) and maintain interest during the training session. These methods may include activities such as small group activities, individual exercises, reflection, case studies, role plays, simulations, and games.

Subject matter expertise: Possesses deep knowledge of training content and applicable experience to draw upon.

Facilitators must have solid background knowledge of the training topic at hand and be able to share related experience to help participants connect workshop content to real-world scenarios. Anecdotes and other examples to illustrate how the content relates to participants' circumstances and work will enhance the learning experience and encourage participants to apply the information and use the tools from the workshop. It is also crucial that facilitators know their topics inside and out, so they can answer participants' questions and guide them toward problem-solving and skill development.

Questioning skills: Asks questions in a way that stimulates participants' understanding and curiosity. Encourages critical thinking.

An effective questioning technique works well to assess participants' understanding of workshop content. It also provides opportunities for them to analyze information and think critically. When participants ask questions, the facilitator is able to see where there may be confusion or a need to review concepts for better understanding and, ultimately, appropriate application. Similarly, when a facilitator asks thought-provoking questions in a way that invites participation, learners can brainstorm solutions to problems or think about situations to help them apply the training content to the issues they deal with on a regular basis.

© 2015 Kimberly Devlin. Used with permission. **CUSTOMER SERVICE** training 3

Assessment 2: Facilitator Competencies, *continued*

Assessment 2: Facilitator Competencies, *continued*

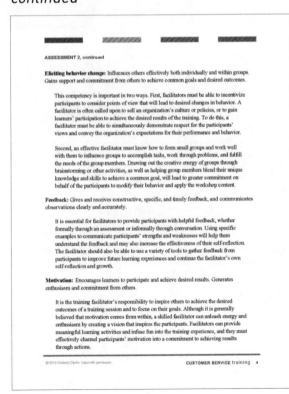

ASSESSMENT 2, continued

Eliciting behavior change: Influences others effectively both individually and within groups. Gains support and commitment from others to achieve common goals and desired outcomes.

This competency is important in two ways. First, facilitators must be able to incentivize participants to consider points of view that will lead to desired changes in behavior. A facilitator is often called upon to sell an organization's culture or policies, or to gain learners' participation to achieve the desired results of the training. To do this, a facilitator must be able to simultaneously demonstrate respect for the participants' views and convey the organization's expectations for their performance and behavior.

Second, an effective facilitator must know how to form small groups and work well with them to influence groups to accomplish tasks, work through problems, and fulfill the needs of the group members. Drawing out the creative energy of groups through brainstorming or other activities, as well as helping group members blend their unique knowledge and skills to achieve a common goal, will lead to greater commitment on behalf of the participants to modify their behavior and apply the workshop content.

Feedback: Gives and receives constructive, specific, and timely feedback, and communicates observations clearly and accurately.

It is essential for facilitators to provide participants with helpful feedback, whether formally through an assessment or informally through conversation. Using specific examples to communicate participants' strengths and weaknesses will help them understand the feedback and may also increase the effectiveness of their self-reflection. The facilitator should also be able to use a variety of tools to gather feedback from participants to improve future learning experiences and continue the facilitator's own self-reflection and growth.

Motivation: Encourages learners to participate and achieve desired results. Generates enthusiasm and commitment from others.

It is the training facilitator's responsibility to inspire others to achieve the desired outcomes of a training session and to focus on their goals. Although it is generally believed that motivation comes from within, a skilled facilitator can unleash energy and enthusiasm by creating a vision that inspires the participants. Facilitators can provide meaningful learning activities and infuse fun into the training experience, and they must effectively channel participants' motivation into a commitment to achieving results through actions.

© 2015 Kimberly Devlin. Used with permission. **CUSTOMER SERVICE** training 4

Organizational skills: Works in an orderly and logical way to accomplish tasks. Ensures that work is correct and complete. Presents ideas logically and sequentially for participants to understand.

The importance of this competency for facilitators is twofold. First, the facilitator must have good work habits and pay attention to detail. With any training event, many factors are necessary to ensure a successful experience. A well-organized training facilitator typically creates well-organized, professional training. Second, it is important for facilitators to present ideas in a logical, sequential order that allows learners to absorb new content easily and also to be able to retrieve it quickly when needed.

Time management: Plans and uses time effectively. Balances important and urgent tasks and can work on multiple tasks simultaneously.

Facilitators do many things in addition to conducting training sessions. They must also budget their time effectively to address other priorities in their work: prepare for the workshop, keep accurate records, analyze assessment data, design new content or activities, and report to the client organization. The most competent facilitators are able to multitask and keep the goals of the participants and client organization in view as much as possible. Good time management helps a facilitator keep track of all there is to do during any given day.

© 2015 Kimberly Devlin. Used with permission. **CUSTOMER SERVICE** training 5

Assessment 2: Facilitator Competencies, *continued*

Facilitator Competencies

Instructions: If using this instrument as a self-assessment, place a ✔ in the box that best describes your skill level for each of the 12 facilitator competencies. If using this form to provide feedback to a facilitator, place a ✔ in the box that best fits the facilitator's demonstrated level of competence in each area that you feel qualified to assess based on your interaction with the facilitator.

COMPETENCY	SKILL-LEVEL DEMONSTRATED			
	Not demonstrated	Infrequently demonstrated	Often demonstrated	Consistently demonstrated
Understanding adult learners: Applies principles of adult learning when designing and delivering training.	☐	☐	☐	☐
Presentation skills: Conveys content clearly to achieve the desired outcomes of the workshop. Encourages participants to generate their own answers by effectively leading group discussions.	☐	☐	☐	☐
Communication skills: Expresses self well verbally and in writing. Responds to nonverbal communication and listens effectively.	☐	☐	☐	☐
Emotional intelligence: Respects participants' viewpoints, knowledge, and experience. Recognizes and responds appropriately to others' feelings, attitudes, and concerns.	☐	☐	☐	☐
Training methods: Varies instructional approaches to address different learning styles and hold participants' interest.	☐	☐	☐	☐
Subject matter expertise: Possesses deep knowledge of training content and applicable experience to draw upon.	☐	☐	☐	☐

Assessment 2: Facilitator Competencies, *continued*

ASSESSMENT 2, continued

COMPETENCY	SKILL-LEVEL DEMONSTRATED			
	Not demonstrated	Infrequently demonstrated	Often demonstrated	Consistently demonstrated
Questioning skills: Asks questions in a way that stimulates participants' understanding and curiosity. Encourages critical thinking.	☐	☐	☐	☐
Eliciting behavior change: Influences others effectively, both individually and within groups. Gains support and commitment from others to achieve common goals and desired outcomes.	☐	☐	☐	☐
Feedback: Gives and receives constructive, specific, and timely feedback and communicates observations clearly and accurately.	☐	☐	☐	☐
Motivation: Encourages learners to participate and achieve desired results. Generates enthusiasm and commitment from others.	☐	☐	☐	☐
Organizational skills: Works in an orderly and logical way to accomplish tasks. Ensures work is correct and complete. Presents ideas logically and sequentially for learners to understand.	☐	☐	☐	☐
Time management: Plans time effectively. Balances important and urgent tasks and can work on multiple tasks simultaneously.	☐	☐	☐	☐

Chapter 13

Handouts

What's in This Chapter

- Forty-one handouts to use in your workshops
- Refer to Chapter 14 for instructions to download full-sized handouts

---

Handouts comprise the various materials you will provide to the learners throughout the course of the workshop. In some cases, the handouts will simply provide instructions for worksheets to complete, places to take notes, and so forth. In other cases, they will provide important and practical materials for use in and out of the training room, such as reference materials, tip sheets, samples of completed forms, flowcharts, and so forth.

The workshop agendas in Chapters 1–3 and the learning activities in Chapter 11 will provide instructions for how and when to use the handouts within the context of the workshop. See Chapter 14 for complete instructions on how to download the workshop support materials.

Handouts Included in *Customer Service Training*

Half-Day Workshop: Service Behaviors That Matter

Handout 1: Hello, My Idea Is . . .

Handout 2: Learning Objectives

Handout 3: I'm Stumped Idea Starters

Handout 4: Keep a Cool Head

Handout 5: Quit Taking It Personally (Q-Tip)

Handout 6: The HELP Process for Customer Interactions

Handout 7: HELP the Customer—Interview Tool

Handout 8: HELP the Customer—Planning Worksheet

Handout 9: HELP the Customer—Observer Worksheet

Handout 10: Interconnected Service Facets

Handout 11: Course Evaluation—Service Behaviors That Matter

One-Day Workshop: From the Customer's Perspective

Handout 12: Service Heroes

Handout 13: Learning Objectives

Handout 14: Participant Journal

Handout 15: Interconnected Service Facets

Handout 16: Do They Agree?

Handout 17: Performance Improvement

Handout 18: The HELP Process for Customer Interactions

Handout 19: HELP the Customer—Interview Tool

Handout 20: HELP the Customer—Planning Worksheet

Handout 21: HELP the Customer—Observer Worksheet

Handout 22: Mistake Proofing to Improve Customer Service

Handout 23: Creating Mistake-Proof Techniques Worksheet

Handout 24: Where and How Can I Help?

Handout 25: Where We Go From Here

Handout 26: Course Evaluation—From the Customer's Perspective

Two-Day Workshop: A Total Approach to Service

Handout 27: Learning Objectives

Handout 28: Now You Know

Handout 29: Interconnected Service Facets

Handout 30 The Root Issue Is?

Handout 31: Performance Improvement

Handout 32: Field Trip Log

Handout 32B: Virtual Field Trip Map

Handout 33: Mistake Proofing to Improve Customer Service

Handout 34: Mistake-Proofing Process Map Elements

Handout 35: Seven-Step Creative Problem-Solving Process

Handout 36: Creative Problem-Solving Worksheet

Handout 37: Next Steps to Improve Our Systems

Handout 38: Keep a Cool Head

Handout 39: Quit Taking It Personally (Q-Tip)

Handout 40: Living My Legacy Worksheet

Handout 41: Course Evaluation—A Total Approach to Service

Handout 1: Hello, My Idea Is . . .

Handout 2: Learning Objectives

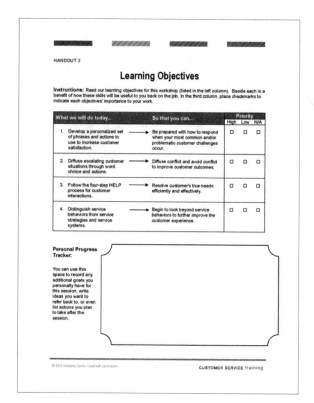

HANDOUT 1

Hello, My Idea Is...

Instructions: As you mingle to meet new people and their ideas, use this worksheet to record.

- The idea
- Who shared the idea
- How you can apply the idea in your service interactions.

An Idea I Met	Who Shared It	How I Can Apply It!
1.		
2.		
3.		

Questions To Ponder

- Were these ideas new to you?
- If not, are you applying them consistently in your service interactions?
- If not, why not? And, what will you do to change that?

© 2015 Kimberly Devlin. Used with permission.   **CUSTOMER SERVICE** training

HANDOUT 2

Learning Objectives

Instructions: Read our learning objectives for this workshop (listed in the left column). Beside each is a benefit of how these skills will be useful to you back on the job. In the third column, place checkmarks to indicate each objectives' importance to your work.

What we will do today...	So that you can...	Priority High	Low	N/A
1. Develop a personalized set of phrases and actions to use to increase customer satisfaction.	Be prepared with how to respond when your most common and/or problematic customer challenges occur.	☐	☐	☐
2. Diffuse escalating customer situations through word choice and actions.	Diffuse conflict and avoid conflict to improve customer outcomes.	☐	☐	☐
3. Follow the four-step HELP process for customer interactions.	Resolve customer's true needs efficiently and effectively.	☐	☐	☐
4. Distinguish service behaviors from service strategies and service systems.	Begin to look beyond service behaviors to further improve the customer experience.	☐	☐	☐

Personal Progress Tracker:

You can use this space to record any additional goals you personally have for this session, write ideas you want to refer back to, or even list actions you plan to take after the session.

© 2015 Kimberly Devlin. Used with permission.   **CUSTOMER SERVICE** training

Handout 3: I'm Stumped Idea Starters

Handout 4: Keep a Cool Head

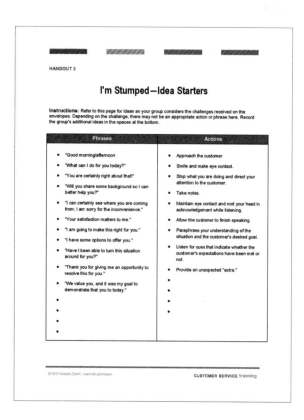

HANDOUT 3

I'm Stumped—Idea Starters

Instructions: Refer to this page for ideas as your group considers the challenges received on the envelopes. Depending on the challenge, there may not be an appropriate action or phrase here. Record the group's additional ideas in the spaces at the bottom.

Phrases	Actions
• "Good morning/afternoon"	• Approach the customer
• "What can I do for you today?"	• Smile and make eye contact.
• "You are certainly right about that!"	• Stop what you are doing and direct your attention to the customer.
• "Will you share some background so I can better help you?"	• Take notes.
• "I can certainly see where you are coming from; I am sorry for the inconvenience."	• Maintain eye contact and nod your head in acknowledgement while listening.
• "Your satisfaction matters to me."	• Allow the customer to finish speaking.
• "I am going to make this right for you."	• Paraphrase your understanding of the situation and the customer's desired goal.
• "I have some options to offer you."	• Listen for cues that indicate whether the customer's expectations have been met or not.
• "Have I been able to turn this situation around for you?"	• Provide an unexpected "extra."
• "Thank you for giving me an opportunity to resolve this for you."	•
• "We value you, and it was my goal to demonstrate that you to today."	•
•	•
•	•
•	•

© 2015 Kimberly Devlin. Used with permission.   **CUSTOMER SERVICE** training

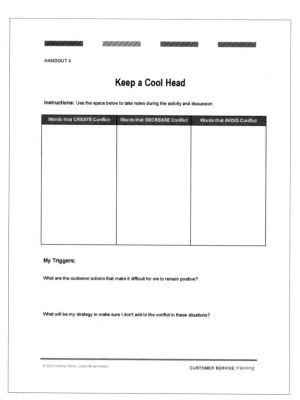

HANDOUT 4

Keep a Cool Head

Instructions: Use the space below to take notes during the activity and discussion.

Words that CREATE Conflict	Words that DECREASE Conflict	Words that AVOID Conflict

My Triggers:

What are the customer actions that make it difficult for me to remain positive?

What will be my strategy to make sure I don't add to the conflict in these situations?

© 2015 Kimberly Devlin. Used with permission.   **CUSTOMER SERVICE** training

Handout 5: Quit Taking It Personally (Q-Tip)

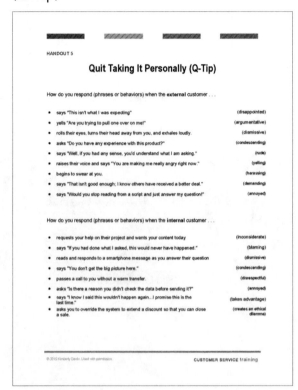

HANDOUT 5

Quit Taking It Personally (Q-Tip)

How do you respond (phrases or behaviors) when the **external customer** . . .

- says "This isn't what I was expecting"   (disappointed)
- yells "Are you trying to pull one over on me!"   (argumentative)
- rolls their eyes, turns their head away from you, and exhales loudly.   (dismissive)
- asks "Do you have any experience with this product?"   (condescending)
- says "Well, if you had any sense, you'd understand what I am asking."   (rude)
- raises their voice and says "You are making me really angry right now."   (yelling)
- begins to swear at you.   (harassing)
- says "That isn't good enough; I know others have received a better deal."   (demanding)
- says "Would you stop reading from a script and just answer my question!"   (annoyed)

How do you respond (phrases or behaviors) when the **internal customer** . . .

- requests your help on their project and wants your content today   (inconsiderate)
- says "If you had done what I asked, this would never have happened."   (blaming)
- reads and responds to a smartphone message as you answer their question   (dismissive)
- says "You don't get the big picture here."   (condescending)
- passes a call to you without a warm transfer.   (disrespectful)
- asks "Is there a reason you didn't check the data before sending it?"   (annoyed)
- says "I know I said this wouldn't happen again...I promise this is the last time."   (takes advantage)
- asks you to override the system to extend a discount so that you can close a sale.   (creates an ethical dilemma)

© 2015 Kimberly Devlin. Used with permission.   **CUSTOMER SERVICE** training

Handout 6: The HELP Process for Customer Interactions

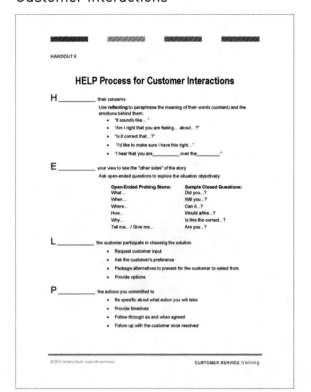

HANDOUT 6

HELP Process for Customer Interactions

H_____ their concerns
Use **reflecting** to paraphrase the meaning of their words (content) and the emotions behind them:
- "It sounds like... "
- "Am I right that you are feeling... about...?"
- "Is it correct that...?"
- "I'd like to make sure I have this right..."
- "I hear that you are_____ over the_____."

E_____ your view to see the "other sides" of the story
Ask open-ended questions to explore the situation objectively:

Open-Ended Probing Stems:	Sample Closed Questions:
What...	Did you...?
When...	Will you...?
Where...	Can it...?
How...	Would at/the...?
Why...	Is this the correct...?
Tell me... / Give me...	Are you...?

L_____ the customer participate in choosing the solution
- Request customer input
- Ask the customer's preference
- Package alternatives to present for the customer to select from
- Provide options

P_____ the actions you committed to
- Be specific about what action you will take
- Provide timelines
- Follow through as and when agreed
- Follow up with the customer once resolved

© 2015 Kimberly Devlin. Used with permission.   **CUSTOMER SERVICE** training

Handout 7: HELP the Customer—Interview Tool

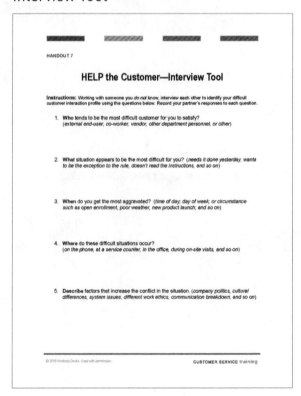

HANDOUT 7

HELP the Customer—Interview Tool

Instructions: Working with someone you do *not* know, interview each other to identify your difficult customer interaction profile using the questions below. Record your partner's responses to each question.

1. **Who** tends to be the most difficult customer for you to satisfy?
   (*external end-user, co-worker, vendor, other department personnel, or other*)

2. **What** situation appears to be the most difficult for you? (*needs it done yesterday, wants to be the exception to the rule, doesn't read the instructions, and so on*)

3. **When** do you get the most aggravated? (*time of day; day of week; or circumstance such as open enrollment, poor weather, new product launch; and so on*)

4. **Where** do these difficult situations occur?
   (*on the phone, at a service counter, in the office, during on-site visits, and so on*)

5. **Describe** factors that increase the conflict in the situation. (*company politics, cultural differences, system issues, different work ethics, communication breakdown, and so on*)

© 2015 Kimberly Devlin. Used with permission.   **CUSTOMER SERVICE** training

Handout 8: HELP the Customer—Planning Worksheet

HANDOUT 8

HELP the Customer—Planning Worksheet

Instructions for the role play will be shared by your workshop leader. To prepare for the role play, use the notes you recorded during your partner interview (about *his* or *her* customer situation) and this worksheet to plan what you will say and do as the service provider during the role play.

Hear their concerns. What reflecting statements might be appropriate in this situation?

Expand your view to see the "other sides" of the story. What strategies will you use to remain open to and learn the different sides to the story?

Let the customer participate in choosing the solution. How will you invite the customer to contribute to the solution? What options will you offer the customer to resolve his or her concern?

Perform the actions committed to. What details will you provide the customer regarding the actions you will take and when you will take them?

© 2015 Kimberly Devlin. Used with permission.   **CUSTOMER SERVICE** training

Handout 9: HELP the Customer— Observer Worksheet

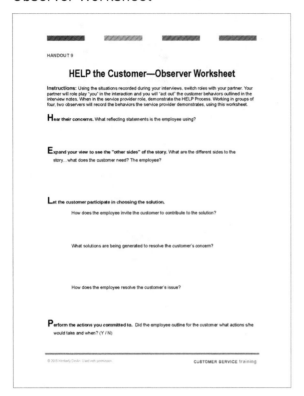

Handout 10: Interconnected Service Facets

Handout 11: Course Evaluation—Service Behaviors That Matter

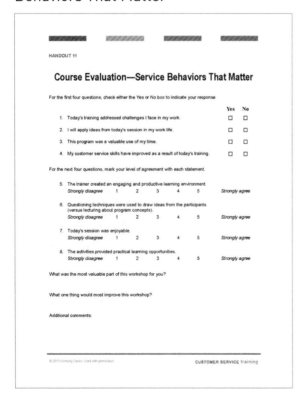

Handout 12: Service Heroes

HANDOUT 12

Service Heroes

PART 1

Instructions: Write your answers to complete these two statements:

- A customer service strength I have is _____ .
- Two ways I demonstrate it are...

PART 2

Instructions: Mingle to meet three new people sitting at other tables. Use this worksheet to record their strengths and what they do to apply it.

Name	Strength	Application Ideas
1.		1. 2.
2.		1. 2.
3.		1. 2.

Questions to Consider:

1. How can you integrate these actions in your service interactions?

2. Which of the people you met may be a good resource for you when facing a challenging situation?

© 2015 Kimberly Devlin. Used with permission.

CUSTOMER SERVICE training

Handout 13: Learning Objectives

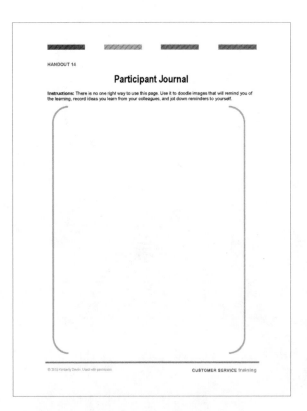

Handout 14: Participant Journal

Handout 15: Interconnected Service Facets

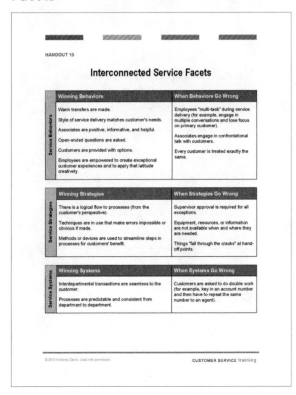

Handout 16: Do They Agree?

Handout 17: Performance Improvement

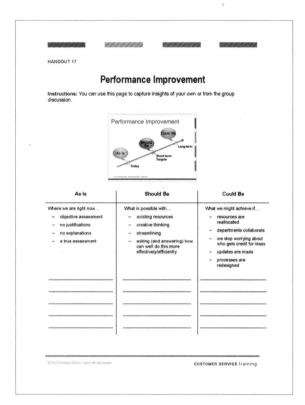

Handout 18: The HELP Process for Customer Interactions

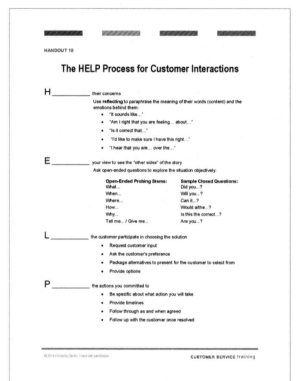

Handout 19: HELP the Customer— Interview Tool

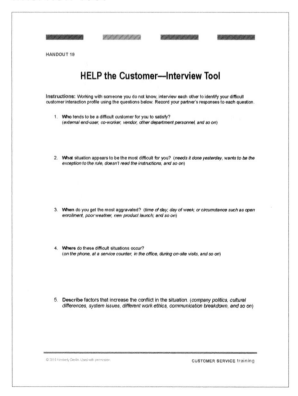

Handout 20: HELP the Customer— Planning Worksheet

Handout 21: HELP the Customer—Observer Worksheet

Handout 22: Mistake Proofing to Improve Customer Service

HANDOUT 22

Mistake Proofing to Improve Customer Service

Mistake proofing serves many purposes. It contributes to safety, profitability, consistency, waste reduction, and more. Our use today will be to create better customer experiences by reducing the likelihood of error, streamlining, simplifying—in short, improving our processes from the customer's perspective! We can do this by building mistake prevention and detection into our processes, creating fail safe techniques to fall back on, and creating a work environment that prevents errors.

Instructions: Use this handout to capture notes and insights from the learning activity.

Mistake Proofing Traits:

1. _____   3. _____
2. _____   4. _____

Techniques	Examples	Add More
Streamline	Eliminate steps, simplify instructions, combine steps	
Color code	Calendar events, to match parts, to distinguish similar materials, to signify a warning	
Templates	Forms/letters, patterns for cutting materials, boards retailers use to fold shirts to a consistent size for display	
Checklists	Client intake, routine tasks, preflight, store opening	
Layout	Designated spots for tools/resources, proximity of items to where they will be used	
Regulate behavior through size/dimension	Arm rests on bus benches and airport seats (limits lying down), counter height of shared courtesy computer stations (limits use), screw hole alignment in assembly-required furniture (only fit one way)	
Correct misinformation	Wrong phone number, outdated forms, obsolete processes, create evergreen materials (i.e., list title of person responsible instead of their name)	
Sequence	Build emails backwards (avoid missing attachments)	
Signage	Educate customer, direct customer, inform customer (billboard with digital display of current wait time at the hospital emergency room)	
Grouping	Bundle silverware in napkin, money wrappers, emergency medical technician (EMT) care kits specific to patient's emergency	
Baiting	Coupons, discounts, promotional products, waivers (of fees, waiting periods, and others)	

© 2016 Kimberly Devlin. Used with permission.   CUSTOMER SERVICE training   1

Handout 22: Mistake Proofing to Improve Customer Service, *continued*

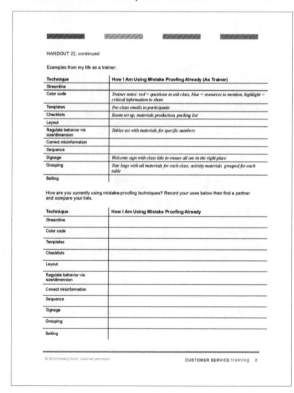

Handout 23: Creating Mistake-Proof Techniques Worksheet

HANDOUT 23

Creating Mistake-Proof Techniques Worksheet

Instructions: Working with a partner, use the questions below to guide you in creating mistake-proof techniques to implement in your workplace. Don't stop at just one! Keep going if you have extra time.

Who is a customer you serve? _____

What is a service they receive? _____

Looking from the customer's perspective, what are the key actions/steps involved in executing the delivery of this service? (NOTE: You might not be involved in some steps.)

Where do you see opportunities to streamline, reorder, simplify, clarify, or otherwise improve the process (above)? What mistake-proof technique will help? Design it below or record what needs to happen to implement the technique.

© 2016 Kimberly Devlin. Used with permission.   CUSTOMER SERVICE training

Handout 24: Where and How Can I Help?

Handout 25: Where We Go From Here

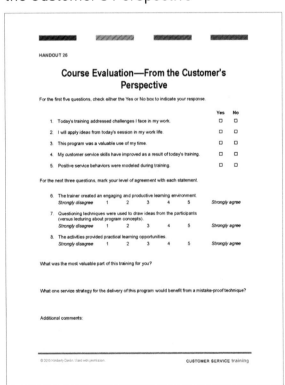

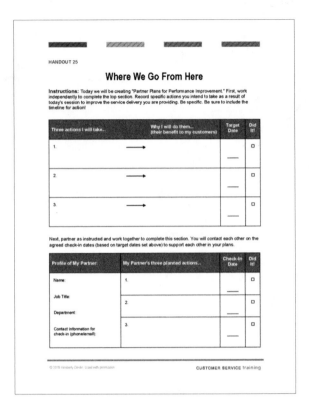

Handout 26: Course Evaluation—From the Customer's Perspective

Handout 27: Learning Objectives

Handout 28: Now You Know

Handout 28: Now You Know, *continued*

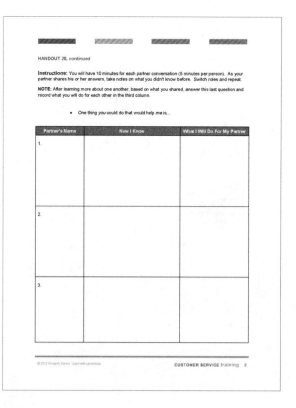

HANDOUT 28

Now You Know

Instructions: Write brief answers (that you are comfortable sharing with others) to the **first four** and **last four** prompts (in bold). Choose **four additional** question prompts and record your answers to them.

1. **My job title is** _____
2. **In five words or less, what I do is...**
3. **Basically, that means that I:**
4. What I like about my job is _____ .
5. My least favorite part of my job is _____ .
6. Something most people do not know about my job is...
7. External customers come to me for (or expect me to)...
8. Internal customers come to me for (or expect me to)...
9. Three big challenges I face in providing excellent service to every customer are:
10. One "go-to" strategy I use with customers that reliably provides a positive result is...
11. It would greatly improve my ability to serve our customers if _____ would _____ .
12. I am passionate about _____ (either personally or professionally).
13. **A professional goal I have (or a professional challenge I'd like to take on) is...**
14. **A personal goal I have (or a personal challenge I'd like to take on) is...**

© 2015 Kimberly Devlin. Used with permission.   CUSTOMER SERVICE training   1

HANDOUT 28, continued

Instructions: You will have 10 minutes for each partner conversation (5 minutes per person). As your partner shares his or her answers, take notes on what you didn't know before. Switch roles and repeat.

NOTE: After learning more about one another, based on what you shared, answer this last question and record what you will do for each other in the third column.

- One thing you could do that would help me is...

Partner's Name	Now I Know	What I Will Do For My Partner
1.		
2.		
3.		

© 2015 Kimberly Devlin. Used with permission.   CUSTOMER SERVICE training   2

Handout 29: Interconnected Service Facets

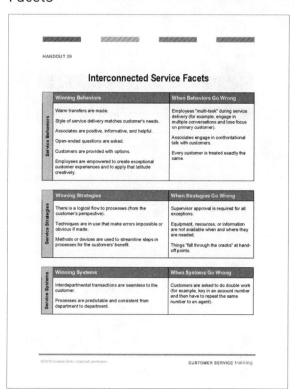

HANDOUT 29

Interconnected Service Facets

	Winning Behaviors	When Behaviors Go Wrong
Service Behaviors	Warm transfers are made. Style of service delivery matches customer's needs. Associates are positive, informative, and helpful. Open-ended questions are asked. Customers are provided with options. Employees are empowered to create exceptional customer experiences and to apply that latitude creatively.	Employees "multi-task" during service delivery (for example, engage in multiple conversations and lose focus on primary customer). Associates engage in confrontational talk with customers. Every customer is treated exactly the same.

	Winning Strategies	When Strategies Go Wrong
Service Strategies	There is a logical flow to processes (from the customer's perspective). Techniques are in use that make errors impossible or obvious if made. Methods or devices are used to streamline steps in processes for the customers' benefit.	Supervisor approval is required for all exceptions. Equipment, resources, or information are not available when and where they are needed. Things "fall through the cracks" at hand-off points.

	Winning Systems	When Systems Go Wrong
Service Systems	Interdepartmental transactions are seamless to the customer. Processes are predictable and consistent from department to department.	Customers are asked to do double work (for example, key in an account number and then have to repeat the same number to an agent).

© 2015 Kimberly Devlin. Used with permission.   CUSTOMER SERVICE training

Handout 30: The Root Issue Is?

HANDOUT 30

The Root Issue Is?

Instructions: Read each of the service interaction situations. Identify the service failure: What went wrong? Determine the root issue that contributed to the service failure: Was it a service behavior, a service strategy, a service system, two of the three, or all of them?

1. *[Replace with an industry-specific example of: employee having a difficult day personally and not being empathetic to the customer]*
   Mike, a long-time resident of the county and a retiree on a fixed income, received his property tax bill—for more than three times the previous year's bill. Reviewing it, he saw that he was now being taxed as if his home were a waterfront property. Wanting his account corrected and an explanation, he went to the tax collector office and assured Sarah, who waited on him, his home had not relocated itself. Sarah responded with "Yeah, this has been happening to a lot of people since we updated the database. There's nothing we can do about it. And I don't appreciate your yelling at me about it."

2. *[Insert an industry-specific example of: employee creating a workaround to account for a system constraint...but missing a critical action]*

3. *[Insert an industry-specific example of: customer asked for one thing, but actually needed something else]*

4. *[Insert an industry-specific example of: the service or product desired is not available]*

5. *[Insert an example of a common service challenge in this organization or industry]*

© 2015 Kimberly Devlin. Used with permission.   CUSTOMER SERVICE training

Handout 31: Performance Improvement

Handout 32: Field Trip Log

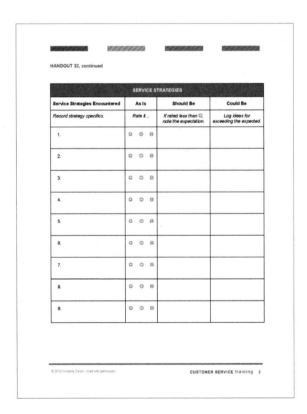

Handout 32: Field Trip Log, *continued*

Handout 32: Field Trip Log, *continued*

Handout 32B: Virtual Field Trip Map

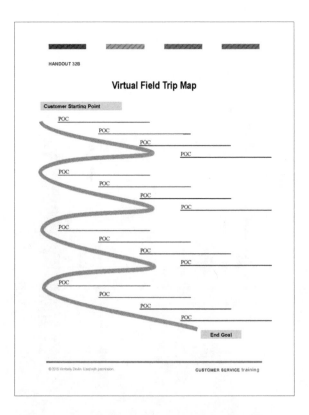

Handout 33: Mistake Proofing to Improve Customer Service

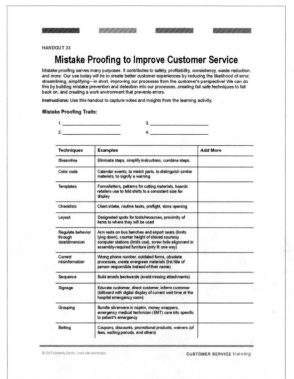

Handout 34: Mistake-Proofing Process Map Elements

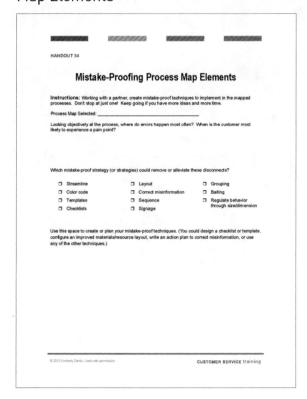

Handout 35: Seven-Step Creative Problem-Solving Process

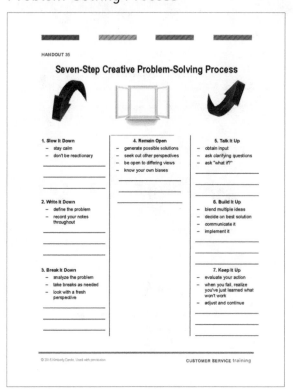

Handout 36: Creative Problem-Solving Worksheet

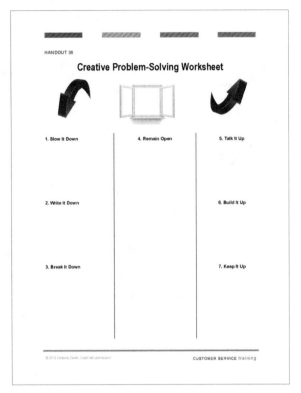

Handout 37: Next Steps to Improve Our Systems

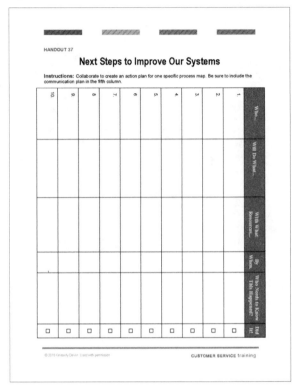

Handout 38: Keep a Cool Head

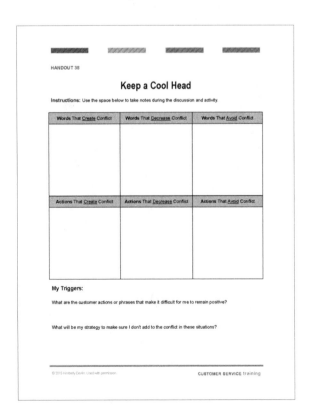

Handout 39: Quit Taking It Personally (Q-Tip)

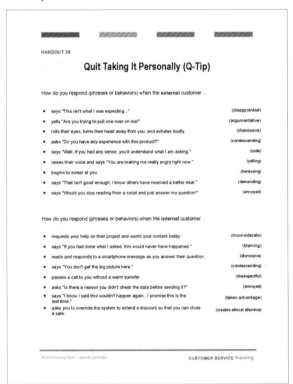

Handout 40: Living My Legacy Worksheet

Living My Legacy Worksheet

Instructions: Consider the questions below to help form a plan for your service legacy. Be sure to be specific in your responses to the last two questions.

On what area(s) do I want to focus my legacy?

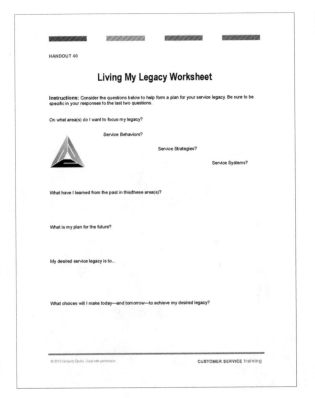

Service Behaviors?

Service Strategies?

Service Systems?

What have I learned from the past in this/these area(s)?

What is my plan for the future?

My desired service legacy is to...

What choices will I make today—and tomorrow—to achieve my desired legacy?

CUSTOMER SERVICE training

Handout 41: Course Evaluation—A Total Approach to Service

Course Evaluation—A Total Approach to Service

For the first five questions, check either the Yes or No box to indicate your response.

		Yes	No
1.	This workshop addressed service challenges this organization faces.	☐	☐
2.	I will apply ideas from this workshop in my work life.	☐	☐
3.	This program was a valuable use of my time.	☐	☐
4.	My customer service awareness has improved as a result of this workshop.	☐	☐
5.	Positive service behaviors were modeled during the workshop.	☐	☐

For the next three questions, mark your level of agreement with each statement.

6. The trainer created a collaborative and productive learning environment.

   Strongly disagree   1   2   3   4   5   *Strongly agree*

7. Questioning techniques were used to draw ideas from the participants (versus lecturing about program concepts).

   Strongly disagree   1   2   3   4   5   *Strongly agree*

8. The activities provided practical application of the concepts and techniques.

   Strongly disagree   1   2   3   4   5   *Strongly agree*

What was the most valuable part of this workshop for you?

How could this workshop be improved for future participants?

Additional comments:

CUSTOMER SERVICE training

Chapter 14
Online Tools and Downloads

What's in This Chapter

- Instructions to access supporting materials
- Options for using tools and downloads
- Licensing and copyright information for workshop programs
- Tips for working with the downloaded files

The ATD Workshop Series is designed to give you flexible options for many levels of training facilitation and topic expertise. As you prepare your program, you will want to incorporate many of the handouts, assessments, presentation slides, and other training tools provided as supplementary materials with this volume. We wish you the best of luck in delivering your training workshops. It is exciting work that ultimately can change lives.

Access to Free Supporting Materials

To get started, visit the ATD Workshop Series page: www.td.org/workshopbooks. This page includes links to download all the free supporting materials that accompany this book, as well as up-to-date information about additions to the series and new program offerings.

These downloads, which are included in the price of the book, feature ready-to-use learning activities, handouts, assessments, and presentation slide files in PDF format. Use these files to deliver your workshop program and as a resource to help you prepare your own materials. You may download and use any of these files as part of your training delivery for the workshops, provided no changes are made to the original materials. To access this material, you will be asked to log into the ATD website. If you are not an ATD member, you will have to create an ATD account.

If you choose to re-create these documents, they can only be used within your organization; they cannot be presented or sold as your original work. Please note that all materials included in the book are copyrighted and you are using them with permission of ATD and Kimberly Devlin. If you choose to re-create the materials, per copyright usage requirements, you must provide attribution to the original source of the content and display a copyright notice as follows:

© 2015 Kimberly Devlin. Adapted and used with permission from ATD.

Customizable Materials

You can also choose to customize this supporting content for an additional licensing fee. This option gives you access to a downloadable zip file with the entire collection of supporting materials in Microsoft Word and PowerPoint file formats. Once purchased, you will have indefinite and unlimited access to these materials through the My Downloads section of your ATD account. Then, you will be able to customize and personalize all the documents and presentations using Microsoft Word and PowerPoint. You can add your own content, change the order or format, include your company logo, or make any other customization.

Please note that all the original documents contain attribution to Kimberly Devlin and this book as the original source for the material. As you customize the documents, remember to keep these attributions intact (see the copyright notice above). By doing so, you are practicing professional courtesy by respecting the intellectual property rights of another trainer (the author) and modeling respect for copyright and intellectual property laws for your program participants.

ATD offers two custom material license options: *Internal Use* and *Client Use.* To determine which license option you need to purchase, ask yourself the following question:

Will I or my employer be charging a person or outside organization a fee for providing services or for delivering training that includes any ATD Workshop content that you wish to customize?

If the answer is yes, then you need to purchase a *Client Use* license.

If the answer is no, and you plan to customize ATD Workshop content to deliver training at no cost to employees within your own department or company only, you need to purchase the *Internal Use* license.

Working With the Files

PDF Documents

To read or print the PDF files you download, you must have PDF reader software such as Adobe Acrobat Reader installed on your system. The program can be downloaded free of cost from the Adobe website: www.adobe.com. To print documents, simply use the PDF reader to open the downloaded files and print as many copies as you need.

PowerPoint Slides

To use or adapt the contents of the PowerPoint presentation files (available with the Internal Use and Client Use licenses), you must have Microsoft PowerPoint software installed on your system. If you simply want to view the PowerPoint documents, you only need an appropriate viewer on your system. Microsoft provides various viewers for free download at www.microsoft.com.

Once you have downloaded the files to your computer system, use Microsoft PowerPoint (or free viewer) to print as many copies of the presentation slides as you need. You can also make handouts of the presentations by choosing the "print three slides per page" option on the print menu.

You can modify or otherwise customize the slides by opening and editing them in Microsoft PowerPoint. However, you must retain the credit line denoting the original source of the material, as noted earlier in this chapter. It is illegal to present this content as your own work. The files will open as read-only files, so before you adapt them you will need to save them onto your hard drive. Further use of the images in the slides for any purpose other than presentation for these workshops is strictly prohibited by law.

The PowerPoint slides included in this volume support the three workshop agendas:

- Two-Day Workshop
- One-Day Workshop
- Half-Day Workshop

For PowerPoint slides to successfully support and augment your learning program, it is essential that you practice giving presentations with the slides *before* using them in live training situations. You should be confident that you can logically expand on the points featured in the presentations and discuss the methods for working through them. If you want to fully engage your participants, become familiar with this technology before you use it. See the text box that follows for a cheat sheet to help you navigate through the presentation. A good practice is to insert comments into PowerPoint's notes feature, which you can print out and use when you present the slides. The workshop agendas in this book show thumbnails of each slide to help you keep your place as you deliver the workshop.

NAVIGATING THROUGH A POWERPOINT PRESENTATION	
Key	**PowerPoint "Show" Action**
Space bar or Enter or Mouse click	Advance through custom animations embedded in the presentation
Backspace	Back up to the last projected element of the presentation
Escape	Abort the presentation
B or b	Blank the screen to black
B or b (repeat)	Resume the presentation
W or w	Blank the screen to white
W or w (repeat)	Resume the presentation

Acknowledgments

First, thank you, dear reader and colleague! Of all the resources and options available, you chose this book. In the same way that I think of clients' needs, constraints, resources, and unique concerns when designing learning events for their use, I thought of you throughout writing this book. As activities unfolded, I would stop to consider reasons they might not work for you, and how to fix that. I pictured you facilitating the workshops and worked to create visuals that would be meaningful to participants and helpful to you—resources that you could stand beside with comfort, confidence, and pride. Wanting you to succeed, I questioned what content may be unfamiliar to you and where you might appreciate examples, stories, or sample language to explain concepts or provide instruction. And now, you are holding this book; so, I thank you for influencing my choices in the workshop designs and in the structure and content of the book itself. I thank you for seeing something in these pages that resonated with you and your needs. Your confidence in my effort is humbling.

My involvement with this book would not have happened if not for a bread trail of incredible professionals at ATD whom I have the good fortune of knowing, including Courtney Kreibs, Pat Byrd, Jennifer Naughton, Bettina Timme, Alicia Cipriani, and others who have given me opportunities to contribute, lead, learn, grow, and influence through CPLP, ATD–CI, and ATD Education. The faith placed in a first-time author by Cat Russo and the guidance and patience of Jacki Edlund-Braun, both of Trainers Publishing House, have been a gift. They have both been vital in my ability to fulfill a longstanding ambition.

It would be short-sighted of me to thank the following colleagues and friends merely for their influence in my ability to write this book. My indebtedness to them stretches far beyond a single project. Without them, I wouldn't be me: Susan DellCioppia, Ronnie Glotzbach, Kathy Shurte, Sarah Shannon, David Gant, Lindsey Forgash, Jim Ash, Tsi Tsi Wahkisi, and Professor Masterson.

To my cheerleaders, deadline watchers, court jesters, and all-around supporters, you make this life of mine meaningful. Christine Trust, sitting here at my desk, I see on my bookshelf every book (and there are many) you ever gave me on writing and publishing. Thank you for planting seeds. Mom and dad, every time I turn around, you are making me a better person—how can

I express the depth of my appreciation for that? Matt Devlin and Kim Devlin, thank you both for freeing up bandwidth at a critical time for me to finalize this project. Nicky Velazquez, I couldn't ask for a better friend (or better-timed encouraging nudges). Kaylon Green, you make me smile every day.

And thank you, Mick, my wonder dog!

About the Author

Kimberly Devlin is both president of Poetic License, Inc., a business communication consulting firm, and managing director of EdTrek, Inc., a training and development consulting firm that caters to the unique needs of the public sector. She has been an independent consultant for more than 18 years helping client agencies realize business objectives through strategic planning, organization-wide training implementations, service standard creation, train-the-trainer certifications, and other initiatives.

She has presented at international and industry-specific conferences, including ATD's International Conference & Expo, ATD's Chapter Leader's Conference, the Office Connection Conference for school district administrative personnel, the Florida Association of Court Clerks' Conference, Florida Gulf Coast University's Developing World Class Employees, the Florida Association of City Clerks' Conference, SUNCOAST League of Cities' Conference, the Florida Association of Code Enforcement Conference, and others. Kimberly has also been featured in *TD* magazine for her status as a Certified Professional in Learning and Performance (CPLP) pilot pioneer.

With a MA in journalism and a BA in English literature from the University of Miami, and her CPLP credential, Kimberly leverages her communication specialist skills and industry-leading training and development qualifications to create highly effective, sought-after learning events. Topics include competency-based designs for leadership at all levels of public sector agencies, effectiveness in business writing, proprietary software and business process training, and others. She also leads world-class learning events for ATD Education. Among her most professionally rewarding projects are developing the skills of other industry professionals through online and instructor-led facilitation of ATD's Training Certificate Program, Master Instructional Designer Certificate Program, and Designing Learning Certificate Program, as well as EdTrek's train-the-trainer certification programs for hand-selected public sector staff. She has recently revised the curriculum for one of ATD's certificate programs and worked closely with ATD and HumRRO staff on CPLP-related projects.

As a writer, instructional designer, facilitator, and consultant, she has provided technical assistance nationally and internationally to organizations as diverse as Lucent Technologies, Avaya, U.S. Marine Corps, Social Security Administration, U.S. Department of Veterans Affairs, ATD–CI, HumRRO, Broward College, Akron Children's Hospital, multiple school districts, Grady Health System and Fulton County in a public/private partnership, defense contractors, as well as city, county, and state agencies across the country. The organizations she serves work in a wide range of fields, including healthcare, pharmaceuticals, insurance, higher education, manufacturing, telecommunications, aviation, and others.

A long-time ATD volunteer, she served on her chapter's board as vice president of professional development from 2007 to 2010, during which time the chapter received national recognition and awards, and has been a volunteer in multiple capacities for ATD–CI since 2007. She is a graduate of Leadership Broward XXIV, where she served as community project chair, and is a former board member of the Association of Women in Communications. Kimberly was the recipient of Avaya Communication's E-Learning Excellence Award for the Caribbean and Latin America Region in 2000.

About ATD

The Association for Talent Development (ATD), formerly ASTD, is the world's largest association dedicated to those who develop talent in organizations. These professionals help others achieve their full potential by improving their knowledge, skills, and abilities.

ATD's members come from more than 120 countries and work in public and private organizations in every industry sector.

ATD supports the work of professionals locally in more than 125 chapters, international strategic partners, and global member networks.

1640 King Street
Alexandria, VA 22314
www.td.org
800.628.2783
703.683.8100

HOW TO PURCHASE ATD PRESS PUBLICATIONS

ATD Press publications are available worldwide in print and electronic format.

To place an order, please visit our online store: www.td.org/books.

Our publications are also available at select online and brick-and-mortar retailers.

Outside the United States, English-language ATD Press titles may be purchased through the following distributors:

United Kingdom, Continental Europe, the Middle East, North Africa, Central Asia, Australia, New Zealand, and Latin America
Eurospan Group
Phone: 44.1767.604.972
Fax: 44.1767.601.640
Email: eurospan@turpin-distribution.com
Website: www.eurospanbookstore.com

Asia
Cengage Learning Asia Pte. Ltd.
Phone: (65)6410-1200
Email: asia.info@cengage.com
Website: www.cengageasia.com

Nigeria
Paradise Bookshops
Phone: 08033075133
Email: paradisebookshops@gmail.com
Website: www.paradisebookshops.com

South Africa
Knowledge Resources
Phone: +27 (11) 706.6009
Fax: +27 (11) 706.1127
Email: sharon@knowres.co.za
Web: www.kr.co.za

For all other territories, customers may place their orders at the ATD online store: **www.td.org/books**.

0215145.62220